The Philosophy of Action

The Philosophy of Action

An Introduction

CARLOS J. MOYA

Polity Press

First published 1990 by Polity Press
in association with Basil Blackwell

Editorial office:
Polity Press
65 Bridge Street,
Cambridge CB2 1UR, UK

Marketing and production:
Basil Blackwell Ltd
108 Cowley Road, Oxford OX4 1JF, UK

ISBN 0 7456 0746 2
ISBN 0 7456 0747 0 (pbk)

British Library Cataloguing in Publication Data
A CIP catalogue record for this book is available from the British Library.

Typeset in 10½ on 12 pt Baskerville
by Hope Services (Abingdon) Ltd.
Printed in Great Britain by
Billings & Sons Ltd, Worcester.

Contents

Contents

Acknowledgements

This book was mainly written during my stay, as an Honorary Research Fellow, in the Philosophy Department of the University of Birmingham in the academic year 1986–7. This stay was possible owing to a Scholarship awarded by the Valencian Council of Culture, Education and Science and a leave from my teaching duties at the University of Valencia.

Very special thanks are due to Dr Christopher Hookway, who encouraged me to get my ideas down on paper and gave me the opportunity to improve them with his patient and insightful criticisms and comments, although his views about human action were – and remain – fairly different from mine. Without him, this work would not have existed. Defects, however, are solely my responsibility. Very helpful and competent remarks were also made by Dr N. Dent. My thanks also to Dr H. Noonan and Mr B. Falk for their help and encouragement, and to the rest of the Department staff for their warm welcome and extreme kindness.

I am also grateful to Professor Donald Davidson who read some parts of the typescript and made invaluable comments on it, though I want to stress the fact that the exposition and criticism of his theory in this book, including possible errors, are my exclusive responsibility. I also benefited from some wise suggestions made by Dr Tom Sorell.

My thanks, finally, to Dr F. Mowtero, V. Raga and to my colleagues in the Department of Metaphysics in Valencia, as well as to my students, from whom I have learnt more than I have been able to teach.

The author and publishers are grateful to the following for permission to reproduce material which originally appeared elsewhere: Basil Blackwell for extracts from A. Rosenberg, *Sociobiology and the Preemption of Social Science*, 1981; and Oxford University Press for extracts from D. Davidson, *Essays on Actions and Events*, 1980, and from M. Bratman, 'Davidson's Theory of Intention' in B. Vermazen and M.B. Hintikka (eds) *Essays on Davidson: Actions and Events*, 1985.

For Milagro and Nuria

Introduction

This book is intended to be an introductory inquiry into central issues in the philosophy of action and some related topics in the philosophy of mind. I have tried to avoid technical expressions, so that it can be read by any educated reader, with no need of a special philosophical training. So, I hope it will be useful not only to philosophy students, but also to students of politics, psychology, sociology and other social sciences who would like to get some idea of what philosophy can contribute to a subject which has a relevant bearing on their disciplines, namely human action. Moreover, it can be read with profit by the general reader with an interest in philosophy. This introductory task is not accomplished, however, from a detached and cold perspective, but from a committed point of view, which takes an active part in the discussion. My aim has been to draw a sort of map that can help the reader to find his or her way through a certain field of problems. But I have not taken up the pen without prejudices. I have dealt with these matters from a sort of obscure feeling that certain ordinary assumptions about human beings are basically true, and I have tried to uncover the foundations of this feeling, to give them form and structure and to turn this structure into philosophical argument. I have made a serious effort not to mistake feeling for argument, nor to present as reasons mere disguised prejudices. I do not think I have settled the questions. If a question is really deep, it cannot be settled once and for all, but only reformulated and argued further. Philosophy progresses through reformulation and arguing. As long as one is doing philosophy, one should not look for a definitely secure position, on pain of finding that the building in which one intended to settle down is now being rebuilt some yards ahead.

WHAT WE DO
v.
WHAT HAPPENS

The starting-point of this inquiry will be action itself. In our everyday life we tend to contrast what we do with what merely happens. This is an important conceptual polarity. It plays a central role in the way we conceive of ourselves and others, as well as in the value we put on our lives. Try to think of the way things would appear to us if we did not distinguish between agents and mere objects, nor between actions and happenings. Could there be meaning and value without agents? If we feel there could not, then this may partly explain why viewing ourselves as agents is more important than viewing ourselves as, say, taxpayers. The idea that we are agents, and therefore that there are agents, is not a mere opinion we can embrace or reject. It is a basic conviction that permeates our life, giving support, and being supported by, other equally basic convictions.

We find an even more direct connection between the concept of action and such concepts as responsibility, blame, good and evil. If there is something we are responsible for, it seems there must be something that is or was up to us, something we could do or could have done. If such words are to have a meaning, not everything should depend on circumstances or mere happenings. We want them to have a meaning, so we want there to be actions.

But is there any action? This question may sound bizarre, for what could be more evident than that? Philosophy, however, cannot allow itself to be satisfied with that level of evidence. It certainly would be false to deny that we do draw a sharp distinction between actions and happenings and that we think there are actions. But that is not a proof of the validity of such distinction or of the existence of actions. We could be wrong. Philosophy of action begins when we stop taking those everyday assumptions at face value.

Whether there are or there are not actions is not something that can be answered by direct observation. Those who doubt the existence of actions are not questioning what everyone can perceive. They are rather wondering whether the concepts we ordinarily use to describe and interpret those observations are appropriate and ultimately consistent. If they are not, then this leads to a negative answer to our question: if action is an inconsistent concept, there cannot be actions, just as there cannot be squared circles. So, analysis of the concept of action itself is a main topic of the philosophy of action.

Suspicions about the ultimate consistency of the concept of action, as well as of the distinction between actions and happenings, are likely to arise from scientifically formed outlooks. If we take science seriously, then we are bound to reflect on the possibility of reconciling scientific and everyday accounts of reality, for they appear to be, if not simply contradictory, at least widely disparate. Scientific perspectives are happy with happenings, being explained by other previous or contemporary happenings with the aid of laws. But if we think of ourselves as agents, we conceive of ourselves as being able to initiate changes, independently of the world's previous history. Agents and actions, then, are likely to face difficulties if they look for a place on a scientific stage.

A suspicious or sceptical attitude towards action can take several forms, ranging from eliminative proposals to more or less radically reductionist ones. To give the reader an idea of what a reductionist attitude is like, let us start with an episode that nobody would hesitate in classifying as an action, say, drinking a glass of water. What right do we have to call this an action, and not a mere happening? Where does the actional character of this episode lie? What did *I* do? The water got into my mouth as an effect of gravity. The water getting into my mouth is a mere happening. This happening, in turn, was caused by the movement of the glass. Where is action in this? Well, one could say, I caused that movement, so I acted. But think that this movement can be said to be properly caused by my arm's and hand's movement, which in turn were caused by some muscles' contractions, which in turn were caused by some neurons' firings, and so on. Action as such seems to dissolve and to be reduced to a sequence of happenings. Our everyday sharp distinction between actions and happenings begins to fade; it seems that we were calling 'action' what is in fact a series of causally related happenings. Appealing to desires will not do, for our desire for water is presumably a state caused by organic deprivation. The chain of causes extends further and further into the past and there appears to be nothing we, as agents, initiate, no action at all, only further happenings. Actions, then, seem to be nothing but specific sequences of happenings. THE REGRESS PROBLEM

A slightly modified version of this sort of argument gives rise to what has been called the regress-problem in action theory. It leads also to scepticism about actions. Its starting-point is the fact that the occurrence of certain happenings is logically implied by many actions. For instance, it cannot be true that I move my arm unless my arm moves. What explains this movement? My moving my arm cannot count as a factual or informative explanation of that happening's occurrence, for they are logically related. We must find some different action to explain that happening. But if this action in turn has a specific happening as an essential part of it, this quickly leads to the need for performance of an infinite number of actions in order to perform any action at all. And, since we are not able to perform an infinite number of actions, we do not act at all. Again, only happenings remain, and 'action' is just a way of referring to happenings. The regress-problem seems to be what prompts some philosophers to postulate basic actions. Chapter 1 deals with this set of topics.

One way of getting around the regress-problem and its resulting scepticism can be to find actions that involve no specific happenings as logically necessary conditions. As I see it, this is an important motivation for developing <u>volitional theories of action</u>, that is, theories that identify actions with such conative mental acts as volitions or tryings. After some years of silence, partly owing to Ryle's sharp attack on volitions, volitional theories have recently rushed with force into the philosophical arena. According to such theories, what we really do is to will the occurrence of a happening, to try for it to occur. Acting is properly willing or trying, it is identical with it, the rest being just causal antecedents and consequents of this one genuine act. It is easy to see how this move is supposed to stop the infinite regress, namely by individuating a pure act of will that involves no physical happening. The reasons why I do not think it succeeds are given in chapter 2, where volitional theories are presented and criticized in some detail.

The strategy I propose in order to avoid the infinite regress and to justify a strong distinction between actions and happenings is also to look for actions that do not involve specific happenings as logically necessary conditions. But instead of adopting an atomistic perspective, searching for small and internal acting episodes such as volitions, my proposal is to view actions as large wholes of everyday behaviour. I propose to examine some specifically human actions, namely those that might be called 'meaningful', owing to their having and transmitting a symbolic content. Think of such actions as marrying, voting or bidding. An examination of them is carried out in chapter 4. My contention will be that such actions are not logically committed to the occurrence of any specific kind of happenings; they show our ordinary concept of action in a pure form, which does not depend on happenings; in this sense, they can stop the infinite regress with no need of volitions.

Meaningful actions, then, are a good starting-point in order to show the consistency of our everyday notion of action as opposed to that of happening and irreducible to it. If we could identify what gives (some) meaningful actions their logical independence from specific kinds of happenings, this would be a major step in clarifying the foundations and justification of our ordinary sharp distinction between actions and happenings. Chapter 5 sets itself this task. Meaningful actions, it is argued, can escape the regress-problem owing to their necessarily intentional character. Meaningful actions being necessarily intentional, intentionality could be raised to a general criterion of agency. This is, in fact, our proposal.

In taking <u>intentionality as a general criterion of agency</u>, our account joins the ranks of such authors as G. E. M. Anscombe and Donald Davidson. But it departs from them with respect to the nature of that criterion, that is, the nature of intentions and intentional actions. Davidson's account of these concepts is causal. Ours is not. Intention, so our account runs, should be understood as a kind of commitment to act and intentional action as behaviour that honours that commitment and does so correctly. A commitment, however, cannot simply occur; it is an essentially active performance. That is why mere happenings cannot give a full account of it. Moreover, if our account is correct, normativity is an essential aspect of intentions and intentional actions. This being so, a factual, causal perspective is likely to find difficulties in dealing with them. But just as causal views deserve a more careful examination, so our account is in need of a no less careful defence. Chapters 8 to 13 deal with these and other related questions.

Chapter 6 places intentions and intentional actions in the context of the whole network of mind. It tries to give an idea of the close relationship between the philosophy of action and the philosophy of mind. They are not separate investigations: agency and mind stand or fall together.

If the philosophy of action opens naturally on to the philosophy of mind, it also has an important bearing on the philosophy of social sciences. If we think that human actions are a central subject of social sciences, philosophical research into the structure and nature of actions cannot but have consequences for our understanding of social sciences themselves. This book sets itself as one of its tasks that of pursuing this other natural extension of the philosophy of action.

At least as old as modern natural sciences are the attempts to shape the scientific study of human beings and their actions on the model provided by those impressively successful bodies of knowledge. The results of such attempts, after some centuries, are rather discouraging. This should not surprise us. There is a real tension between a scientific view and explanation of the world, inspired by the natural sciences, and the everyday conception of ourselves and our fellows. An impartial examination of the character and constraints of the latter suggests that it might not be just the undeniable complexity of human affairs or mere lack of talent or intellectual genius that lies behind the meagre results of the naturalistic programme in the field of social sciences. Chapter 7 tries to uncover the roots of this tension between scientific and everyday views of human beings and the obstacles that stand in the way of an assimilation of the latter to the former; it also outlines some programmes in the philosophy of mind that aim at reducing or overcoming the conflict.

This book approaches the issue focusing on one particular aspect: the nature of intentional action and its explanation. Antinaturalism has traditionally emphasized the differences between intentional actions and physical events, as well as between their respective explanations. The distinction between understanding and explanation in the hermeneutic tradition of the nineteenth century, or that between reasons and causes in the Wittgensteinian school, are a sign of this attitude and were meant to lead to a sharp distinction between social and natural sciences. Naturalism, on the contrary, has come to insist on their basic similarity, despite some superficial differences of procedures or interest.

Chapter 8 discusses P. M. Churchland's attempt to show that explanations of actions in terms of their reasons are causal in character and show the same logical structure as scientific explanations of physical events. A second proposal on these general lines is discussed in chapter 9. According to this proposal, human actions could be explained and predicted in the context of an empirical nomological frame inspired by modern decision theory. Actions would be a function of previously fixed causal factors, namely the relative desirabilities an agent assigns to several possible outcomes and the probabilities he or she assigns to several possible conditions.

Explanations of intentional actions by means of reasons show normativity in that they present the action as a logical, or at least reasonable, consequence of having those reasons. This feature was turned by some Wittgensteinian philosophers into an interesting, even if not fully clear, argument against the causal character of reasons. This piece of reasoning came to be called 'the logical connection argument'. Sketchily stated, it holds that, if cause and effect relate to each other in a merely factual, contingent way, then, if reasons and actions show a logical, not merely factual, connection, reasons cannot be causes of actions, and explanations by reasons cannot be a species of causal explanation. There is a short step from this to the autonomy of social sciences. Donald Davidson came to be widely known through a 1963 paper called 'Actions, Reasons, and Causes', where he resisted the conclusion of the logical connection argument while accepting some of its premises. This was the starting-point of a sophisticated and challenging causal theory of intentional action, that has aroused general attention and interest. Chapter 10 tries to give a clear and faithful account of this Davidsonian theory in its original form. I hope it will prove useful as an introductory interpretation.

According to causal theories of intentional action, if one has appropriate reasons for doing something and if these reasons cause one to do that, what is done is an intentional action. The causal route, however, can be such that both conditions are met without the effect being an intentional action. This obstacle in the way of causal theories of action is known as the problem of wayward or deviant causal chains. The possibility of these chains suggests, of course, that normal cases of intentionally acting, where they do not appear, cannot be accounted for solely in those causal terms. Wayward causal chains are, therefore, a general problem for causal theories of intentional action; they do not affect just bizarre or peripheral cases of behaviour. Chapter 11 presents several ways that causal theories have tried out to neutralize this problem. It also implies that each new attempt leads, potentially, to a progressive abandonment of the structural traits of those theories.

The several attempts to cope with wayward causal chains from a causal perspective have the virtue of bringing to light some requirements of a correct account of intentional action. They illuminate with special clarity the normative aspects that constitute it. So, our discussion helps also to refine our analysis of intentional action and to defend it against criticism. This analysis, which is carried out in chapter 12, stresses explicitly those normative traits which prevent causal theories from giving a correct and complete account of intentional action. This chapter goes further in examining the concept of intention and its varieties. Future intention is crucially central in our view of agency. Future intention should be understood, as outlined above, as a kind of commitment on the part of an agent to make its content true. This view, which is then defended against objections, places intentions alongside decisions and promises – contrary to other accounts, such as Davidson's, that classify them among pro-attitudes. Agency, it is argued, has at its core this ability to commit oneself to do things in the future. A more or less clear awareness of this ability, which we do possess, lies behind that sharp distinction between actions and happenings which shapes our view of ourselves as agents. Future intentions, it is further claimed, cannot be dispensed with in a correct account of agency: they are irreducible to other states, such as beliefs and desires.

Chapter 13 presents Davidson's theory of intention and intentional action as it results from his developing and modifying his initial account of those concepts. This sophisticated Davidsonian theory is evaluated by considering some objections to it. This gives the occasion for further defence of our own claims about intention and intentional action.

Finally, chapter 14 draws a sort of loop in order to revisit the problem with which the book began, namely the tension between our ordinary concept of agency and a scientific perspective on the world. This is a version of an old philosophical question, namely whether free will and determinism are compatible. A final Conclusion ties together the different lines of argument that have been developed throughout the book.

Before finishing this Introduction, it may be worth calling the reader's attention to two different senses of the term 'intentional', which will be much used in this book. According to its first, ordinary sense, it means roughly 'purposeful' or 'intended', and applies mainly to actions and activities we can refrain from doing or decide to do. In its second, technical sense, the word is used to refer to that feature of mental states by virtue of which they can be said to have a content or object which they are about. In this sense of the word, such mental items as beliefs, hopes, decisions, aimings, intentions, and so on, are intentional. All of them have a content which they are about, namely what is believed, hoped, decided, aimed at, intended, and so on. A hope, for instance, is intentional in the latter sense, but not, usually, in the former. The two senses, however, are not so disparate that there is no systematic relationship between them. I think there is such a relationship. It can be stated by saying that in order to be able to perform intentional actions an agent must be able to have intentional states; that is, intentionality in the technical sense is a necessary condition of intentional action and, therefore, acting intentionally is a sufficient condition of having intentional states. The two senses of the term 'intentional' will be distinguished here through the substantives it qualifies. It will have its ordinary sense when applied to actions and its technical one when applied to mental states or to the mind. The same thing will happen with the word 'intentionality', though we will find this term most often in relation to the mind or mental states. This does not mean that some items cannot be intentional in both senses. If, for instance, one decides to engage in thinking about some subject, this thinking is intentional in both senses. And intentional actions can be considered also as intentional in the technical sense, that is, as having a content or expressing it.

One of the main purposes of this inquiry will be to uncover the deep structure that lies behind what we call, in everyday life, 'intentional action'. Linguistic intuition retains an important role: it is by appealing to it that we can appreciate whether a particular analysis of intentional action is ultimately sound; it will not be such if, for example, it classifies as intentional (or unintentional) actions that would clearly not be such according to that intuition. This, of course, does not imply that we are going to remain at this level of undifferentiated intuition. We are not doing lexicography, but philosophical analysis. The mastering of that intuition by competent speakers is simply not enough to solve philosophical worries or to answer philosophical questions. Moreover, we will not be taking as decisive the fact that, by ordinary pragmatic standards, we would not find it appropriate to use the term 'intentional' in some contexts: if, for instance, I am having a cup of tea, I would find it strange if someone were to ask me whether I was doing that intentionally; but for all that it is simply true that I was.

1

Actions and Happenings

1.1 Agency

One of the most fundamental distinctions in our world-view is the one we draw between what we do and what happens to us, between actions and mere happenings. We engage in a lot of activities: reading, walking, working, etc. But we are also subject to numerous contingencies: we fall ill, lose our jobs, fall over, etc. This distinction is essential if we are not to view ourselves as just helpless victims of the world's general evolution. We have a consciousness that at least some things – even if few – are in our power, depend on us; we think we can somehow influence the course of the events by acting, instead of just suffering it; we think we are agents, and not just passive beings.

We can ask ourselves what is implied in the idea of agency and what kind of justifications we have for it. As with other basic convictions, it seems to us that nothing could be truer than that, but at the same time we feel we cannot provide, apart from our conviction, good reasons in support of it. Moreover, the idea of agency conflicts with our nowadays equally basic conviction that the universe is a network of causally related events where no room can be found for agents, for beings capable of initiating *new* causal chains. The problem is that even the smallest gap in this causal network would mean its complete collapse.

I think that every attempt to account for actions within this deterministic picture, that is, every attempt to consider actions as nodes of that causal network, will destroy what is specific about agency: actions will appear not just as opposed to non-actional events, but as kinds of events typically having certain kinds of causes. Actions will not appear as one element of a basic, twofold *distinction*, but as one of the items of a manifold *classification* of events. We will not be distinguishing between actions and non-actions, but differentiating between actions, eruptions, falls, storms, etc., so that the distinction between an action and an eruption will not bear more significance than the distinction between, say, an eruption and a storm.

None the less, the problem of agency seems to be somehow related to certain natural facts, notably the fact that animals exhibit a natural, non-learnt ability for spontaneous movement, as well as an equally natural ability to engage in teleological behaviour. These abilities are clearly shown from birth by healthy human beings. And in a sense they constitute the natural basis of our condition as agents: human beings can perform an enormously wide range of actions, but the process of learning and socialization that leads to this ability rests on the fact that they can perform certain bodily movements *without* learning, that is, spontaneously.

I do not see any clear reason to deny that most of our spontaneous movements are actions, but I do see reasons to deny that the significance and justification of the distinction between actions and non-actions can be formulated and captured by conceiving it in terms of the distinction between spontaneous and teleological movement and, say, reflex or mechanical movement. It is all too easy to account for this distinction by appealing to the particular organization of the matter that constitutes living bodies. And, therefore, this way leads, not to a distinction between actions and non-actional events, which is what we are considering, but to a classification of spontaneous bodily movements as a special kind of event at the same level as several others. This result, instead of making us think that our belief in agency is a mere illusion, should warn us against thinking that we are really getting at what lies at the very heart of the problem we are concerned with.

What worries us about agency and turns it into an important notion is not, I contend, the fact that certain living beings are able to move spontaneously while other beings are not, but, if we want to remain at the level of movements, that we, human beings, seem to be able to perform these movements *at will*, that, independently of the past history of the universe, we can, now and here, stand up or remain sitting, according to our will. What is important about agency is what connects it with such notions as will and freedom.

1.2 The Search for Agency

I am walking to the University, as I do every day. Suddenly, I stumble on a stone and I am about to fall. The first sentence describes an action of mine. The second, something that happened to me. I seem to have no doubt about that. I *know* that stumbling and being about to fall was not an action of mine, and I *know* that walking to the University was. I think everybody knows with certainty, in most cases, when an event was his or her action and when it was a mere happening. But most of us would find serious difficulties if asked how we know that and how we distinguish between what we do and what happens to us, and, in general, between actions and happenings.

Let me try to bring out some of the characteristics that seem to distinguish actions from happenings. In the above example, the first thing that distinguishes the two cases is the element of surprise. My stumbling came as a surprise, as something unexpected, while my walking was no surprise for me. But we can easily find cases of happenings where this element of surprise is not present. Suppose that I know about the financial difficulties my firm is going through and that I am afraid I am going to lose my job. If I lose my job, this is something that happens to me, but it has not come as a surprise. On the other hand, some of the things I do can surprise me. Suppose I am trying to hit a difficult target and do not think I will be able to succeed. If I hit the target, I can be surprised, but that is something I did, an action of mine. What about being intentional as what characterizes actions? In the above example, my walking was intentional, but my stumbling was not. Leaving aside the question of what 'intentional' means, this trait, taken by itself, would exclude those things we do unintentionally. Marrying his mother was something Oedipus did, though it was not intentional. If intentionality is to play a role as a criterion of agency, it needs at least more qualifications. Consider, however, that what we do unintentionally has, intuitively, some of the traits of what happens to us. Experience tells us about what happens to us, but also about what we do unintentionally. Oedipus discovered he had married his mother, but he did not discover he had married Jocasta. Equally, in our example, I knew I stumbled by experience, but I did not know by experience that I was walking to the University. In fact, when we first think of the distinction between actions and happenings, we tend to think of the contrast between intentional actions and mere happenings, not of the contrast between unintentional actions and mere happenings. This points to a special privilege of intentional actions that will reveal itself as an important insight into the nature of agency. However, even if we restrict ourselves to intentional action, non-experiential knowledge of what we do intentionally is not a sufficient criterion of action, because we have such a knowledge of our hopes, desires, intentions, etc., which are not actions. Moreover, this criterion applies only to one's own actions, for we know what other people are doing by observation. But this does not prevent us, in most cases, from being certain that other people are performing actions.

Let us assume, however, that some of these criteria, or a combination of them, work and are in fact used to distinguish actions from happenings. One could accept this and still hold that these criteria do not prevent actions from being a special kind of happenings. The real distinction we would be drawing is not one between actions and happenings as exclusive categories, but one between actions and *other kinds* of happenings. Our distinction, that is, could be drawn within the realm of happenings; it would not take us beyond it. Our pre-theoretical, intuitive distinction between actions and happenings is no proof of its having the strength our natural attitude tends to assume. Nothing so far excludes the possibility that what is implied in it is much less than what we would be inclined to think. Actions could be, after all, characteristic sequences of happenings in us. Let us see how this might be argued for. Compare these two cases:

(1) A person takes a gun, aims carefully at the target, pulls the trigger, and fires the gun.
(2) The person gets home and puts the gun on the table. While he is putting it down, the gun, unexpectedly, fires.

Now, starting from our intuitive distinction between actions and happenings, we would agree, I hope, that in the first example shooting the gun was an action, while in the second the gun's firing was a happening.

We have, then, the fact that in the first case,

(a) Someone fired the gun,

while in the second case,

(b) The gun's firing happened or the gun fired.

What distinguishes (a) from (b)? The problem in drawing the distinction is that a happening of the specific kind conveyed by (b) is also involved in (a), for if someone fired the gun, a gun's firing took place. In fact, 'someone fired the gun' logically implies 'the gun fired', for unless the gun's firing happened it could not possibly be true that someone fired the gun. The converse, however, does not hold: 'the gun fired' does not logically imply 'someone fired the gun', as the second example shows. So, an action of the kind described by (a) involves essentially (logically) a happening of the kind described by (b), in the sense that if this happening does not take place, the action is not performed, but if the happening takes place, the action may or may not be performed. The happening, then, is a necessary, but not a sufficient, condition of the action.

If the gun's firing occurs, then (b) is automatically true, but not (a). Something must be added to the gun's firing in order for (a) to be true. This missing element is what would bring agency into the picture. A natural suggestion would be that in the first case, but not in the second, the gun's firing was brought about or caused to happen by someone. In (b) the firing simply happened. In (a) it was brought about or caused to happen. The action, then, would be properly the bringing about of the gun's firing, the causing it to happen. So, an action of the kind described by (a) could be conceived as the bringing about of a happening.

This view of certain actions as the bringing about of a happening or as causing something to happen has wide acceptance. Useful as it may be, this formulation does not succeed in capturing what is specific to action, for surely not every bringing about of a change, not every causing something to happen is an action. For instance, in our second example the firing of the gun brought about the bullet's lodging in the wall, but there was no action there. Or the rain caused a flood to happen, but there was no action there either. In both cases we have simply a causal chain of happenings. Moreover, if I ask someone to fire the gun, I caused the gun's firing to happen, but I did not fire the gun. So, the way in which a change or happening is caused to occur or brought about is essential for the causing or bringing about to be a case of action.

So, if we allow 'someone fired the gun' to mean 'someone brought it about that the gun fired' we will have to specify the way in which he brought it about for that equivalence to be right. If, *ex hypothesi*, 'someone fired the gun' describes an action, the specification will have to refer to some action of that person. Otherwise we should say that someone fired the gun if he fell on the gun and this went off. And the specification would be: 'by pulling the trigger'. So, 'someone fired the gun' would mean 'someone brought it about that the gun fired by pulling the trigger.'

But pulling the trigger essentially involves a happening, namely the trigger's getting pulled, in the same sense in which firing the gun does. If the trigger does not get pulled, it cannot be true that someone pulled the trigger. And then we could apply to 'someone pulled the trigger' the same argument as to 'someone fired the gun.' And we would have to find another action such that the person in question brought it about that the trigger got pulled by performing that action. But then, if the same argument applies to this other action, we are clearly facing an infinite regress, for we would have to perform an infinite number of actions in order to perform any action at all. And, if this is so, we do not act at all, for we cannot perform an infinite number of actions.

1.3 Basic Actions

This is the point where the need for basic actions arises. Let us quote
Danto, who first introduced this concept in the theory of action. We
need some actions which are not cases of bringing something about or
causing something to happen,

> for suppose every action were a case of the agent causing something
> to happen. This means, each time he does a, he must independently
> do b, which causes a to happen. But then, in order to do b, he must
> first independently do c, which causes b to happen . . . This quickly
> entails that the agent could perform no action at all. If, accordingly,
> there are any actions at all of the sort described by 'causing
> something to happen', there must be actions which are *not* caused to
> happen by the man who performs them. And these are basic
> actions.[1]

So, we can analyse 'someone pulled the trigger' in terms of 'someone
brought it about that the trigger got pulled by moving his finger.' And
what about 'moving his finger'? This, according to Danto, could be a
basic action, provided that the agent did not bring about the
movement of his finger by doing anything else, for instance moving it
with his other hand. According to Danto,

$Bam \rightarrow Aam \wedge \neg \exists b : Abm \wedge Cba.$

> a is a *basic action* of m only if a is an action and there is no action,
> distinct from a and performed by m, which stands to a as cause to
> effect. If b is the effect of an action distinct from itself, and b is
> performed by m, then b is a *nonbasic* action of m. Raising his arm is a
> *basic* action of m, if m does not cause his arm to rise; if he does cause
> it to rise, then it is a nonbasic action.[2]

In our example, supposing that the person in question did not move
the finger by doing any other action, his moving the finger was a basic
action. We could not analyse it in the terms in which we analysed
'someone fired the gun' or 'someone pulled the trigger.' We cannot say
that 'someone moved his finger' means 'someone brought it about that
his finger moved . . .', because if he fired the gun by pulling the trigger
and pulled the trigger by moving his finger, he did not move his finger
by doing anything else, but, let us say, 'directly'. Basic actions, then,
are designed to stop the infinite regress and to allow for the existence of
any other action. In order for 'someone fired the gun' and 'someone
pulled the trigger' to be descriptions of actions, a description of a basic
action must be true of that person. Basic actions are, so to speak, the
source of agency; they transmit agency to other things we do. That is

why Danto says that 'if there are any actions at all, there are basic actions.'[3]

As I shall try to show, I do not think that basic actions can solve the regress-problem. If they illuminate the structure of human agency, it is by pointing to what we called the natural conditions of agency. Consider that the ability to move spontaneously and teleologically is presupposed in every process of teaching and learning how to perform new actions. Think of someone who is explaining to another person how to use a gun. This latter person has to *know how* to do certain things, for instance to move his or her fingers. *This* cannot be taught, but is presupposed in teaching. And unless the person in question can make certain movements spontaneously (that is, without learning), he or she will not be able to learn, for example, how to fire a gun. Some of these movements we perform from birth; others we acquire naturally as we grow up; and others we learn, but only by training or practice. We share this natural ability with other animals. We display a natural ability to move our bodies, and to move them teleologically. How to perform these movements is something that cannot be explained in the way, say, in which how to play chess can be. This suggests that no concepts are involved in their performance. No norms seem to govern their performance; one simply moves one's arms or does not move them, can or cannot do it, but there is no point in criticizing that movement as rightly or wrongly made, unlike what happens with, say, playing chess.

But Danto wants basic actions to do more than this. He wants them to be those actions by virtue of which any other action can be performed, for they avoid the need to perform infinite actions in order to perform any action at all. I do not think that basic actions in Danto's sense can do this work. Recall that the problem of infinite regress started from the fact that certain happenings were essentially (logically) involved in the performing of certain actions. I cannot be said to have fired the gun unless the gun fires nor can I be said to have pulled the trigger unless the trigger gets pulled. But then, for the same reason, I cannot be said to move my finger unless my finger moves. Now, 'the firing of a gun', 'the pulling of a trigger' and 'the moving of a finger' can describe mere happenings. In fact, my finger can move without my moving it, owing, for instance, to a spasm. There is, then, a difference between:

(a') Someone moved his finger, and
(b') Someone's finger moved

because, if the finger moves, (b') is *ipso facto* true, but not (a'). However, if (a') is true, (b') has to be true. So, what does (a') add to (b')? It is natural to think that when (a') is true, oneself brings about the movement of one's finger, whereas when (b'), but not (a'), is true, it is not oneself who brings about that movement. But, since the movement of the finger is a happening, the element of action has to be in the bringing about of that movement. This bringing about has to include an action. So far, then, the regress has not been stopped. But now the problem is that there seems to be no action we perform in order to bring about the movement of our finger. Therefore, we face a dilemma: either the cause of that happening is the agent himself, and we embrace a conception of action in terms of agent-causation, or the cause of that happening is another happening, and we get very close to dissolving actions into mere sequences of happenings.

The problem with the first horn of the dilemma is not that it is false, but that it does not go beyond the unanalysed and intuitive conception of action: to say that in acting the agent is the cause of his own actions is really not very different from saying that acting is not merely suffering changes, but initiating them, which is in turn the very notion of agency that a theory of action is supposed to clarify. Causing one's own actions is not a clearer notion than acting. We do not know what 'causing' means here. So far, then, this first horn of the dilemma does not exclude the possibility that 'acting' could be analysed in terms of the second. This latter amounts to the following: there is a difference between (a') and (b'); but a happening of the kind described in (b') is logically involved in (a'); the difference between (a') and (b') will lie in the way in which that happening is brought about; but there seems to be no further action by means of which we bring about the movement of our finger; the difference, then, may simply lie in the causal (neurological, muscular) sequence that gives rise to the movement of the finger in each case. So, we would be describing as actions what are simply specific configurations of causal sequences of mere happenings. The 'action' of firing a gun would be a causal sequence of happenings:

> 'normal' neurological and muscular processes – the movement of the finger – the pulling of the trigger – the firing of the gun.

The distinction between actions and happenings would then be nothing but a convention to refer to different kinds of causal sequences of mere happenings. We would say that we moved our finger when the causal sequence leading to the movement of the finger was normal or standard, and we would say that our finger moved (owing, for example, to a spasm) when the causal sequence was abnormal or non-standard, in a purely statistical sense.

A way out could be found if we were able to identify some action by means of which we bring about the movement of our finger but such that, in turn, does not essentially involve a happening (as moving the finger does) with respect to which it would make sense to ask how it was brought about. Here is where <u>volitional theories</u> enter into the picture. This is the answer that could be offered: when moving our finger is an action, we bring about the movement of our finger by ⟨*willing*⟩ it to move or ⟨*trying*⟩ to move it. This is *how* we cause the movement of our finger, and this is what accounts for the difference between (a') and (b'): in (a'), but not in (b'), that person willed his finger to move or tried to move it. In order for volitions or tryings to be able to stop the infinite regress and to avoid the collapse of actions into mere happenings, two things should be shown concerning them: first of all, volitions or tryings should not essentially involve happenings, so that the difference we found between (a') and (b') would not arise in this case; and, secondly, volitions or tryings should match our intuitive idea of action, they should be shown to be actions.

If both conditions are met, volitions and tryings would be the answer to the question with which we started this chapter: they would be what distinguishes (a) and (a') from (b) and (b'), the mark and source of agency. If they are mental, as they seem to be, they will account for that knowledge we seem to have when we say with certainty that, say, stumbling on a stone was not an action, but something that happened to us: we did not will the stumble or try to stumble, and we know we did not with the same certainty with which we know that we desire something or that we are in pain. From this point of view, moreover, moving the finger would not be, contrary to Danto's contention, a basic action, for we cause the movement of the finger to happen by willing it to move or trying to move it. <u>Willing and trying would be the proper basic actions, the only ones we do not perform by doing anything else.</u>

2

The New Volitional Theory

The old volitional theory, which dates back to British empiricism, conceived actions reductively in terms of non-actional, causally related events, namely volitions and bodily movements. An action would be a pair of events, the first of which causes the second one, neither of them being itself an action. There seems to be no means by which *we* can move our bodies at will, in the usual sense. Moving our bodies at will means that a mental event, a volition, occurs and causes a movement in our bodies. That mental event is in turn caused by motives, desires, etc. Willing to move our bodies is, properly speaking, a mental *happening* caused by some motive or desire, which in turn is a happening, a state we happen to be in. That mental happening, through a chain of nervous and muscular events, gives rise, causally, to a movement in our bodies, and, according to, for example, Mill, in the same sense of 'causally' as that in which cold causes ice. There is, then, no important sense in which actions and happenings differ, for actions are but causal sequences of happenings.

This reductionist account of actions clashes violently with the central place we give to our view of ourselves as agents and to the distinction between actions and happenings. It has been abandoned by the New Volitional Theory, according to which when we act, what gives rise to movements in our bodies is not itself a happening, but an action. Conations (volitions, willings, tryings) *are* actions, not happenings.

We shall refer to the views of three representatives of the New Volitional Theory: Hugh McCann, Brian O'Shaughnessy and Jennifer Hornsby.

2.1 Hugh McCann: Basic Actions Are Volitions

McCann starts from the assumption that most actions have both
results and causal consequences.[1] Results are what we have called
happenings which are essentially (logically) involved in actions.
'Results . . . are events which are necessary for those actions whose
results they are. But . . . they are never sufficient for those actions.'[2]
The result of shooting Smith is that Smith is shot and the result of
shutting the door is that the door shuts. These results are necessary for
the actions of shooting Smith and shutting the door to take place, but
the facts that Smith is shot and that the door shuts do not imply that
those actions took place, they are not sufficient for them to occur.
What McCann calls the result-problem is that of specifying sufficient
conditions for an action to occur when an event which is necessary for
its occurrence has taken place, or, in McCann's words: 'It is the
problem of providing an account of how it is, when events and
processes qualify as results of human actions, that they do so qualify.'[3]
Besides results, actions can have also consequences. Consequences,
unlike results, 'are not intrinsically tied to the action. Rather, they are
caused by it.'[4] For instance, if the door's shutting wakes John up,
John's being awake is a causal consequence of the action of shutting
the door. McCann's characterization seems to imply that actions do
not cause their results, but only their consequences. Now, the result of
an action A qualifies as such a result if it is caused by (is a causal
consequence of) an action B of the same agent 'which is in some sense
"other" than A.'[5] For instance, Smith's being shot qualifies as a result
of an action A of the agent P if it is caused by an action B of the same
agent, say by P's pulling the trigger. Pulling the trigger does not cause
the *action* of shooting Smith, but the result of that action, and makes it
the result of an action of P, namely P's shooting Smith. But action B
transmits, so to speak, agency to action A by causing its result. That
Jones shot Smith means that Smith's being shot was caused by some
action of Jones, namely by his pulling the trigger. Unless this last
action had taken place, Jones could not be described as shooting
Smith. That this is an action depends, then, on a causally more basic
action of Jones. But then, if this latter action has in turn a result and
requires a causally more basic action to bring about that result, we are
starting the infinite regress we are familiar with, since 'one would have
to bring about an infinite series of further changes in order to bring
about any change or set of changes at all.'[6] Unless we can find a way
out of this regress, there cannot be any actions at all.

Volitions provide this way out. First of all, volitions are thoughts,
are mental processes. As such, they are intentional: they have a
content or intentional object which, according to McCann, is

propositional in character, namely that a result of a specific kind occurs. For example, the volition that causes the result of my action of raising the arm has as its content that the arm's rising occurs. Being propositions, contents are not themselves results, for results are changes or happenings. Since I can will my arm to rise without my arm rising (due, for example, to a paralysis), my arm's rising is not the result of my volition, but only a causal consequence of it. Being thoughts, volitions have no results, but only causal consequences, so that the result-problem does not arise in them and the threat of infinite regress can be prevented. Secondly, volitions, besides being thoughts, are executive, actional in character, they are executive acts with respect to intentions and desires. The content of intentions and desires are descriptions of actions: I have the intention of raising my arm. Volitions execute intentions by bringing about the result of the intended actions, namely the arm's rising in the above example. Volitions are conations or initiations of those movements that, by being so caused, qualify as results of actions. They are, then, the causally more basic actions. Without them, there could not be actions at all, since they transmit agency to other actions by causing their results. Without them, nothing could qualify as the result of an action, and there would be only happenings and no actions.

Volitions are actions because, according to McCann, they share the main intuitive features of actions excepting that of having a result: they are behaviour, they are intentional, we are responsible for them and we control them.

The advantage of McCann's conception of basic actions over Danto's is, apparently, that a volition cannot occur without someone willing, whereas a bodily movement can occur without someone's performing it. If volitions are actions, they are pure actions, involving no happening as a result.

This means that in the case of volitions we do not find a difference between:

(1) Someone wills his arm to move, and
(2) Someone's volition of his arm to move takes place,

because the second sentence has the same content as the first. It does not report a happening, but an action. A volition cannot occur without someone willing. A volition, that is, does not involve essentially a happening. It is a pure action. That is why it can stop the infinite regress. To will one's arm to move is, then, different from moving one's arm in this respect: this latter action essentially involves a happening, and this happening (the movement of the arm) can occur without someone moving the arm. That is why I think that Melden's criticism of volitions, according to which 'there would seem to be a difference between the occurrence of an act of volition and my performing such an act . . . If so, willing the muscle movement is not enough; one must will the willing of the muscle movement, and so on ad infinitum' was not right,[7] as McCann himself points out. But this advantage can be paid for too expensively, for if volitions involve no happening, how can they cause happenings, results of actions such as the rising of one's arm? This is one aspect of the general problem of interactionism between mind and body raised by this kind of theory. Volitions are thoughts, are mental, but they cause movements of the body, which are physical happenings.

McCann's theory was designed to solve the result-problem and the infinite regress implied in it. But it seems to give rise to a much more difficult one: the classical problem of interactionism. But are volitions really purely mental actions? Volitions are thoughts, McCann says. But let us quote some of their other features: 'Volition', McCann points out, 'is execution: to will the occurrence of a change is to enter upon the act of bringing it about.'[8] And later we read: 'Especially useful [as evidence of the existence of volitions, C.M.] is the testimony of victims of paralysis as to what they do in trying to perform bodily movements. Such attempts appear to consist in volitional acts, in which case volitional theory is the key to solving this puzzle about action too.'[9] Now, if a volition is 'entering upon the act', is 'trying to perform bodily movements', it cannot be in the same sense a thought having a content: it is merely the initiation of the act, it is an act in the *same sense* in which to move one's body is. Volitions are the performing of the first stages of the movement, and so they involve physical happenings. An analogue of the case of paralysis is the situation in which we are trying to raise a very heavy weight without succeeding: if what we are performing here are volitions, then we are calling physical efforts, contracting of muscles and so on, volitions. If we do not exercise our physical strength, we are not 'entering upon the act' of getting the weight raised. Of course, our thoughts are perhaps concentrated on the weight, on its resistance, on our pulling. This can also be an aspect of 'entering upon the act' of raising the weight, but surely it is not the same thing as pulling and exercising our strength. To put both things together and to label that composite 'volition' does not succeed in making the idea of a pure mental action causing physical happenings intelligible. So, volitions can only solve the result-problem if they do not involve physical happenings; but if they do not involve physical happenings they cannot be 'executive'; to be executive, volitions have to involve essentially physical happenings; and if they do, then the result-problem remains open. In the case of raising the weight, the physical happenings involved – tensing of muscles, etc. – can also occur with no action, as a result of a spasm. Only by viewing volitions as thoughts can we avoid this regress; but then the weight will remain where it is for ever (leaving aside telekinesia), that is, no happening will be caused by volitions and no action will be performed. Setting about acting ('entering upon the act', 'executing') is a physical process and involves physical happenings as results, even if the process is not completed; otherwise one is not setting oneself to act, but merely thinking of it or having the intention to do so. And postulating new volitions that make those happenings the results of actions will only take the problem one step back.

2.2 Brian O'Shaughnessy: Trying, Mind and Body

O'Shaughnessy shares with McCann the view that most actions are related to non-actional events or, as he says, 'act-neutral events' such as arm-risings. He shares also the view that the occurrence of these act-neutral events is never sufficient for an action to be performed. So, what is specific about actions is just that they are the bringing about of those events by an agent. 'All physical action involves the bringing about of act-neutral bodily events.'[10] An action is never identical with the occurrence of these act-neutral bodily events, it is the bringing about of these events. Now, there is a sense in which these events can at any time fail to occur. This basic uncertainty is concealed by the general reliability of the world, of which the fact that usually our bodies do not fail is only one aspect. And this general reliability of the world conceals also the fact that, whenever we perform a physical action, we *try* to perform that action, and that trying is just what *we* contribute to the action, the rest being up to the world. We are not omnipotent, but we are not completely powerless either; acting is something other than the occurrence of happenings, and in acting we contribute to that occurrence by *trying*.

The same event of trying occurs both when we fail and when we succeed in bringing about the act-neutral event. This presence of trying is concealed by the fact that we generally succeed, so that we reserve the word 'trying' only for those cases where we failed or where failure was foreseeable. But since failure is always a possibility, we also try when we succeed. 'Consider the case of a man who believes but is not quite certain that his arm is paralyzed; suppose him asked at a signal to try and raise his arm. At the given signal he tries, and to his surprise the arm moves; but a moment later he tries again and thinks he has succeeded, only to discover on looking down that he has failed.'[11] Now O'Shaughnessy contends that in both cases there was an episode of trying which was an event, an action and an event-action of the same kind, namely of the kind captured by the description 'trying to raise his arm': 'On each occasion that description has application, and the agent knows so independently of knowing whether his arm moved.'[12]

Therefore, in the dubious paralytic's case, 'the same act-event occurred, both when the arm rose and when it did not. Therefore, trying and arm rising must be *two* events and two *distinct* events. But now trying must rate as a psychological event . . . Therefore, when this man succeeded in raising his arm, a psychological event, freely chosen and intended, occurred side by side with another event, a distinct event, a merely physical and act-neutral event, the event of arm rising.'[13] The same thing applies, according to O'Shaughnessy, to the case of normal physical action. Now, this is what raising one's arm, when this is an action, and an intentional one, involves: 'When a man intentionally raises his arm, trying to raise the arm causes the act-neutral event of arm rising . . . I think we can take this to be the sense of the perfectly harmless and intuitively obvious truth, that, when a man raises his arm by intent, then *he* brings about the movement of his arm. We can now say *how* he brings this about: it is by trying.'[14] These last words show that tryings play quite a similar role to McCann's volitions. Being what we ultimately do in bringing about the event of arm rising, they are also the causally basic actions we perform. We raise the arm *by* trying to raise it. Even if O'Shaughnessy does not refer to the result-problem, I think it is fair to say that tryings parallel volitions in being supposed answers to that problem.

Trying shows the following features: it is an event; it is an action; it is mental in showing intentionality, that is, directedness towards a content; it is an intentional action ('. . . if I tried to perform an intentional action, then I must have intended to try');[15] and, finally, it is essentially a cause of a bodily event.

Being mental, and having physical effects, trying is the point where mind reaches the body, a mental 'pineal gland': '. . . Trying, in being essentially a cause of a physical phenomenon *and* a linchpin of consciousness, serves as a crucial bridge function between mind and body, not unlike that allotted by Descartes to the pineal gland.'[16] Trying relates to the rest of the mind via its relation to intending. This relation can be expressed by a psycho-psychic law of this form: 'If a man at an instant in time realizes that that instant is an instant at which he intends to perform action x, then logically necessarily he begins trying to do x at that very moment of realization.'[17] On the other hand, trying relates to the bodily event in terms of psycho-physical laws of this form: 'In a body in a normal state, world permitting, necessarily trying is a sufficient condition of arm rising.'[18] According to this model, this is how the act of intentionally raising one's arm can be analysed: 'The act of raising an arm is a complex event constituted out of two causally linked simultaneous events that were "made for each other"',[19] namely an event of trying and an event of arm rising.

This completes our exposition of O'Shaughnessy's views. Now, we can go on to disentangle and criticize them.

First of all, I think that the notion of trying, as characterized by O'Shaughnessy, makes sense only if applied to bodily movements, to basic actions in Danto's sense. As a matter of fact, O'Shaughnessy discusses mainly this case, but there are in his paper hints that other, non-basic actions are envisaged. The psycho-psychic law speaks about 'action x', and this presumably ranges over more than merely moving the body. And, on the other hand, one of his examples concerns the situation of starting a car, which is a non-basic action. As I said, I think that his notion does not apply to this last kind of action. The reason is that 'trying to . . .', when it is followed by a description of a non-basic action, itself describes an action in the ordinary sense, not an episode of trying as characterized by O'Shaughnessy. For instance, trying to start a car is doing such things as taking the key, putting it into the lock, turning it, etc. And if trying to start a car is identical to those actions, it is not an extra action beyond them. So, trying in O'Shaughnessy's sense can only be trying to move one's body. In other words, the 'intentional object' of O'Shaughnessy's tryings can only be (descriptions of) bodily movements. This restriction is strange enough, since it does not apply to other intentional states, such as intentions, desires or beliefs. And it does not apply to tryings in the ordinary sense either, for besides trying to move my body I certainly can try to start a car or to sing a song. 'Trying', in O'Shaughnessy's sense, cannot mean what it ordinarily means, it is a new kind of intentional state. But in this technical sense it cannot be what is referred to in the psycho-psychic law. This law assigns the same intentional object ('action x') to the intention and the trying. But, as objects of intentions can be much wider than moving our bodies, if the object of the intention is the object of the trying, 'trying' cannot have, in the psycho-psychic law, the meaning O'Shaughnessy gives to it, but its ordinary meaning, according to which trying to do something is acting intentionally so that, world permitting, one can achieve what one intends to, for instance starting the car. Trying, then, as characterized in the psycho-psychic law, is just doing those things one believes will lead to the intended result or to the intended action. This intended result or intended action, namely the object of the intention, is also the object of those acts by which one tries to achieve it. And if the intended action is to move (a part of) one's body, as it sometimes is, trying is just starting intentionally to move (that part of) one's body.

So, as conveyed by the psycho-psychic law, 'trying' means simply acting intentionally or starting so to act. Suppose a man is sitting. He feels a pain in his arm, he feels too warm and a fly is disturbing him. He intends to relieve the pain, to refresh himself and to get rid of the fly by raising his arm. He raises his arm and, in doing so, he is trying to relieve the pain (a), to refresh himself (b) and to put away the fly (c).

Here, trying a, b, and c is raising his arm intentionally. And, if he succeeds, he relieves the pain intentionally, refreshes himself intentionally and gets rid of the fly intentionally. Raising his arm was due to his intention to a, b, and c, and was identical to trying a, b, and c. This does not mean that, besides raising his arm intentionally, he performed three other *particular event-actions* called 'tryings'. He simply tried to achieve three different things with *one* action. This is how trying appears from the point of view of the psycho-psychic law; from this law, it does not follow that there are particular act-events called tryings which are different from and correspond to each of our successful intentional actions. Here, trying a, b, and c were identical to one intentional action, namely raising the arm.

Now, if trying is to be a particular, intentional, internal, psychological act-event, not identical to an intentional, overt action in the ordinary sense, then it can only be trying to move (parts of) one's body. In the above example, since raising the arm was intentional, there must have been another particular act-event of trying, different from trying a, b or c, namely trying to raise the arm, where 'trying' means something different from what it means in 'trying a, b or c'. This different sense of 'trying' is conveyed by the psycho-physical law: 'In a body in a normal state, world permitting, necessarily trying is a sufficient causal condition of arm rising.' Here, 'trying' refers to a particular, internal act-event, uniquely located in time, that causes the arm rising, whereas, from the point of view of the psycho-psychic law, trying, *malgré* O'Shaughnessy, did not identify particular act-events.

In the context of the psycho-physical law, then, trying refers just to an event which exists only as cause of a bodily movement. Does in this context 'trying to raise the arm' refer to a particular, intentional act-event, as O'Shaughnessy asserts? If it refers to a particular, intentional act it refers just to the particular act of raising the arm, or, more exactly, to the first stages of that act, not to an act different from it. Raising the arm is a process. It takes time. It involves thousands of events constituting a causal chain. Trying to raise the arm, if it is an intentional act, is just to initiate this chain intentionally. This is what a paralytic is doing when he is trying to move the arm. Somewhere in the causal chain there is a break, and the arm does not move. If someone, after an accident, tries to move his leg and his leg does not move, this does not mean that, since he is engaged in an activity and he does not move the leg, he is performing some mental act. He is performing *physical* acts, involving physical events, namely those physical acts that, before the accident, would have given rise to the leg's movement. What gives his activity its mental aspect is that he *intends* to move his leg and is *conscious* of his intention and of his efforts, physical efforts, as directed to the intended action of completing the movement of his leg. Between intention and overt physical action we do not need an intermediate trying, for trying is just starting the action.

Well, how do we initiate the chain that ends in the overt movement of our bodies, how do we start the action? We *know how* to initiate the chain, we know how to start the action. We have not learnt how to move the arm, we have been moving the arm from birth and, since we move it from birth we know how to move it. The ability of spontaneous bodily movement is a natural, unlearnt ability in healthy human beings and other animals. And in a *certain sense*, not in the important philosophical sense O'Shaughnessy gives to it, whenever animals and human beings move, they *try* to move. Trying is acting physically. Only when we engage in it as consciously fulfilling an intention does it take the appearance of something psychic. What is psychic is not the trying itself, but the *consciousness* of making an effort *now* directed to some previously *intended* action. The two things are different, for we find this trying in animals, but not consciousness of time nor future-directed intention. In the case of O'Shaughnessy's paralytic, we find both things united. But not by building a composite out of these two things and labelling it 'trying' have we discovered a mental act causing physical movements or a mental 'pineal gland'. Trying is exercising a natural ability to move; and a wounded lion tries to move in the same sense in which an injured person does; trying is starting the movement and all healthy animals know how to do that. But starting the movement *now*, when noticing that now is the time of the *intended* action, involves much more than a natural ability; it is acting intentionally in a strong sense, and most healthy animals cannot do that. While the first sense of 'trying' is conveyed in the psycho-physical law, the second is conveyed in the psycho-psychic law. 'Trying', then, has different senses in O'Shaughnessy's paper and the same meaning is not preserved when we go from the psycho-psychic law to the psycho-physical law. This, of course, destroys its supposed character of a pineal gland.

Trying was meant to refer to a particular, mental act which mediates between intention and action. But, after scrutiny, we have found no such act. In the psycho-psychic law context, trying is simply acting intentionally in the ordinary sense; in the psycho-physical law context, trying is simply starting to move, and so, moving (in its first steps). The latter explains why O'Shaughnessy says, strangely enough, that trying and arm rising are *causally* linked *simultaneous* events. They are simultaneous because trying is just moving, and moving implies logically that something moves.

Neither 'by willing' nor 'by trying', then, provides a satisfactory answer to the regress generated by conceiving actions as bringing about mere happenings. Despite appearances, volitional theories do not go beyond basic actions in Danto's sense, and if these do not solve the result-problem, neither do willing nor trying. If trying is starting to move, this logically implies that something has started to move, which can happen with no action taking place, as is the case with spasms.

In fact, trying to move follows the natural ability to move, and not conversely. Someone who is paralytic from birth cannot try to move. He simply does not know how to try, because he lacks the ability to move. Trying, then, does not identify a mental cause of the movement, but simply points to the fact that, since we move naturally, we know how to start to move. Imagine the following case:[20] from a certain instant on, when we try to raise our right arm, our left arm rises; during some period, when I want to raise my left arm, I try to raise my right arm and my left arm rises; I think, however, that, after that period, we would no longer try to raise our right arm to raise our left one; we simply would try to raise our left arm, that is, trying to raise our right arm would turn simply into trying to raise our left arm. This, if right, shows that trying to move follows our natural ability to move, it does not precede nor cause our movement, it *is* moving, exercising that ability.

2.3 Jennifer Hornsby: Actions Are Tryings

We shall refer briefly to Hornsby's views,[21] for in a sense they develop O'Shaughnessy's insights into tryings and most of the criticisms we made to his views also apply to her's. Hornsby, like McCann and O'Shaughnessy, starts from a view of action which has its roots in the idea of an action as the bringing about or causing of a non-actional event: 'Actions are people's doings of things, and what is done is never an action.'[22] We should seriously doubt whether this view of actions can avoid the infinite regress we have found unsolved in Danto, McCann and O'Shaughnessy. We will find it unsolved in Hornsby as well. Maybe something is wrong with this idea; if nothing else, at least the fact that it begs the question. For, as we saw, the idea that an action is the bringing about of a change is simply false unless corrected with 'by acting'. And then, when it is true, it is question-begging. Besides that, however, it prompts the search for actions at more and more basic levels where no happening is involved, but this search has, up to now, proved useless. In Hornsby's case, this search leads again to tryings:

> We can ask whether there are descriptions of actions so basic that they *are free of any specific commitment to consequences like the body's movings$_1$ or the muscles' contractings$_1$* [My emphasis. The index '$_1$' refers to the intransitive use of the expression, stressing the fact that non-actional events are referred to. C.M.]. Is there any type of events

instances of which can be shown to occur before the muscles contract, and instances of which can be shown to be actions? I shall answer these questions 'Yes' in this chapter. Every action is an event of *trying* or attempting to act, and every attempt that is an action precedes and causes a contraction$_I$ of muscles and a movement$_I$ of the body.[23]

Since an event which causes a contraction$_I$ of muscles and a movement$_I$ of the body occurs presumably inside the body, actions are internal events, in the specific spatial sense that they occur inside the body: 'I do claim that all actions occur inside the body. And that summarizes the principal thesis of this essay.'[24] Hornsby's position, however, is not so eccentric as it might appear to be, since she thinks that the concept of action is a causal one, so that actions are described and attributed in terms of their overt, non-actional effects. So, we can perfectly well say that someone moves his arm or kills someone, even if what we are doing is to describe his action in terms of the effects (the movement of the arm or the death) of the internal event of trying that caused, through several links, those consequences.

Hornsby contends that her position is free from dualistic problems. She departs from McCann and O'Shaughnessy in holding that tryings are physical events: 'Any dualist who wants to introduce a purely mental item into my account of action would need to look back beyond the trying (which is the action, and is something we know is physical) . . . A theory that identifies actions with tryings has no need to posit anything more than physical events.'[25] Now, if tryings are physical, they surely involve non-actional, physical happenings. Hornsby wants her notion of trying to be free of any commitment to consequences like the body's movings$_I$ or the muscles' contractings$_I$. But, if tryings are physical, and they cause the body's movings$_I$ or muscles contractings$_I$, then they are committed at least to, for instance, neurons' firings.$_I$ Are, then, neurons' firings$_I$ actions? Presumably not, because they can occur with no action taking place. But notice what Hornsby says: 'A person's action of ϕ_T-ing [e.g. raising the arm, the index $_T$ stands for "transitive", C.M.] may be identified with an event that causes a ϕ_I-ing [e.g., the arm's rising, C.M.].'[26] Then, according to this claim, we are led to the conclusion that actions can be mere happenings of neurons' firings$_I$, for neurons' firings$_I$ can cause an event of ϕ_I-ing (the arm rising) and, if they do, they are actions. But then, if in a spasm my arm rises and this is caused by some neurons' firings in my brain, then a spasm is an action of raising my arm, which is undoubtedly false. However, it is implied by that claim. We can concede that in a spasm there was no trying. Are we going to say that only those physical events that are tryings and cause ϕ_I-ings are actions? This leaves us with an unanalysed notion of trying which rests upon that of action itself, instead of clarifying it. The idea that actions are tryings does not lead us in that case much further than to the idea that actions are active, and not mere happenings, which is not very illuminating. Are we going to say that actions are the bringing about of such happenings as neurons' firings? Here we are caught in the endless regress we have found before, since neurons' firings can be brought about by no action, and we should find a new action that brings about those happenings, and so on. So, Hornsby's notion of trying has not proved able to avoid the infinite regress that threatens the possibility of actions.

2.4 Summary

The New Volitional Theory has not been able to account for the possibility of the distinction with which we began, namely the distinction between actions and mere happenings. It has not been able to identify actions that do not essentially involve the occurrence of happenings. If volitions and tryings are not physical, we face the problem of interactionism: how can purely mental acts cause physical happenings? If, to avoid this problem, tryings are conceived as physical (Hornsby), then they involve essentially physical happenings or they are even simply identified with physical happenings, so that the distinction between actions and happenings has been destroyed. So far, then, the New Volitional Theory has not been able to solve the regress-problem. Looking for basic actions at deeper and deeper levels, it has found only further happenings which cause our bodies to move. So far, its difference from the old volitional theory has been shown to be a mere appearance.

However, we have learnt something: the deep insight into agency that, despite other problems, we find in some of these works – especially in O'Shaughnessy's – rests, it seems to me, on the correct view that agency relates essentially to the *mind*, that only beings having minds can be agents.

We shall try to exploit these insights from a new starting-point. Before that, however, we shall refer to some questions about the ontology of actions that, even if involved in the problems treated in this chapter, we have left here, for the sake of the argument, untouched.

3

Some Remarks about the Ontology of Actions

Consider, again, a rather bloody example: at a certain instant, John, who takes a gun, moves his finger, pulls the trigger, shoots James, and kills James.

The question is now: how many particular actions did John perform? The answer depends, partly, on the ontological attitude one adopts towards actions. If one is inclined to say that John performed four *particular* actions, namely moving his finger, pulling the trigger, shooting James, and killing James, one is probably inclined to think of particular actions as exemplifications of act-properties by particular agents at particular times and to think that properties are real entities. This ontology contains, then, particular objects (including agents) and abstract objects, namely properties (including act-properties such as pulling triggers or shooting people). One is probably sympathetic with Alvin I. Goldman's views.[1] According to Goldman, a particular act or act-token 'is the exemplifying of an act-property by an agent at a particular time'.[2] Moving one's finger, pulling triggers, shooting people, killing people, are act-properties. In the above example, these properties are exemplified by John's moving his finger, pulling the trigger, shooting James, and killing James. These exemplifications are different act-tokens or particular actions of John, according to Goldman's criterion of individuation of particular actions: 'Two act-tokens are identical if and only if they involve the same agent, the same property, and the same time.'[3] In the above example, those four act-tokens are not identical, for, even if they involve the same agent and (perhaps) the same time, they do not involve the same property. None the less, these four acts are closely connected by a relationship of causal generation. Each act-token (except one) is causally generated by a previous one, and the order in which they causally generate and are causally generated can be discovered by testing which 'by'-relations hold between them. For instance, if 'John shot James by pulling the trigger' is true, but 'John pulled the trigger by shooting James' is not, then pulling the trigger causally generates shooting James, but not conversely. The relation of causal generation holds between two act-tokens when the first causes an effect which is necessary for the second one to be performed. In McCann's terms, an effect which is necessary for an act to be performed is the result of that act. So, the relation holds between two act-tokens when the first one causes the result of the second. For instance, John's shooting James causally generates John's killing James in that it causes James's death. The relation of causal generation is asymmetric, irreflexive and transitive.[4] It is asymmetric: if act-token A causally generates act-token B, this latter does not causally generate the former. It is irreflexive: act-token A does not causally generate itself. It is transitive: if act-token A causally generates act-token B, and act-token B causally generates act-token C, act-token A causally generates act-token C. In our example, then, from Goldman's point of view, there are four act-tokens, or particular actions, of John, united by a relation of causal generation: John's moving his finger causally generates John's pulling the trigger, which causally generates John's shooting James, which causally generates John's killing James. In terms of the 'by'-relation: John kills James by shooting him, shoots him by pulling the trigger, and pulls the trigger by moving the finger. This last is a basic action. Moving the finger is not causally generated by any other action.

We can represent this in a diagram: the diagonal line (\) means 'causes', the vertical arrow (↑) expresses the relationship between an act and its result, and the horizontal arrow (→) means 'causally generates':

John moves the finger	→	John pulls the trigger	→	John shoots James	→	John kills James	*Act-tokens*
\		↑	\	↑	\	↑	
		the trigger's pulling		James's being shot		James's death	*Effects*

This diagram corresponds, roughly, to McCann's conception, except that in McCann's case there would be a different basic action starting the chain, namely John's willing that his finger moves, an action with no result 'by which' John brings about or causes his finger's moving, which so qualifies as a result of an action of John, namely John's moving his finger.

In Danto's case, however, things would be rather different. The causal relation expressed by the diagonal line would hold between the actions themselves. The basic action of John's moving his finger would cause the non-basic action of John's pulling the trigger, and so on.

According to another view, held notably by Donald Davidson (who is indebted to G. E. M. Anscombe) our example would be analysed differently. John would not have performed four particular actions, but only one, which we can describe truly in four different ways, according to its effects. This analysis rests on a different ontology, which contains, besides particular objects (including agents), particular events (including actions). A particular action is not the exemplifying of a property, but a particular, spatiotemporally located, unrepeatable event, which can receive several descriptions, some of which are, characteristically, in terms of its effects. The idea, to apply this to our example, is that after having pulled the trigger (or, for that matter, after having moved his finger) John did not perform any other particular action in order to shoot James and to kill him. Simply, what he did had as causal consequences that a trigger got pulled, that a bullet entered James's body and that James died, and because it had these consequences we can say that John pulled the trigger, shot James, and killed him.

We do not need a relation of 'causal generation', but only an ordinary causal relation holding between particular events. The diagram would take this form (the arrow ($\rightarrow$) means 'causes' and the vertical arrow ($\uparrow$) can be read as 'allows the description'):

'John moves his finger'	'John pulls the trigger'	'John shoots James'	'John kills James	*Action-description*
$\uparrow$	$\uparrow$	$\uparrow$	$\uparrow$	
John's finger's moving	$\rightarrow$ the trigger's moving	$\rightarrow$ James's being shot	$\rightarrow$ James's death	*Effects*

We should recall that the action is conceived as a particular, spatiotemporally located event, with the same merit as a particular physical object ('that table there'). If we forget that, we will find it very strange that John's pulling the trigger should be the same action as John's killing James. We could ask: well, if pulling a trigger and killing someone are not the same thing, how can those two actions be the same? If we recall that John's action is a particular event, this should be no problem. Being square and being yellow are not the same thing. But this does not imply that one and the same particular table cannot be both square and yellow. In the same sense, one and the same particular event, John's action, can be both a pulling of a trigger and a shooting of James. The question was confusing properties and particulars.

Equally, Davidson's conception does not amount to saying that, for example, playing the piano, building a house, reading or signing a contract *reduce* to moving our bodies, to basic actions. From the fact that what John did can be described as moving his finger it does not follow that the rest of the descriptions can be reduced to this, any more than from the fact that a particular table can be described as square it follows that the rest of its properties can be reduced to its form. Even if each particular action can be described in terms of bodily movements, this does not imply that actions are 'simply' or 'nothing but' bodily movements. But, conversely, all this in turn does not affect the fact that a particular action can be (described as) a bodily movement, nor the fact (if it is one) that, as the diagram suggests, in tracing back the causal consequences of something done by someone, we can always find a bodily movement.

The decisive point seems to be, then, the ontological question concerning actions and events as true particulars, that is, the contention that, besides persons and physical objects, the world contains also such things as shootings, strollings and storms. The main Davidsonian arguments favouring the existence of events are semantic ones. According to him, we need to quantify over events to give a correct account of the logical form of action sentences, especially those that involve adverbial modification, as well as to make sense of causal speech. I cannot enter into a detailed exposition of his arguments. I shall restrict myself to some remarks about action sentences.

Consider this sentence:

'John was walking absent-mindedly at seven.'

This simple action sentence poses a lot of problems to a conception such as Goldman's. According to his view, this sentence would say that there is a property (Goldman needs quantification over properties), namely walking, such that John exemplified that property at seven. But what about 'absent-mindedly'? It seems that walking absent-mindedly is not the same property as walking. Then, this sentence would say, besides, that there is another property, namely walking absent-mindedly, such that John exemplified that property at seven. Then, since we have two properties, John was doing two different things, namely walking *and* walking absent-mindedly. This seems quite strange, indeed. Perhaps Goldman could avoid this by treating 'walking' as a three-place predicate; one place for the agent, another for the manner, and another for the time. But then he faces another problem. From 'John was walking absent-mindedly at seven' we can infer 'John was walking.' However, if we take 'walking' as a three-place predicate, this inference cannot be made. Davidson's suggestion is that we can cope with both difficulties by holding that this sentence says the following: that there was a particular event which was a walking, was by John, was absent-mindedly carried out, and took place at seven. We quantify over events, not properties. And by so doing we avoid the conclusion that John was performing two particular and different actions and we justify the desired and obvious inference from 'John was walking absent-mindedly at seven' to 'John was walking.' Davidson's idea is that the sentence deals with a particular event, of which many things are asserted, just as a sentence like 'this table is white and square' deals with a particular object, of which many things are predicated. From 'this table is white and square' we can infer 'this table is white'; and from 'John was walking absent-mindedly' we can infer 'John walked.' Both sentences deal with (quantify over) particulars, a particular table and a particular walk.

Besides this, the context where we typically speak about what was done intentionally and what was not – contexts of justifications, excuses and responsibility – are those in which, according to Davidson, we have to take seriously the idea of one and the same particular action having several descriptions. Suppose that, in the example with which we began, after shooting James and killing him, John starts crying 'I did not know the gun was loaded.' John is saying that he moved his finger and pulled the trigger intentionally, but that he did not shoot James nor kill him intentionally. This does not mean that besides moving his finger and pulling the trigger there was another action, that of doing it intentionally, which was not present in shooting James and killing James. It means that John, in pulling the trigger, did not know he was shooting James, because he believed the gun was unloaded. It means that <u>his action, what he did, was intentional under some descriptions and unintentional under other descriptions. For Davidson, the notion of 'intentional action' is not extensional, that is, it does not determine a *class* of particular act-events. To be intentional is not a property of actions, but only of actions under descriptions</u>. 'How many intentional actions did John perform?' cannot be answered in the sense in which 'How many actions did John perform?' can. The answer to the latter question is: one, with many causal consequences, and so, with many descriptions. But if the answer to the latter question is 'one', the answer to the former cannot be 'two', for this would be inconsistent. The answer is: his action was intentional under two descriptions. The same applies to the locution 'trying to x'. It is not extensional, and does not succeed in identifying a class of particular events. In our example, John was trying to move the finger and to pull the trigger, but not to shoot James or to kill him. This, incidentally, explains some of the difficulties we found in O'Shaughnessy's conception of tryings as identifying particular act-events, and the ambiguity we discovered in this notion.

If Davidson's view can cope with some problems, Goldman could reply that his own view is better at dealing with others. Here are some objections that could be raised from a Goldman-like perspective. If actions are particulars, uniquely located in time, how can 'John pulled the trigger' and 'John killed James' refer to the same particular action, if the second occurred later than the first? The Davidsonian answer could run on the following lines: what happened later was the event of James's death; this does not mean that the action of killing James occurred also later than the action of pulling the trigger; John's contribution to James's death had finished when he completed his act of pulling the trigger; if James dies as a causal consequence of this action, then this action can receive a new description as 'killing James'; but this does not mean that 'pulling the trigger' and 'killing James' refer to different particular actions; they refer to the same particular act-event, uniquely located in time. The paradox expressed by 'How can John kill James before James dies?' is only apparent. The answer is: by doing something that causes James's death. If what he did caused James's death later, what he did can *then* be described as 'killing James'. But what he did, his action, occurred before that. A second objection can be as follows: if John shoots James by pulling the trigger, but he does not pull the trigger by shooting James, that is, if the relation of causal generation is asymmetrical, how can both be descriptions of the same particular action? They must be describing different act-tokens. Let us quote Anscombe to answer: 'One might as well argue that because the US President is the US Commander-in-Chief by being President, while the Commander-in-Chief is not the President by being the Commander-in-Chief, the President and the Commander-in-Chief can't be the same man.'[5]

If McCann's ontological views (and, perhaps, O'Shaughnessy's) are akin to a Goldman-like perspective, Hornsby's are explicitly Davidsonian. Since there are similarities between McCann, O'Shaughnessy and Hornsby about the nature of actions and, moreover, big differences between Davidson's and Hornsby's views of agency and actions, this suggests that ontological theses about actions ('What kind of entity is an action?') do not have a *direct* bearing on the question of what an action is and what distinguishes actions from mere happenings. Furthermore, while Davidson and Goldman disagree quite deeply about the ontological status of actions, their views about what an action is show important similarities: both share a causal theory of action, for instance. Questions about ontology and questions about the nature of agency are largely independent. From a Davidsonian perspective, for instance, since both actions and happenings are particular events, their distinction is still to be dealt with. Equally, from a Goldman-like position, if act-tokens are exemplifications of properties, nothing has yet been said about what distinguishes them from other, non-actional exemplifications of properties, such as, for example, a particular storm. The relationship between the two issues is indirect. Davidson, for instance, would contend that a causal conception of actions could not do without (or would do better with) conceiving actions as particular events.

From our point of view, this brief excursus into the ontology of actions will help us in our analysis of agency, by sparing us *ad hoc* digressions when some ontological question is at issue. Let us then go back to the problems we were dealing with, namely the distinction between actions and happenings and its conditions of possibility.

4

Meaningful Actions

What McCann called the 'result-problem', and in general the problem of infinite regress that Danto, McCann, O'Shaughnessy and Hornsby attempted to solve by different conceptions of basic actions, seems to arise because it is said:

(1) That most actions have results, that is, non-actional or act-neutral events that are necessary, but *not sufficient*, for the corresponding action to take place.
(2) They are not sufficient because they can also occur while no action has been performed. That my finger rises does not imply that I raised it; I can suffer a spasm. That James dies does not imply that someone killed him.
(3) The proper element of agency in action is, then, the causing or bringing about of that event by an agent.
(4) This causing or bringing about, to avoid the infinite regress, has to be, ultimately, a pure action, with no result, that is, an action essentially involving no specific happening. Because if it has a result, it would still make sense to ask how (by *doing what*) the agent brought about that result.
(5) These pure actions will be the basic actions we perform. Without them there would be no actions at all.

It is clear that Danto's notion of basic action, even if useful in some respects, does not fulfil these requirements, for basic actions in Danto's sense have results that can occur non-actionally, namely bodily movements₁. McCann's volitions are purely mental actions, but this view faces the problem of dualism, namely how the purely mental can have physical causal consequences. These basic actions can be conceived as physical, as in Hornsby's case, but then they must involve events (neurons' firings, for instance) that could take place with no action being performed. Finally, these basic actions could be conceived as uniting the mental and the physical, as the point where mind and body interact, as is the case with O'Shaughnessy's 'tryings'. But we saw that these 'tryings' did in fact split between ordinary intentional actions and the first stages of bodily movements.

So, in the end, infinite regress has not been avoided by these theories, which, moreover, lead to more and more eccentric and counter-intuitive views of (basic) actions: as acts of will, as mental pineal glands or as events occurring inside the body.

A way out of this puzzle could be found if we were able to identify examples of *ordinary actions essentially involving no specific happenings*. This would allow us to deny the premises that gave rise to this seemingly hopeless regress back to more and more basic actions. If we can identify examples of actions having those characteristics, the appeal to volitions or tryings would no longer be necessary to solve the result-problem. Now, I think *there are such actions*, though, as far as I know, this fact has not been noticed. I am thinking of some of those actions we can call 'meaningful', actions that can be said to have a meaning or a symbolic content, such as bidding in an auction, holding a lecture, voting, making a chess-move, signalling for a turn when driving or greeting a friend. Now, what is the difference between this kind of action and the examples of actions we have been analysing so far, such as raising one's arm or killing someone? These latter actions have results, namely one's arm rising or someone's death, that, being happenings, can occur with nobody's raising his arm or killing someone, so that we need an action by means of which the agent brought about that result. On the contrary, these meaningful actions do not have results in that sense; their 'results' cannot, *strictly speaking*, occur without the action of which they are results being performed, because these 'results' are actions, not mere happenings. An offer, a lecture's having been held, a vote, a chess-move, a signal for a turn, a greeting, are, respectively, the 'results' of making an offer, holding a lecture, voting, making a chess-move, signalling for a turn and greeting a friend. But think that there is no real difference of content between the members of the following pairs of sentences:

(1) – Someone made an offer, and
    – An offer took place
(2) – Someone held a lecture, and
    – A lecture took place

whereas there *is* a real difference of content between the members of the following pairs:

(3) – Someone killed Smith, and
   – Smith's death took place
(4) – Someone raised his arm, and
   – An arm's rising took place.

If the second members of pairs 3 and 4 report happenings that are necessary, but not sufficient, for their first members to be true as descriptions of an action, the second members of 1 and 2 report actions, not happenings, so that their truth entails the truth of the first members. Even if sometimes some movements can be *mistakenly* taken as offers or greetings, they are not such if someone does not make an offer or greet someone. These meaningful actions, then, seem to be pure actions, essentially involving no specific happenings, and they can stop the infinite regress that threatened the possibility of action. Besides that, contrary to volitions or tryings, they are clear-cut, ordinary and intuitive examples of actions. Appealing to these actions can solve simply and straightforwardly the regress-problem that basic actions were unable to solve and can short-circuit the move towards such strange actions as volitions or tryings, for a meaningful action is *not* the bringing about of a happening. An event of signalling for a turn, voting or marrying someone is actional, it refers essentially to an action, whereas an event of one's arm rising does not need to refer to an action. The work that moving the body (Danto), volitions (McCann) or tryings (O'Shaughnessy) were supposed to do, but were not able to do, can be done by these meaningful actions, and be done much better and without the huge costs of those other notions.

Remember that, so far, we have been analysing as paradigms of actions mostly cases that could be understood in terms of bodily movements (basic actions in Danto's sense) and their causal consequences. Killing someone, for instance, is making some movement that causes that person's death, such as, say, moving the finger and pulling the trigger of a gun. In fact, a well-trained non-human animal, able to perform the requisite movements, could kill someone by pulling a gun's trigger. Moreover, with no training, lions, tigers or wolves can kill people. One difference between such actions and meaningful ones is that non-human animals (excepting perhaps extraterrestrial intelligent beings), even if well-trained, cannot, strictly speaking, perform the latter ones. They can, by training, *imitate* the *movements* human beings make when performing them, but they cannot perform them in a strict sense, whereas a lion can, strictly speaking, kill people, and not merely imitate a killing. Meaningful actions seem to be, then, specifically human.

We have said that basic actions in Danto's sense pointed to the fact that unlearnt, natural abilities for spontaneous movement and teleological behaviour, common to human beings and other animals, were natural conditions of agency. With meaningful actions we have reached a different level, not shared by non-human animals. We can give a characterization of meaningful actions that parallels and contrasts with the one we gave of basic actions in chapter 1. First of all, even if each *particular* meaningful action can be given a true description in terms of bodily movements, meaningful actions, as a *type* of actions, do not consist merely of the performing of bodily movements, for a non-human animal whose behaviour could receive that same true description in terms of bodily movements would not be performing that meaningful action. Secondly, how to perform them is something that *can* be explained by linguistic means, such as the rules of elections or of auctions, even if it is not necessary that they are so learnt. This suggests that mastery of certain concepts is involved in their performance. They require learning and socialization. And, thirdly, their performance is subject to rules and norms: besides being able to signal for a turn while driving or to bid, one can do those things rightly or wrongly. Doing them can be right or wrong ('that was not the right moment to bid'), and they can be performed rightly or wrongly ('and, besides that, your bid was stupidly high'). They can be evaluated and criticized from several points of view.

We were saying that the interest of these examples of meaningful actions lies in the fact that the events that are necessary for them to be performed ('making an offer' logically implies 'an offer has taken place') are *also* sufficient ('an offer has taken place' logically implies 'someone made an offer'), that is, they cannot occur without being actions. They are, then, a good starting-point to analyse agency. The conditions that allow the performance of such actions will provide a good insight into the nature of agency.

The interest of meaningful actions could be challenged by an argument based upon Davidson's (and Anscombe's) ontological views about actions. The argument could run on the following lines: think of a particular meaningful action, such as John's signalling for a turn at t by raising his arm; this is a particular act-event; at t, John did not perform two different particular actions, but only one, which can be described as 'raising his arm' and as 'signalling for a turn'; then, his signalling for a turn at t was (identical to) his raising his arm at t; you contended that the results of meaningful actions could not occur without there being an action of which they are results; but John's raising his arm at t has the result that his arm rises, and this can occur with no action of raising the arm being performed; and, since John's raising his arm at t was (identical to) his signalling for a turn at t, it seems that this meaningful action has a result that can occur with no action being performed.

The proper answer to be given is this: results of actions, according to McCann's definition, are events that are necessary, but not sufficient, for those actions whose results they are; if, however, in a Davidsonian vein, we take actions to be particulars, then results are properly events that are necessary for certain *descriptions* to be true of someone's action; according to McCann's definition, the arm's rising is not the result of John's action under the description 'signalling for a turn'; it is not necessary for such a description to be true of John's action, since, for instance, John can signal for a turn by switching on a flashing light; John's arm's rising is the result of John's action under the description 'raising his arm'; there is, instead, no specific happening that must occur for the description 'signalling' to be true of John's action; the only event that is necessary for the truth of this description is a signal by John; this event, however, is not a result, for it cannot occur without John's signalling; it is not only necessary, but also sufficient for that description of John's action to be true, and, therefore, it is not a result, according to the definition given; the argument, then, does not succeed in falsifying our claim.

Nevertheless, the argument reveals a temptation to make of Davidson's ontological claims more than they are, namely a tool for reducing actions to bodily movements (basic actions in Danto's sense), and so to turn those ontological claims into contentions about the nature of actions as being 'nothing but' bodily movements. Of course, if actions are 'nothing but' or 'ultimately' or 'in the last instance' bodily movements, my claim about meaningful actions will not hold, since meaningful actions are actions, and bodily movements have results that can occur without one's moving the body. This temptation can be encouraged even by some Davidsonian texts such as the following: 'We must conclude, perhaps with a shock of surprise, that our primitive actions, the ones we do not do by doing something else, mere movements of the body – these are all the actions there are. We never do more than move our bodies: the rest is up to nature.'[1] I think, then, that even though something was said in the preceding chapter, it is worth showing in more detail that Davidson and Anscombe's ontological claims do not imply reductionist consequences.

The claim that actions are particular events, and that one and the same action can have several descriptions, among which we will find one in terms of bodily movements, is not intended to mean that there is a privileged description of actions – namely their descriptions as bodily movements – that gives the 'real' nature of actions. I think that this non-reductionist view is the one intended by Anscombe and Davidson, despite other differences between them. Let us quote Anscombe:

> I have on occasion stared dumbly when asked: 'If one action can have many descriptions, what is *the* action, which has all those descriptions?' The question seemed to suppose to mean something,

but I could not get hold of it. It ought to have struck me at once that here we were in 'bare particular' country: *what* is the subject, which has all these predicates? The proper answer to 'What is the action, which has all these descriptions?' is to give one of the descriptions. Any one, it does not matter which; or perhaps it would be best to offer a choice, saying 'Take whichever you prefer'.[2]

I think this quotation is expressive enough of the non-reductionist aim of Anscombe's claim. The claim, however, gives rise to identity-statements that can generate confusions. Think of an example of meaningful action: at t, A extends his arm out of the car's window and signals for a turn. Anscombe and Davidson would claim that A has not performed two actions, but only one, which can be described as 'extending his arm' and as 'signalling for a turn'. But this can also be expressed in identity statements, namely that A's extending his arm and A's signalling for a turn are the same action, or that A's extending his arm is (identical with) A's signalling for a turn. So stated, the claim can begin to raise problems. One may wonder how both actions can be the same, since not every extending of one's arm is a signalling for a turn. And from this wondering there is only one step to thinking that the claim is reductionist. But in the premises that led to this conclusion there was a confusion, namely the confusion between sense and reference. That A's extending his arm (at t) is A's signalling for a turn (at t) means only that both descriptions *refer* to the same particular action, not that both descriptions mean the same or have the same *sense*. This latter claim is reductivistic; the former is not. The difference between the two claims can be shown easily in this example: if someone says 'A black horse was the winner of the last Grand National' he is not saying that 'black horse' means 'winner of the last Grand National', but only that both descriptions refer to the same particular animal. And if one is worried about how A's extending his arm (at t) can be A's signalling for a turn (at t), one should also be worried about how a black horse can be the winner of the last Grand National.

This answer is, I think, right, but it is a bit tricky, since it conceals the fact that the identification of actions is far less clear than the identification of objects. If someone were in doubt about what I was referring to when saying that it was a black horse and the winner of the last Grand National, I could bring the animal in question to that person and tell him: 'to *this*'. But no similar proceeding would be available if someone were in doubt about what I was referring to when saying that it was an extending of the arm and a signalling for a turn, if not for any other reason at least for the reason that the action in question, but not the animal, is now over. But, leaving this aside, if we accept that actions are particulars – and we were referring briefly to some arguments in favour of this in the preceding chapter – the answer is all right. It points also to a related mistake or confusion lying behind that worry: the confusion between types and tokens (or between properties and particulars). Two *different* action-types (namely extendings of arms and signallings for turns) can be instantiated by the *same* action-token or particular action (A's action at t), just as two different properties (such as being a black horse and being the winner of the Grand National) can be possessed by the same particular (the animal in question). Now, Anscombe and Davidson's claim is *not* intended to involve the identity between types of actions. It says only that one and the same particular action can fall under different action-types (and so have different descriptions). This claim does not imply, so understood, that, say, playing chess is (or is nothing but) moving pieces of wood, but only that *in some concrete circumstances* and on some particular occasions, moving a certain piece of wood *is* a chess-move.[3]

Anscombe and Davidson's ontological claims do not imply that meaningful actions are (nothing but) bodily movements. Therefore, they do not threaten my contention about meaningful actions and I can consistently accept those claims and make this contention, keeping in mind that results of actions are events that are necessary for certain *descriptions* of a particular action to be true.

Of course, if we think of particular actions in Goldman's vein, as *being* exemplifications of properties, to say that A's extending his arm at t is identical to A's signalling for a turn at t will *ipso facto* lead to an identification of these act-properties or act-types and will have reductionist consequences. Goldman can avoid reductionism by saying that in extending his arm at t and in signalling for a turn at t, A has performed *two particular actions*. Davidson and Anscombe can avoid reductionism with no need to say that. I think that Davidson and Anscombe's position has many advantages over Goldman's and is better at solving problems. So, I accept that position.

My contention about meaningful actions as being able to stop the infinite regress is an indirect criticism of the need for basic actions in order to account for the possibility of any actions at all. Viewing any action as receiving its actional character from a basic action distorts the character of agency in that it puts the very core of agency in what is simply a natural condition of it: the unlearnt ability for spontaneous and teleological behaviour. That emphasis on basic actions favours the view that moving the body is the paradigm of action. In Danto's theory, the focus on basic actions as the very source of agency goes hand in hand with a positivistic view of actions as built up out of these elementary action-atoms, and Danto himself pointed to the parallel between the role basic actions play in the theory of action and the role elementary propositions play in a positivistic theory of knowledge.[4] My own view is that actions are holistic phenomena and that we get a better insight into their nature by starting from high-level actions, such as meaningful ones. My criticism of the need for basic actions also involves a criticism of volitional theories in so far as these insist on elementary 'actions' (volitions, tryings) as being the source of the actional character of any other actions. We do not need volitions or tryings in order tó account for the possibility of actions. Meaningful actions play much better the role that volitions or tryings were supposed – but were not able – to play. Finally, my criticism of the need for basic actions also involves an indirect undermining of causal theories of action. As we shall see, causal theories of action view actions in terms of their typical causes: actions are those items of behaviour that are caused by certain antecedent events, characteristically beliefs and desires. This being so, basic actions, being bodily movements, are reasonably simple physical events to be included in a causal scheme, especially if we conceive beliefs and desires, at the same time, in physicalistic terms, as being neurophysiological states. This is why basic actions, in Danto's sense, have a relevant place in some causal conceptions of action.

Now, in order to account for meaningful actions in a causal frame, basic actions – in Danto's sense – must be shown to play an especially relevant role in them. The problem, however, is that, even if certain bodily movements are needed to perform a meaningful action, bodily movements, and in general physical happenings, are not essentially involved in them in the way in which they are in such actions as raising one's arm (the arm rising) or in killing someone (someone's death). Even if one signals for a turn by raising the arm, the arm rising is not essential for the action of signalling, for one can signal in many other ways. Recall how Goldman and Davidson would analyse an action such as John shooting James at t. Leaving aside their differences in ontological views, the notion of basic action plays an essential role both in Goldman's and in Davidson's view of such an example. For Goldman, John's action of shooting James at t is causally generated from a *basic action* of John, through a chain of intermediate actions and results. For Davidson, this action is identical to a *basic action* of John, which we describe as John shooting James by focusing on one of its effects. But this pattern does not seem to work in the case of a particular meaningful action such as Jack's signalling for a turn at t. From a Goldman-like perspective, signalling for a turn was not causally generated from extending the arm in the way in which John shooting James could have been causally generated by John pulling the trigger or moving the finger. From a Davidsonian perspective, John signalling for a turn at t, even if it is identical to John extending the arm at t, does not seem to receive that description from an effect of the arm's extension.

The most outstanding attempt to maintain an especially relevant place for basic actions in meaningful ones is Goldman's notion of conventional generation. According to Goldman, even if meaningful actions are not *causally* generated from basic actions, they are none the less *conventionally* generated from them. So, Goldman would analyse meaningful actions in essentially the same terms as instrumental actions such as shooting someone, and would maintain for the notion of basic action the same *special* relevance in both cases. We can then analyse Goldman's view of meaningful actions in order to see if it succeeds in displaying what is involved in them.

According to Goldman, an act-token such as A's signalling for a turn at t generates from a basic act-token such as A's extending his arm at t by means of a convention. Or, in other terms, A's extending his arm at t conventionally generates A's signalling for a turn at t. 'Conventional generation', Goldman points out, 'is characterized by the existence of rules, conventions, or social practices in virtue of which an act A' [say, signalling for a turn, C.M.] can be ascribed to an agent S, given his performance of another act, A [say, extending his arm, C.M.].'[5] This allows Goldman to trace back meaningful actions into basic ones, since at the end of a chain of conventional generation we find a basic action (in Danto's sense, that is, a moving of the body). So, actions such as shooting someone and actions such as signalling for a turn receive a parallel treatment, being given a common foundation in basic actions.

According to this position, then, a convention makes it possible that, by extending his arm out of the car's window, A be signalling for a turn. What kind of convention will do the trick? Well, a convention establishing that extending one's arm out of the car's window will mean or has to be interpreted as signalling for a turn. In Goldman's words: ' "Extending one's arm out the car window while driving counts as signalling for a turn." This rule indicates that the significance or force of extending one's arm out the car window is that of signalling for a turn.'[6] Fine. 'Convention' is here understood in an ordinary sense, as an agreement, tacit or explicit, which in principle could be replaced or modified. For instance, one fine day several people sit around a table and agree that extending one's arm, etc., will mean signalling for a turn. They publish it in a booklet and that rule is from then on taught in every driving school. And now it seems that that convention generates, from a basic action or bodily movement, a meaningful action. Basic actions are still the source of all subsequent actions, including meaningful ones. Thanks to that convention A can now signal for a turn by extending his or her arm, and every driver can.

But, unfortunately for this nice picture, something has been left out of their booklet, something has been forgotten. Nowadays, drivers extend their arms out of their car windows and 'signal' for a turn. But, when the junction comes, they drive straight on. It seems then that a new 'convention' should be added to the effect that when one signals for a turn by extending the arm one ought to turn. But that is not a convention in the same sense in which the first was. To see this, consider that the first convention could well be changed. It could be established that signalling for turns should be done by, say, showing a red piece of wood. But the second 'convention' could not be changed by establishing that signalling for a turn will not *commit* the one who signals to do the turn. This would not be a new convention about how to signal for a turn, but simply a destruction of the action of signalling for a turn. 'Signalling for a turn' would lose its *meaning* under the new 'convention' and that would amount to the non-existence of that kind of action. But that means that signalling for a turn, as a meaningful action, is not generated from a basic action by means of a convention, as Goldman holds, but, on the contrary, it must have a meaning before any sense can be made of a convention in Goldman's (that is, in its ordinary) sense. So, it is a convention, in the sense of being a mere result of an agreement, that extending one's arm counts as signalling for a turn, but it is *not* a convention that signalling for a turn *commits* one to make the turn. The convention requires, for its mere possibility, that this second relationship holds. What I am contending is that the notion of commitment is logically prior to the notion of convention, in that it does not make sense to speak about establishing a convention if people are not able to commit themselves to future actions. So, if a meaningful action involves commitment, we cannot account for it by appealing to conventions. A meaningful action, then, cannot be 'generated' from a basic action plus a convention in any illuminating sense.[7]

Meaningful actions imply, then, the existence of subjects able to *commit* themselves to do things *in the future*. I shall contend that this notion of commitment is essential to our notion of agency and to the important sense of the distinction between actions and happenings. It constitutes an essential part of our idea of ourselves as agents, as beings who are able to change the world and not mere victims of its evolution. And the reason why it cannot be accounted for in terms of basic actions is that it is a *normative* notion. If I signal for a turn and do not turn, I am doing something *wrong*. And nothing in the natural ability of human beings for spontaneous and teleological movement can account for this evaluation.

If the performing of meaningful actions involves commitments, we can begin to understand why meaningful actions are pure actions, essentially involving no happenings. Part of the point in conceiving some actions as the bringing about of happenings is that these happenings could take place as mere effects of other happenings. But there is no specific happening whose occurrence is necessary for an action of signalling for a turn to be performed. Now, a signalling for a turn is essentially an action in that it involves a commitment to make the turn, and a commitment is not a happening nor *a fortiori* a happening that could take place as an effect of other happenings: it is essentially actional, it has to be *done* by an agent, and by an agent who is conscious of his or her being so. And here lies also the reason why meaningful actions do not receive their actional character from basic actions. The mere ability to perform basic actions – the natural ability for spontaneous, that is, not learnt movement – is not sufficient to ensure the ability to perform meaningful actions. If meaningful actions involve commitments, in order to perform them an agent must also possess a sense of coherence and of being subject to norms. Think of an auction. Completely paralysed persons can bid if they find the way to make it known that they commit themselves to pay the agreed price. But clearly mad persons, even if they raise their arms in an orthodox way, say by imitating other people, even if they retain all of their ability for spontaneous movement, cannot be bidding; the fact that they are mad excludes them from bidding, in so far as it excludes their ability to commit themselves to act in a way that is coherent with what they are doing now. For this same reason, I do not think that Davidson can be right in saying that we never do more than move our bodies and that the rest of the actions we ascribe to people are actional descriptions of effects of those basic actions. This Davidsonian claim was made, we should recall, in the context of a reflection upon the relationship between an action and its causal consequences. And I think that it cannot be transferred to the case of meaningful actions. It can be plausible to consider the action of stopping the car as being really an actional description of a causal consequence of pressing the pedal, and, in the end, of moving one's leg, but it is not plausible to consider the action of signalling for a turn as being really an actional description of a causal consequence of extending one's arm. If it were really true that moving our bodies is the only thing we do, we could not perform meaningful actions. If, besides the ability to move spontaneously and teleologically, we did not have the ability to commit ourselves to do things in the future, we could not be doing such things as signalling for a turn or bidding. So, unless we are prepared to deny that human beings can do such things, we should concede that they are able to do something other than move their bodies and cause changes with these movements, namely – at least – to commit themselves to act in definite ways in the future. And committing ourselves is something we do, and we do it in many ways, either implicitly or explicitly. It is an activity and is essentially so.

So, the appeal to meaningful actions has allowed us to find quite an elegant and simple way out of the regress-problem that threatened the possibility of actions, by identifying actions that do not essentially involve happenings. Volitions and tryings are not needed to account for the possibility of actions. Our strategy will be to examine what is implied in meaningful actions in order to find a clue to what characterizes actions in general. This will be our concern in the next chapter.

Let us close the present chapter with two remarks.

First, I suggest that our ability to commit ourselves to do things in the future is an essential part of agency and of our consciousness of being agents. If that is true, agency cannot possibly be analysed or reduced to mere events, since only persons, beings having minds, can have such an ability. It is *me* who is committing myself to do something, and nôt something that happens in me, even if what happens can and should have a bearing on my engaging in one direction or another, and so it is me who is the source of those future actions. This is the real point behind Chisholm's notion of agent causation,[8] according to which it is the agent himself, and not his motives, desires or whatever, who is the cause of his actions.

Second, one might be tempted to say that, after all, without basic actions there could not be meaningful ones, and so, if basic actions can be shown to collapse into non-actional events, so can meaningful ones as well. This argument, however, is a *non sequitur*, for it goes from a causal sense to a conceptual sense of 'condition'. That suitable causal relations governing our motion hold is something we suppose or take for granted when we engage in meaningful actions. And the failure of this condition is not a mistake in the performance of the action (think of someone who, after signalling for a turn, gets suddenly paralysed). This shows that the condition does not belong to the nature of that kind of action, even though many actions we perform would lose their point if the failure were not to be the exception. It is in this sense that we, as agents, depend on nature and are powerless against a sudden reversal of certain natural relations. But these are not constitutive of meaningful actions in the way in which norms and commitments are. This difference shows itself also in the 'multiple realizability' of meaningful actions: a person unable to extend his or her arm can still be signalling for a turn by other means, but a person who is unable to understand what a norm is cannot. Basic actions are instrumental to meaningful actions; norms are not.

5

Agency and Intentional Action

In this chapter we are trying to move from the notion of meaningful action to a general criterion of agency and of the distinction between actions and mere happenings.

The first thing I want to consider is the possibility that my case concerning meaningful actions as instances of pure actions, essentially involving no happenings, could have been overstated. Is it really true that no meaningful action raises the result-problem, that no meaningful action involves a specific happening? I do not think it is. If we look carefully at those actions that can be said to have a meaning, a symbolic content, we can find some cases of them that raise the result-problem, as they essentially involve happenings. Sports provide a good number of examples. Think for instance of scoring a goal in football. Scoring a goal is not simply introducing a ball into a frame of wood. When the ball is introduced in the frame in certain circumstances – when a match is taking place, etc. – and according to certain rules, that fact has the meaning of being the scoring of a goal, it has a symbolic content. But this meaningful action essentially involves a happening, namely that a ball gets into a frame of wood. Unless this happening occurs nobody can be said to have performed the action of scoring a goal. Similar examples could be found in golf, basketball, etc. This happening could take place with no action of scoring a goal being performed: this will be the case, for instance, if no match is going on. It could take place even with no action at all being performed, for instance if the wind blows the ball into the frame. This parallels the case of such actions as raising the arm or shooting someone, which are not necessarily meaningful actions. There are differences as well: in order for there to be an *action* of scoring a goal, that happening has to be not only brought about, but brought about in certain circumstances and according to certain rules. These differences are due to the meaningful character of scoring a goal, that seems to be related to the rules that govern football. Introducing a ball into a frame has the meaning of being the scoring of a goal only if it is performed according to certain conventions governing and constituting the game of football.

Now, how does this affect our line of argument so far?

First of all, it does not undermine our contention that Goldman's notion of conventional generation is not able to account for meaningful actions. A basic action plus a convention does not generate a meaningful action. The core of our criticism was that the notion of commitment was logically prior to that of convention: conventions would not exist without commitments to behave in certain ways in the future. This is related to the Wittgensteinian distinction between acting following a rule and acting merely in accord with a rule. A meaningful action requires not merely that what is done be in accordance with a rule, but that the agent be following a rule in doing it. And following a rule implies the understanding by the agent of what actions are and are not coherent with acting in a certain way at the present moment. This is why following a rule is related to the notion of commitment: to act following a rule in the present commits the agent to certain other actions in the future. Commitments, however, are involved in many different ways in meaningful actions. For instance, Goldman's example of signalling for a turn while driving or the case of bidding in an auction involve commitments to specific actions, namely turning and paying a certain amount of money. If an agent does not understand that his extending or raising his arm now is related in that way to those future actions, he cannot be properly said to be signalling or bidding. There are other meaningful actions, such as greeting someone or making a move in chess that do not involve commitments to specific actions in the future. These actions include our example of scoring a goal. But it is still essential in order to perform these latter actions, to have a sense that certain ways of acting in the future are coherent or incoherent with performing such actions now. Certain odd ways of acting would raise doubts concerning the truth of the ascription to an agent of actions such as greeting someone, making a chess move or scoring a goal. In this sense, then, the performing of those actions involves negative commitments not to do certain things, even if not positive commitments to perform specific actions. This difference, I believe, is related to the fact that signalling for a turn or bidding in an auction constitute cases of announcing or communicating an intention. And I will be contending that an intention has as its content a specific action and is a way of committing oneself to make that content true, that is, to act in that specific way. The other meaningful actions we are considering are not cases of announcing or communicating an intention and they do not involve commitments to specific actions, but only unspecific and negative commitments not to do certain things. This is related to the general fact that the performing of meaningful actions involves the possession of certain conceptual capacities and of a sense of coherence, so that beings lacking these, such as non-human animals, cannot perform them. In general, then, the notion of commitment is prior to that of convention, and our criticism of Goldman's account of meaningful actions still stands.

Secondly, and more importantly, the fact that certain meaningful actions do raise the result-problem and essentially involve happenings does not undermine the core of our argument so far, namely that we can find cases of ordinary actions that do not raise the result-problem, and that the appeal to volitions and tryings can be disposed of in order to avoid the infinite regress. What the example of scoring a goal suggests is rather that the property of being pure actions and not raising the result-problem, which we find in such actions as signalling for a turn, greeting or making an offer, is not (or not only) due to their meaningful character, for scoring a goal is also a meaningful action but lacks that property.

Cases of pure actions, essentially involving no happenings, are useful as a means of leading to a general criterion of agency, in so far as they exhibit agency in an especially clear-cut way. If we can display what it is that gives them the character of pure actions, this could help us to establish what is involved, in general, in other events being cases of acting. As we have pointed out, this cannot be the fact that they are meaningful or have a symbolic content, or at least this cannot be the whole reason, as the example of scoring a goal shows. To isolate the required factor, let us compare the action of scoring a goal with actions such as marrying or signalling for a turn. Scoring a goal involves essentially the happening that the ball gets into the frame. Now think of the following case: while trying to defend his own goal against the other team, a player kicks the ball, trying to get it far away from his goal, but he does it in such a way that the ball acquires a strange effect, floats back and gets into the player's own goal. Well, he scored a goal, he scored an own goal, but of course – we suppose – he did that unintentionally. He brought about the happening that is essentially involved in scoring a goal, and so he performed the action of scoring a goal, but he brought it about without intending to do it, in a way that was a surprise for him. Now, it seems that when actions essentially involve happenings, the possibility that the agent should bring about that happening in unexpected and unintended ways, similar to those in our example, cannot be excluded. These actions, then, can be unintentional. But if certain actions do not essentially involve specific happenings, this possibility is not open. No specific happening has to be brought about, and so it cannot be brought about in unexpected and unintended ways in such cases as signalling for a turn, making an offer or marrying. If this is so, it seems that we have got the clue to the question of what it is that gives to these actions the character of pure actions: pure actions are such in virtue of there not being the possibility that they be unintentional, or, in other words, in virtue of being *necessarily intentional*. There is no such thing as greeting, signalling for a turn or marrying unintentionally. To do it intentionally is a necessary condition of greeting, signalling for a turn or marrying, but not of shooting a gun, killing someone or scoring a goal.

We can try now to raise the character of being intentional to a general criterion of agency and of the distinction between actions and mere happenings.

If what gives to pure actions this character is the fact that they are necessarily intentional, perhaps intentionality, in a weaker modality, can be considered as a general criterion of agency.

But we have to be careful in stating this criterion in detail. As Anscombe and Davidson pointed out, 'intentional action' and 'doing x intentionally' are not extensional expressions, but intensional ones. The way in which an action is described affects the truth value of attributions of intentionality to that action. This affects what we were calling pure actions in the following way: to say that, for example, marrying is necessarily intentional is to say that, in order to truly attribute that action to someone, this person has to have performed that action intentionally under the description 'marrying'. What he did intentionally under the description 'marrying' could receive other true descriptions (for instance, expelling air from his or her mouth while saying 'yes') under which it could be unintentional. And in general it is true that what a person does intentionally can receive other true descriptions under which it is not intentional. In order to attribute intentionality to an action it is essential to take into account the description of the action under which intentionality is attributed.

Keeping this in mind, think now of a case of action (or, better, of an action-description) different from a pure action (or, better, a pure action-description), such as shooting someone. This action, unlike marrying, is not necessarily intentional, and this means: in order to truly attribute that action to someone, this person does not need to have done that action intentionally under the description 'shooting someone'. What is needed, then, for an attribution of that action to be true? Think of the following example: someone stumbles inadvertently on a loaded gun and the gun goes off, hurting someone. In this case, it would not be true to say of this person that he or she performed the action of shooting someone. Now think of a different case: a person is playing with a gun and, while doing so, he inadvertently pulls the trigger and the gun goes off, hurting someone. In this case, it could be true to say that this person shot someone. What distinguishes these two cases? In the first case, there is no description of what the person did under which it was true that it was intentional. Shooting someone was not an action of his; it was an unfortunate happening. But in the second case, there is a description of what he did, namely 'playing with a gun', under which what he did was intentional. This description was not 'shooting someone'. But shooting someone was an action of his, and the reason is that it was intentional under another description. In this case, the happening (a bullet entering someone's body) that is essential for an action of shooting someone to be performed was brought about by the agent, although in an unexpected, unintended way. Shooting someone was an action of his, although an unintentional one. More exactly: 'shooting someone' is a true description of what he did, although 'shooting someone intentionally' is not. This last contention could not possibly be true in the case of a pure action: 'marrying' cannot be a true description of what someone does if 'marrying intentionally' is not.

We can try to formulate a general criterion of agency in the following terms: we said that pure actions were necessarily intentional under those descriptions; we can say now that actions are, as a matter of fact, intentional under some description; more precisely, a certain piece of behaviour is an action if, and only if, it is intentional (or intentionally performed) under some description. If a certain piece of behaviour is not intentional under any description, we are then faced with a case of a mere happening, not a case of exercise of agency.

The relationship between agency and intentionality has been emphasized by several authors, such as Anscombe and Davidson, and I consider it as basically correct. But I think that we have *derived* that relationship, and its associated criterion, through a – successful, I hope – attempt to cope with the regress-problem that threatens the very existence of actions.

We cay try to bring out this relationship in more detail. The relationship between agency and intentionality is not that of identity. Not every action is an intentional one. We must provide room for non-intentional actions, or for non-intentional true descriptions of actions. But we can say, in a first approach, that there are non-intentional actions, or non-intentional true descriptions of actions, only because there are intentional actions, or intentional true descriptions of actions. This relationship between agency and intentional action can be pursued at the level of action-types as well as that of action-tokens. As to the first, if we go through action-terms or action-expressions,[1] we shall find among them some which can be truly attributed to an agent only by attributing intentionality to him in his performance. This group includes pure action-terms we have referred to above: 'marrying', 'signalling for a turn', 'greeting', 'making a chess-move', etc. It also includes such pure action-terms as 'lying' or 'conspiring', usually mentioned in this group. These types of actions do not essentially involve happenings as results. Besides this, we shall find a group of action-terms whose attribution to an agent does not imply either intentionality or non-intentionality; they are, so to speak, neutral concerning intentionality. Think, for instance of such action-terms as 'offending', 'kicking', 'shooting', 'pulling a trigger', etc. This group includes all basic action-terms, in Danto's sense. Concerning these terms, however, we can properly say that unless the kinds of actions they refer to could be performed intentionally, they would not count as *action*-terms. Anscombe expresses this relationship nicely: 'For example, "offending someone"; one can do this unintentionally, but there would be no such thing if it were never the description of an intentional action.'[2] The relation between agency and intentionality is reflected in the fact that we do not find any term which implies non-intentionality and which counts as an action-term. Concerning this relationship between action-types and intentional action we can say, then, that in order for a term to count as an action-term, the type of activity referred to must be such that at least some people can perform it intentionally. At the level of action-tokens or concrete, spatiotemporally located actions – the level in which we formulated the criterion above – if we adopt Anscombe and Davidson's view of actions as particulars capable of receiving several descriptions, we can express the relationship by saying, with Davidson, that 'an event is an action if and only if it can be described in a way that makes it intentional.'[3] Hornsby expresses this view in the following way: 'If we go through a list of things that were done when there was someone's action – a catalogue of the different kinds that subsume this action of his – then we shall find at least one thing in the list such that we can truly say "He did that intentionally".'[4] If, for instance, Mary is jumping on the sofa and she breaks it, even if she did not break it intentionally, breaking the sofa was her action, because it was intentional under the description 'jumping on the sofa'.

How does this work in dubious cases? Think, for instance, of the question 'Is sneezing an action?'. Distinguishing between the level of types and that of tokens can help here, as in most other cases. The question, so formulated, involves an ambiguity, since 'sneezing' can be understood both as an action-term and as a non-actional event-term. It is an action-term in so far as sneezing can sometimes be done intentionally. It is a non-actional event-term in so far as most often sneezing simply happens to us. So, there is no general answer, at the level of types, to the question 'Is sneezing an action?', but only a vague one such as 'It can be.' However, there are answers in concrete cases, at the level of tokens. For instance, Smith's sneezing at t *was* an action since he did it intentionally (say, as part of a plan to attract the waiter's attention), but Jones's sneezing at t' *was not* an action, but something that happened to him, since he did not do it intentionally.

According to this criterion, moreover, those bodily movements performed in performing a meaningful intentional action, such as buying a book, would count usually as actions. Or, for example, expelling air from our mouth is something we do in speaking, it is an action, since there is a description of it, namely 'speaking', under which it is an intentional action. But expelling air from our mouth is not an action of ours when sleeping or in normal breathing, since there is no such true intentional description. And, finally, it is an action, and an intentional one, if it is intentionally done under that description (in order, for instance, to blow out a candle or for its own sake).

Now, from this criterion of agency that relates it to intentional action, there are some descriptions of actions which are in some sense privileged ones, namely those under which the action was intentional, since these descriptions allow the rest of actional descriptions to be true. This privilege of intentional action and of descriptions of actions as intentional shows itself in the fact that intentionality is *supposed*, unless there is a statement to the contrary, in current descriptions of actions, so that if we do not describe an action as intentionally performed, we normally add a suitable qualification to make it clear.[5] On the other hand, we do not normally say 'A did x intentionally', or 'on purpose'. But not because it is *false* in most circumstances to say so, but because it is *redundant*, and, for this same reason, misleading, so that when we say 'A did x intentionally', our hearers are invited to think that there was some hidden or additional purpose with which that action was performed, that is, that the action was intentionally performed in the sense of being part of a plan or a means to achieve something special (usually something mischievous), instead of being something the agent simply intended to do for normal reasons or for its own sake. So, if someone who does not know Oedipus' story is told that Oedipus married his mother, he is probably induced to think something that is false, namely that Oedipus did it intentionally. A non-misleading description of that action should include a qualification, such as 'with no intention' or 'involuntarily'. Moreover, in this case, if our contention about pure actions is right, since marrying is a pure action, in order for 'Oedipus married his mother' to be true, there has to be a description in terms of 'marrying' of what Oedipus did under which his action was intentional; and so there is: Oedipus married Jocasta, or the queen, intentionally.

So far, our investigation of agency has led us to the notion of intentional action. This path has allowed us to avoid what seemed to be a blind alley, namely the search for basic actions, by finding some intuitively and ordinarily clear types of actions, which fulfil the conditions that basic actions in Danto's sense, or in the sense of the

New Volitional Theory, should – but couldn't – meet. Pure actions, we said, were necessarily intentional under such descriptions. Actions are those events that are intentional under some description. Obviously, our next question will be: What is an intentional action?

Think again of our example of unintentionally scoring a goal. What we do unintentionally has something in common with what merely happens to us, namely that we can discover or find out that we were doing it or that it happened to us. The unlucky goal-scorer discovered that he had scored an own goal, but he did not discover that he had kicked the ball. This last action was intentional. This fact is what Anscombe emphasized by saying that we know what we do intentionally in a non-observational way. We know observationally what we do unintentionally – we find ourselves doing it – as well as what happens to us. This feature, common to unintentional actions and happenings, is related, I think, to the fact that certain happenings are essential for certain actions to be performed. As we have a physical body, its movements can bring about those happenings through unforeseen and unexpected ways, as when someone causes somebody's being shot when playing with a gun. This is the reason why we cannot discover or know observationally that we are doing pure actions, such as signalling for a turn or marrying, because those actions do not essentially involve happenings. I can discover that I am, absent-mindedly, extending my arm out of the car window, but not, properly speaking, that I am signalling: I discover myself doing something – extending my arm – that can be mistakenly, and dangerously, taken as a signal, and so I stop doing it immediately if I did not intend to signal. These differences in knowledge can give us a first clue to the nature of acting intentionally. Why did the unlucky goal-scorer discover, or know observationally, that he had scored an own goal? Because, so to say, that action was not depicted in the content of his intention. He intended to send the ball far from his own goal. Why did he not discover, or know observationally, that he was kicking the ball? Because doing that was depicted in his intention, and he was matching that picture in kicking the ball. Let this serve as a first – and somehow metaphorical – approach to the question of what an intentional action is.

In this chapter we shall try to answer, tentatively, this question by focusing on intuitively clear examples of intentional (meaningful and non-meaningful) actions and trying to display what is involved in them.

Suppose I am driving home from my workplace in another town. As the junction leading to the village where I live approaches, I extend my arm out of the window to signal for my turning. I turn at that junction. As I get to my village, I see a neighbour and I greet him by raising my arm. We can focus on these three examples of acting: my signalling for a turn, my turning, and my greeting a neighbour. From the description we understand that these were things I did intentionally. Why do we understand that? What makes them intentional actions of mine? Think of my signalling for a turn. My aim is to get home. Achieving this aim involves a certain action-plan, which in this case seems to be quite a detailed one, for I know the way home by heart; every day I make the same trip. This action-plan includes turning at the junction mentioned. And the Highway Code says that a turning must be announced or signalled previously. So, since I intend to turn at the next junction, I announce it by extending my arm out of the window, following the Highway Code. Do I have the intention to signal? I think I do. And the pattern of relations in which I intend to signal is that I intend to turn and I believe that signalling makes my turning easier or safer; so, I intend to signal. That is, the intention to A an the belief that B is a convenient way to A usually implies the intention to B. A similar pattern applies to turning: I intend to turn because I intend to get home and I know that turning is a means of getting home. I could equally well say that I turn for the same reason: a reason to *do* something is also a reason to *intend* to do it. My signalling for a turn intentionally involves at least four aspects: in doing it I am following a plan; I am following certain (traffic) rules; I am following my intention to signal; I am commiting myself to turn. Think now of turning. It too has also several aspects, which, however, differ a little from the last ones: I am still following a plan to get home; I am not following the Highway Code in the same sense in which I was in signalling, for the Highway Code does not require turning at this junction; but I am still following the Highway Code concerning the way turnings should be made, for instance not moving into the wrong lane; I am following my intention to turn, which in this case was explicitly announced in signalling, and in following that intention I am fulfilling my commitment to turn; if turning is intentional under the pattern of a plan to get home, it is related, in terms of coherence, to further actions leading to that end. What about greeting my neighbour? I am not following a plan to get home, but perhaps I am still following a certain pattern directed to be on good terms with my acquaintances; I am following certain social rules; as soon as I saw my neighbour I might form the intention to greet him, and so in greeting him I followed or fulfilled that intention; finally, greeting my neighbour does not involve commitments to specific actions, but perhaps it still involves negative commitments, as we pointed out above.

Think now of another case. While driving I feel uncomfortable and I sit well back, changing my position. This was also an intentional action. I wanted to feel more comfortable and I did it in order to feel so. This action was intentional just in the sense of being purposive, of tending to an end, namely to be comfortable; it was perhaps the display of a routine pattern of behaviour when I feel uncomfortable while driving; there was no rule I was following nor any commitment, even negative, to future actions. I do not see any reason to deny the intentionality of this action. But I want to say that the range of intentional actions human beings can perform could never be explained with this kind of intentional action and this sort of intention. My intention to get home or my intention to turn involve a certain kind of rational commitment: if I have those intentions I ought to engage in certain appropriate actions on pain of incoherence. We could call these intentions 'future intentions'. My intention to sit well back does not seem to involve such a commitment: it is just reflected in the action at that very moment. We could call this an 'immediate intention'.

So far, then, we have found several elements present in several intentional actions. Here is a brief list: aims, beliefs, plans, rules, future intentions, immediate intentions. How do they differ and what role do they play in acting intentionally? In the first of the above examples, my aim is to get home. An aim, however, is inert unless I *intend* to achieve it by acting. The intention to get home is something more than that aim and seems to be indispensable for acting intentionally. Something similar happens with plans and rules. Plans and rules are standards. But unless I intend to meet those standards by acting, they are still inert. So, what does the intention add to those standards? Turning at the junction that leads home is part of the plan to get home. The *intention* to turn is something more: it is to *commit* oneself to meet that standard. This distinguishes intentions from aims, rules or plans, from mere ideals, in a neutral (not necessarily moral) sense. Only when one commits oneself to act so as to match an ideal has one formed an intention. Intentions, I contend, are not mere desires, aims, plans or rules: they are *commitments* to act so as to match their content (the desired, aimed at, planned action). Aims, plans, rules, can remain inert. Only by constituting (part of) the content of an intention do they become efficacious as guides to action. And as contents of intentions they are the standard one commits oneself to meet by *intending* to act in a certain way. And one acts intentionally when one adjusts and controls one's behaviour so as to match that standard. We can try to summarize all this in the following tentative definition of intentional action: one acts intentionally (under the description D) if, and only if, in acting one is following an intention to act under that description. Keeping in mind the need for intention, we can also say, harmlessly, that acting intentionally is acting following a plan, or rule, or pursuing an aim. Intentional action, as we understand it, involves commitments and is a normative concept. The notion of commitment we are referring to is a normative one: a commitment is something more than a disposition or tendency to do something, for if there is no incoherence in not displaying a disposition, there is some incoherence in not fulfilling a commitment, there is something wrong in it, at least in that it affects the intelligibility and rationality of our behaviour. Intentions involve this kind of commitment; they are not mere dispositions or tendencies to act.

Acting intentionally is a very complex process. Intentions having a propositional content (say, that I get home, that I turn at such and such a junction) need to be specified by indexical intentions. For instance, if I intend to turn at the junction leading to my village, this intention is specified, when the junction approaches, in an intention to turn at *that* junction.[6] This process of specification adjusts the general, rough content of our intentions to reality and to changing circumstances, and so it contributes to the fulfilment of our commitments. Without this process our activity would be too rigid to deal with the complexity of circumstances and their change. Also involved in the process of intentional action is a continuous processing of information coming from the environment and from our own body. However, it would be a mistake to think that intentional action can be identified with these processes, since they are just at the service of meeting the standard, of fulfilling the commitment. The presence and importance of these processes, which can be fruitfully studied by physiologists and psychologists, cannot undermine or replace the normative core of intentional action.

Something similar could be said about immediate intentions and routine patterns of behaviour, as shown in our example of sitting well back when feeling uncomfortable. They are present in complex intentional actions, involving plans, rules, aims, etc., as well as in relatively simple ones, such as that of the example. They seem to be necessary for a successful development of the action. Consider that, if each of our movements were to be fully under conscious control, few of our actions could meet relatively complex standards. In the example of driving home, when I approach the junction, my intention is to turn at that junction; but I leave the details to the routines created in my previous training as a driver. However, these abilities, related to training and to spontaneous movement, do not undermine the normative character of intentional action either, for they serve precisely as instruments to the fulfilment of our commitments.

Now, if an action reflects or meets *only* an immediate intention, as in the example of sitting well back, and does not involve nor serve future intentions, it is intentional in a minimal sense. A creature which is able to perform only intentional actions in this minimal sense is a creature which is not able to have future intentions, and so, which is not able to commit itself to future actions. But this ability is essential to the range of intentional actions a human agent can perform. Imagine a person who could have only immediate intentions, but not future intentions. This person would not be able to take part in most common human enterprises and activities. He or she would not be able to decide between several future courses of action. He or she would show purposive and spontaneous behaviour, but not full-blooded intentional actions in which one is acting following a standard previously depicted. So, the line between immediate intentions and future intentions gives access to full agency. Having intentions, as commitments to do things in the future, is essential to agency, to being a full-blooded agent. To commit oneself is the core of agency. This, however, does not undermine the fact that showing purposive behaviour and immediate intentions is the natural basis on which future intentions and full-blooded intentional action develop in human beings by learning and socialization. A being showing no spontaneous interest in its surroundings would lack an essential condition to learn basic concepts involved in intentional action and to develop the ability to commit itself to act. Spontaneous teleological behaviour is a natural condition of human agency. But, again, this does not mean that what is involved in the latter can be understood only in terms of the former.

This ability to commit oneself has its simplest expression in having an intention (now) to do something (later). This allows our conception of intentional action to cover other intuitively obvious cases of intentional action: everybody would agree that I am acting intentionally when I am consciously fulfilling, with this action, a decision, a vow or a promise. But if one is doing this one surely is following an intention to act under a certain description, and so one is acting intentionally under that description, for a decision, a vow or a promise to do A implies an intention to do A (but not conversely). So, these cases are covered by our conception of intentional action.

Our next chapter will deal with the context that makes intentions possible.

6

The Intentionality of Mind

The core of agency is commitment. To be an agent is to have the ability to commit oneself to do things in the future. And the simplest expression of this ability is to have an intention to act. In order to act intentionally, in its full-blooded sense, one has to be able to intend. But an intention is not a state you could be in with no further requirement. Intentions can exist only in the wider context of a mind. This mental context, with its inherent constraints of rationality and coherence, supports our commitments to act when we have an intention or make a decision. This context is, therefore, also needed to act intentionally. The main fault of atomistic views of agency is precisely to forget this context and to think of actions as isolated items able to sustain themselves.

In order to get a grip of this context, we can start by asking which conditions are implied in a person's having an intentional state, such as an intention. These conditions are also conditions of intentional action. Now, the point is that a person simply cannot have just *one* intentional state, such as an intention, unless he or she can be described as having many others. And 'cannot' has to be understood here in its logical modality. A person cannot truly be said to have the intention of turning unless he has, for instance, some beliefs about the fact that a junction is coming, that he is approaching it, that he is driving, etc. Each of these beliefs, in turn, is related to indefinitely many others, as well as to plenty of other states. The relationship we are pointing to is normative, not merely factual: you must have one belief if you really have another; it is not just a fact that you have both of them. What is involved here is the normative notion of coherence and its essential link to notions such as belief, intention, and so on: one cannot straightforwardly and consciously believe both A and not A, nor have the intention to do A and not to do A, nor follow at the same time two incompatible plans, nor decide to do A and not to do A. The point is that being coherent is somehow implied in calling something a belief, intention, plan or decision. To believe A and not A is not just to believe something *contradictory*: it is not to *believe* anything at all. This does not mean that people cannot have incoherent or contradictory beliefs, but that in order to have some incoherent *beliefs* most of their beliefs must be coherent. Cases of incoherence can arise only against a background of coherence. A massively contradictory system of beliefs, intentions, plans, etc., is simply inconceivable as such, there is no such thing. If most of someone's beliefs, intentions, etc., were incoherent, we would lose the necessary basis to attribute them to him: he simply would not count as having such states. So, if we are to have just one of those intentional states, we have to have a mostly *coherent view* of the world. Having one intentional state entails, as a condition of possibility, a whole system of intentional states, the whole intentionality of mind. Certain emotions are also built into this network: if, for instance, a person is firmly convinced that a junction is coming, he or she should be surprised if it is not so.

We shall try to bring out the main features of mind as constituted by that network of intentional states. Its first feature is suggested by the words 'intentional' and 'intentionality'. These words come from the Latin word *intendere*, which originally meant something like 'to aim at'. From this point of view, intentionality means something like 'directedness' towards a content (the 'intentional object'), that which those states are 'about'. This is the point of sometimes calling them 'propositional attitudes', if their content is understood as a proposition (what is believed, intended, desired, etc.); they are attitudes (believing, intending, desiring) towards that proposition. This is perhaps a rough and not very illuminating characterization, but it can be useful as a starting-point. What should be kept in mind is that the relationship of directedness is not external, but internal or constitutive. This is not the case with a material object. A stone can be directed towards a window and an arrow towards a certain target. But they are still a stone and an arrow if they are not directed towards anything. A desire, an intention, a hope or a perception are not such types of states unless they are about something, their content, and, moreover, they are partly individuated by that content as being the tokens they are. Their relations of incompatibility are partly determined by logical relations among those contents, as happens with believing that p and believing that not-p.

This leads us to the second feature of intentionality: its *normativity*. The very existence and true attribution of intentional states is subject to normative constraints, to requirements of coherence. There is something wrong, for instance, with believing that p, believing that p implies q and not believing that q, or with seriously believing that it is completely impossible for you to do something and having the intention to do it, or with deciding to do something and believing that you will not do that even if you can, or, to come back to one of our examples, with signalling for a turn and not making a turn when the junction comes. The degrees of wrongness range from plain contradiction to mere oddity: anyway, something has to be done to remedy the fault if someone insists that, none the less, he believes that so and so, or has the intention to do such and such, etc., where these beliefs or intentions seem to be odd or contradictory, since, as we pointed out, unless you meet some normative constraints you cannot count as having such beliefs or intentions, or ultimately as having beliefs or intentions at all. A massively contradictory network of intentional states in a subject is not conceivable; there is no such thing; a merely odd one needs at least some adjustment or justification. So, normativity belongs to the nature of intentional states: they must respond to it in order to be such states. The notions of 'right' and 'wrong' belong to the very nature of intentionality; they do not apply to it from an external point of view, as when we say that something is wrong with our car's engine. An important point about conceiving the mind in terms of intentionality is that intentional states are not entities, but relations to a content. We should then bring the subject into the picture, since it is he or she who relates to a content in believing, intending or wanting it. None the less, norms are not up to the subject: he has to obey them if he is to count as having a mind. Now, if we bring the subject into the picture, the feature of normativity can be expressed in terms of *commitment*: having one intentional state commits someone to having indefinitely many others as well, on pain of having none, of having no mind at all. And this commitment also extends also to overt actions (something has to be done to remedy the fact that you decided to go to the concert and none the less you went to the pub) and, by means of them, to the configuration of the external reality we deal with in acting (well, at least you had to believe that there was a concert somewhere in order for such a decision to make sense, and that belief commits you to the existence of concerts as real events that happen in the world). If this is so, I consider it implausible that the relationship between an intentional state and the intentional action that arises from it can be fully captured in purely factual, non-normative terms, such as Humean causal relations. For these same reasons I think that dispositional analyses of mental terms, according to which they are dispositions to other mental states and to behaviour, are not right, since the term 'disposition', as understood in these analyses (behaviourism is the paradigmatic example), falls very short of the normative character that pervades mental states.

A third feature of intentionality, closely connected to the second one, is its *holism*. Intentional states are essentially a network, a whole system. They are not discrete, separate items: the existence of one of them has necessary implications for the existence of others. There could be, say, just one mountain in the world, but there could not be just one belief, or one intention, or, to put it in less objectivistic terms, nobody could have just one belief or one intention.

An additional feature of intentionality concerns its *subjectivity*, its essential reference to a subject's point of view about the world. We have stressed above the subject's liability to norms. Now we have to insist upon its being properly a subject, a being who has a perspective of its own and conceives the world from a particular point of view, different from that of any other subject. This perspective expresses itself in those beliefs, desires, decisions, plans, etc., that constitute *one* network of intentional states, that of a particular person. This is partly the point of referring to the contents of intentional states as 'intentional objects', and not simply as objects or reality. It is not that we do not relate to the real external world in believing, intending or hoping, but that we relate to it in this network of states *sub specie subjecti*, not *sub specie aeternitatis*. If Oedipus had had a view of the world *sub specie aeternitatis* he would not have had the intention of marrying the queen. This essential reference to the subject is included in Anscombe's view that actions are intentional under descriptions. We engage in actions under descriptions we know or believe apply to them and to reality, but that means: from our own perspective or point of view about the world, which is a partial one. Oedipus' action was intentional under the description 'marrying the queen', not under the description 'marrying his mother'; and this means; he engaged in that action from a perspective of his own, according to which 'being the queen' was true of the person he married, but 'being his mother' was not, though he was mistaken about the latter. The 'intentional object' of Oedipus' decision or intention was not a strange, intermediate entity which was somehow in his mind; it was a real person, only conceived from his own perspective. So far, intentionality includes not only 'directedness' towards an object, but also the subjectivity of this directedness.

That is why, finally, intentional states, as well as the words 'intentional' and 'intentionally' as applied to actions, give rise to *intensional or referentially opaque contexts*, where truth is not always preserved if we substitute for one expression another expression referring to the same object, event or action. This happens with such expressions as 'A believes that . . .', 'A intends . . .', 'A intentionally did . . .', 'A decided . . .', etc. So, for instance, 'Oedipus married the queen' and 'Oedipus married his mother' are both true (recall, however, the misleading effect of the latter sentence), 'the queen' and 'his mother' referring to the same person. But the second one ceases to be true if we insert in both sentences the adverb 'intentionally'. Examples are easy to construe. This feature has been viewed as a major obstacle in the way of every attempt to construe human sciences on the model of natural sciences. Alexander Rosenberg states nicely why it is so. Let us transcribe quite a long quotation of his:

> It seems an indubitable fact that mental states have content; in the case of desires and beliefs, they have propositional content . . . States like belief and desire are accordingly called propositional attitudes, and they are described as reflecting the property of intensionality. Now one test of intensionality is that statements attributing intentional properties to particular items, like psychological states to human beings, are incapable of absorption into the extensional logical apparatus that seems to suffice for analysing and regimenting the statements and inferences of mathematics and the natural sciences. A simple illustration of this recalcitrance of intentional discourse is provided by the following seemingly valid inference from apparently true premises to a presumably false conclusion:
>
> Lady Astor desired to sail on the largest ship afloat in 1912. The largest ship afloat in 1912 was identical to the ship that struck an iceberg, sank, and caused Lady Astor's death.
>
> Therefore,
>
> Lady Astor desired to sail on the ship that struck an iceberg, sank, and caused her death.
>
> Since the conclusion is false, and the inference-form unexceptional, the premises must be ill-formed for purposes of logical manipulation.[1]

Rosenberg's final conclusion, however, is not the autonomy of sciences dealing with intentionality, but their impossibility as sciences.[2] We shall examine later this position, which connects closely with eliminative materialism, that is, with the denial of any respectable reality to intentional states and attitudes.

Having presented the main features of the intentionality of mind, we can now return to the issue that led us to this, namely agency. Let us recall briefly how we got here.

We started asking about the justification of our ordinary strong distinction between actions and happenings and our associated belief in the existence of actions as different from mere happenings. This belief was threatened by the logical involvement of specific happenings in the performing of many actions and the related problem of infinite regress. In order to stop this regress and to justify our belief it was necessary to find actions with no specific happenings logically involved in them. The search for those actions, however, seemed to lead only to further happenings occurring inside our bodies, so that actions appeared to reduce to chains of causally related happenings. This, according to our analysis, was the case with Danto's basic actions, as well as with volitions. Giving up the search for actions at more and more basic levels as hopeless, we suggested instead that we should look for the required actions at a higher level. We found that some meaningful, specifically human actions met the conditions required to stop the regress and to justify our belief in the existence of actions and their sharp distinction from happenings. So taking these actions as a clue to the nature of agency, we found that their regress-stopping virtues seemed to be rooted in their being necessarily intentional and this suggested that being intentional – under some description – could be a criterion of agency, connecting with the view of Davidson at this point. By studying some intuitively obvious cases of intentional actions we went on to state a tentative definition of acting intentionally where the notion of intention, understood as a commitment to act, played an essential role. We asked then for the conditions that must be met in order for someone to have an intention and so to be able to act intentionally, and this question led us to the whole network of the intentionality of mind and its features.

Intentionality of mind seems to be at the root of someone's being able to do such apparently simple things as signalling for a turn. We can now draw, as a conclusion, a largely holistic and normative conception of agency: agency in its important sense, that is, as a real ability for a being to influence some aspects of the world's evolution according to his or her own will, instead of merely suffering it, has as a necessary condition the whole intentionality of mind, with all its features, so that it requires a true attribution to that being of a network of intentional states governed by norms and being an expression of its subjective perspective on the world, which involves in turn its ability, on pain of coherence, and even of mindlessness, to commit itself to accept its being in many other intentional states as well as to behave in certain ways in the future. We can also state this relationship by saying that the true attribution to a being of the performance of just one intentional action is a sufficient condition to truly attribute to that being the whole network of intentionality, and so a mind.

This full-blooded agency we are referring to relates to having intentions and performing intentional actions in a specifically strong sense of these words, already pointed to. Recall, in effect, that in the preceding chapter we distinguished a strong from a weak or minimal sense of these terms. In the weak or minimal sense an action was intentional in being the expression of an immediate intention, such as the intention to sit well back when we feel uncomfortable or the intention to drink now from this glass before me. These intentions are intentions in a minimal sense in that they do not involve a commitment to future actions, but, let us say, they issue directly into actions. This kind of intention is linked to our spontaneous teleological behaviour: little babies, as well as animals, show such intentions. In this sense animals can have intentions and perform intentional actions. Think of a dog approaching its food or of a cat running after a mouse. I do not see any reason to deny them the intention, respectively, of getting the food and catching the mouse,[3] or to deny that they are acting intentionally. But I see reasons to distinguish these senses of 'intention' and 'intentional action' as being much weaker – even if not totally unrelated – than they are as applied to, say, the intention to marry someone in two years' time and marrying that person then. In this last sense, 'intention' means not only 'directedness' or 'aiming at', but also 'commitment' to an action, consciousness of that commitment and responsibility for it. This commitment, consciousness and responsibility are not only attributed to the agent, but also accepted and taken on by him. The second aspect is absent from animals' intentions. Non-human animals show, so to speak, scattered features of intention and intentionality, but by no means all the features we distinguished in these notions. And we should expect them to show those features, since the whole network of human intentionality starts from and supposes, for it to be fully developed, that primary, non-learnt directedness, concern and interest in external objects that human beings share with other animals. The difference could be expressed by means of an example: we can now have the intention to do something, say, next year, we can commit ourselves now to doing something in the future; but a dog or cat cannot; we can say of a dog that runs after a ball that its intention is to catch the ball, but we cannot say of it that it has now the intention to catch the ball in two days' time. Normativity is absent from non-human animals, but is essential to human beings. Similar remarks would apply to the expression 'intentional action' when applied to non-human animals and to human beings. The clearest case is provided by meaningful intentional actions. Norms and commitments are essential to an agent's performance of such actions. A human being can signal for a turn; a dog cannot, even if we can find in animal behaviour scattered and primitive features of human meaningful intentional actions, as happened with intention and intentionality. Unless we specify to the contrary, we shall speak of intention and intentional action in its strong, fully developed sense. I think, then, that our conception of agency can account reasonably well both for animal purposive behaviour and for the intuitive, ordinary difference we draw between human and non-human animal actions.

Before concluding this chapter, I would like to account, from the vantage-point we have reached, for the notion of basic action. Surely a bodily movement, say, raising one's arm, *voluntarily performed*, is an action, and indeed an intentional one, according to our definition, since it follows an intention. And we must concede that it is. Why, then, could we not try to build the notion of agency on such examples of action, which are the clearest and simplest? Well, there have been several attempts to understand agency starting from these intentional basic actions: classical British empiricism (including John Stuart Mill) is an example; Hornsby's (and Prichard's) theory of action is another.[4] An apparent advantage of such attempts is the simplicity of the model of action they start from: a voluntary bodily movement; every non-paralysed person can perform it; you just sit comfortably, thinking about agency, and say to yourself 'I can raise my arm by just wanting to; now I want to, and I raise it'; and so you do. What I contend is that the apparent advantage of this starting-point is precisely its worst disadvantage. The reason for my contention should by now be clear: precisely because we start from this extremely simplified model of action and from that purified, 'armchair' situation, we are leaving behind us, forgotten and concealed, the whole context that makes that very model and situation possible, namely the whole network of intentionality. For *wanting* to raise one's arm and then consciously *raising* it is only possible in this way for beings that are able to commit themselves to do things, to fulfil these commitments, to follow norms and rules – in short, for beings endowed with all the features of intentionality. A dog simply cannot move *like that*. Despite its apparent simplicity, that model is extremely sophisticated by being so purified: wanting to raise one's arm is something that rarely happens except when we are thinking philosophically about actions. We want lots of things, but usually not *that*. We simply move, as other animals do. But now, since all the context of intentionality has been left behind, ignored, we try to account for that situation in its own simplified terms, and what arises then is a forceful tendency to analyse those actions as just external effects of internal causes, call them volitions, acts of will, tryings or anything similar. But now, since the external effect is a movement of the body, we face a dilemma: either the internal cause is our will – our mind – and then we fall into the trap of Cartesian interactionism and are forced to explain how something purely mental can cause a physical event; or, to escape from this, we come to accept that something which causes a physical event has to be a physical event, something happening inside our bodies, presumably neurophysiological events, and by so doing we drop agency or reduce it to mere happenings. What we call our will, however, cannot be isolated as a discrete event, but exists only in its relationship to the network of intentionality, which is what makes possible intentional basic actions of the sort envisaged by these analyses and which, however, has been ignored by them: a distorted picture must, therefore, arise from them. The temptation to misrepresent the will is nicely uncovered by the following text of Anscombe: 'People sometimes say that one can get one's arm to move by an act of will but not a matchbox; but if they mean "Will a matchbox to move and it won't", the answer is "If I will my arm to move in that way, it won't", and if they mean "I can move my arm but not the matchbox" the answer is that I can move the matchbox – nothing easier.'[5] I think, moreover, that this quotation points rightly to the role played in agency by spontaneous movement.

7

Intentionality and Science

The features of intentionality contrast sharply with a scientific view of the world. The continual efforts to accommodate intentionality within such a view, after 400 years of impressive progress in the natural sciences, have not yet produced anything other than promising programmes of investigation, soon replaced by new ones. None the less, phenomena such as biological teleology, that a hundred years ago would have been considered as inexplicable by laws, seem to have been brought by molecular biology under the scope of strict laws, similar to those of other natural sciences, if not totally reduced to the physico-chemical level. Recent developments in philosophy have made us very healthily reluctant to legislate about the future from supposedly conceptual, necessary truths. We do not know whether new analyses of the mental will prove able to do the trick. But the recalcitrance of intentionality to be integrated into the scientific picture of the world is, up to now, an undeniable truth, and we should not rule out the possibility that it could, in time, prove to be a necessary truth.

This recalcitrance is deeply rooted in the features of intentionality. First of all, intentionality is not just a fact *in* the world, but a *view* of facts and of the world according to which we conceive ourselves and other persons in terms which are prima facie different from those of the strict sciences. Science, for instance, depicts the world as a network of causally related events, whereas we consider ourselves, intuitively, as agents, as beings able to *initiate* causal chains. Accordingly, science has not only to account for a fact, but also to prove that the intentional view is false, a mere illusion, or, at least, to show that the prima facie difference is a mere appearance under which hides a substantial similarity. Nor is the relationship between intentionality and science parallel to the relationship between biology and teleology or to the relationship between modern chemistry and phlogiston theory, that is, it is neither parallel to that existing between a theory and a fact nor to that existing between two rival theories within a certain field of inquiry. The view of ourselves and other persons as agents is not equivalent to the view of combustion processes in terms of the phlogiston theory. Lavoisier's theory and the phlogiston theory shared enough assumptions and proceedings to enable the former to replace the latter. But the tension between an intentional perspective on human beings and a scientific view of them seems to be deeper. We have seen that there is a systematic relationship between the concepts of action, intention and intentionality. So, in viewing ourselves and others as agents, we adopt a perspective that includes all that network of concepts. We conceive of agents as having a subjective point of view of the world and acting according to it; we grant them this point of view in attributing to them beliefs, desires, hopes, intentions, values, and so on; and we take this subjective perspective into account in explaining what they do; this is why these states can be falsely attributed when we shift to a perspective other than the agent's; mental concepts, in other words, introduce intensional contexts; finally, intentional states are subject to overall normative constraints of coherence and are holistically attributed.

At first sight, these traits of an intentional perspective on human beings and their actions contrast sharply with the requirements of a scientifically shaped perspective on them. Consider, for example, that while the former does not seem to use laws, laws are essential to the latter, according to an orthodox empiricist conception of science, as well as to scientific practice itself; empirical fields are conceived by science as governed not by norms, but by laws, whose discovery is one of its central tasks; in connection with this primacy of laws, science does not grant its objects a subjective point of view; on the contrary, it is just because scientific objects are denied this subjective perspective that they can be seen as law-governed and predictable by means of laws; moreover, since laws are factual statements, not logically necessary ones, attribution of a certain physical property to an object does not logically imply its having other determinate properties; just the contrary seems to happen with attribution of a determinate mental property to an agent, in virtue of the normative and holistic aspects of intentionality.

There appears to be, then, a not inconsiderable tension between intentionality and science. Can this tension be overcome, so that human minds and actions can be accounted for from a scientific perspective? Scientism, as distinct from science, answers 'Yes' to this question. Scientism is the view that the method of natural science, especially of physics, is the only fruitful and legitimate method in the pursuit of knowledge, so that it should shape the investigation of all kinds of reality, including the objects of humanities, psychology and the social sciences. The core of scientism is the thesis of the unity of science on the pattern provided by physics. In some of its classical forms, this thesis can be said to consist of two separate claims, namely physicalism, according to which every kind of reality worthy of this name is composed of or ultimately reducible to physical states, objects and events, that is, states, objects and events of the kind accepted by physics; and the thesis of extensionality. This latter is the claim that the universal language of science will be, when completed, a purely extensional one.[1] Physicalism and extensionality are separate claims in that they do not logically imply each other, so that a physicalist is not logically committed to being an extensionalist as well, and vice versa. A purely extensional language is such that the truth of its statements depends only upon the extension – as opposed to the intension or sense – of its predicates. The extension of a predicate is the class of objects to which that predicate applies. The extension of predicates determines the truth of the simplest sentences, namely those stating that a particular object has a certain property. The truth of complex sentences is determined by the truth value of the simple sentences they are composed of, according to the logical form of their composition. In an extensional language, then, a singular term can be replaced by another coreferential term with no change in the truth value of the initial sentence; a general term can be replaced by another coextensive term with no change in the truth value of the sentence that contains it; and a component sentence can be replaced by another having the same truth value with no change in the truth value of the initial composed sentence.

Now consider that our everyday discourse about actions, agents and their mental states, which is also partly shared by current social sciences, is a paradigmatic case of a non-extensional language. It may be true that someone believes that his neighbour owns an old car while not being true that he believes that his girlfriend's lover owns one, even though 'his neighbour' and 'his girlfriend's lover' refer to the same person. And notice, moreover, that we do not spontaneously think of beliefs, desires, hopes or intentions as being physical states or properties, as on the contrary we do of such properties as height or weight. Apparently, then, our ordinary discourse about actions, agents and mental states challenges the unity of science programme on both of its claims, namely extensionality and physicalism.

What can be done in order to bring human action and mind under the unity of science? Faced with the mentalistic and intensional language of both everyday understanding of agents and actions and current social sciences, those philosophers and social scientists who are committed to the scientistic programme, or who at least sympathize with it, have taken several attitudes and embraced several research programmes, whose features combine in different ways so as to give rise to several variations. Since, as we have seen, it is mental discourse that stands in the way of a natural-scientific treatment of agents and actions, we should not find it strange that coming to terms with mental states and properties will be a central concern of these proposals. The ways of doing so may range from reduction to sheer elimination of the mental.

A well-known proposal on these scientistic lines is behaviourism. According to this latter, psychology should explain human behaviour by having recourse to physically describable stimuli, such as flashing lights, sounds, punishments or rewards, not to mental states or processes. Behaviour in turn should be understood as a set of responses, consisting of the physical movements of organisms, to such stimuli. Behaviourism, then, honours not only physicalism, but also extensionality, for physical events and movements can be described in an extensional language. Taking physical events as the only legitimate range of variables in psychology, human behaviour could be explained and predicted in much the same way as any other physical event, on the condition that laws could be found that relate such variables, namely stimuli and responses. Laws can be found that relate such happenings as intense visual stimuli and eyelid movements, or acoustic stimuli and salivation. Notice, however, that neither response is an action. They are just reflex movements, mere happenings. But behaviourist psychology certainly wants to explain and predict more than reflex movements. It surely wants to explain and predict complex intentional behaviour. Prediction of complex intentional actions in terms of laws that relate physical stimuli and responses would require, it seems, law-like or logical equivalences between those physical descriptions and intentional descriptions of behaviour. It would require a reduction of mental intentional concepts to physical behavioural ones. There are strong reasons for thinking that those equivalences cannot be formulated. First of all, they cannot be found if our contention is right that specifically human, meaningful actions do not logically imply specific kinds of happenings. There is no hope of finding a finitely specifiable set of physical conditions and movements that matches up an action concept such as buying food or greeting a friend. Consider, moreover, that attributing to someoe the performance of an act of buying food implies the attribution to him or her of a complex set of intentional states. These states should also be given behavioural equivalents in which no intentional state should be mentioned. What physical behaviour could be an equivalent of, say, believing that a grocer's is nearby? Suppose we adopt the following, seemingly desperate proposal: believing that a grocer's is nearby is to emit the sound 'Yes' as a response to the acoustic stimulus 'Do you believe that a grocer's is nearby?'. But that is only true if our subject understands this latter sound as a question, intends to answer that question, and so on. Understanding and intending, however, are good examples of the intentional concepts our behavioural analysis was supposed to get rid of.

In fact, the behaviourist programme for psychology is, nowadays, widely acknowledged as a failure. This failure has prompted other scientistic attempts. Identity theory is one of those. Unlike behaviourism, it has not developed in a psychological context, but in a philosophical one.[2] According to identity theory, mental states and processes are identical to physical (neurophysiological) states and processes, in the sense that a description such as 'John's belief that today is Thursday' has the same referent as a description of some state of John's nervous system, even if the speaker's intention is not to refer to the latter, just as someone who uses the word 'water' refers in fact to H_2O, even if he does not know that water is H_2O and so has no intention to refer to H_2O. Identity theory can give a straightforward account of how our mental states can give rise to physical changes, such as bodily movements: they can do that for the simple reason that they are physical processes themselves.

The generic claim of identity between mind and body can be variously specified. In some of its forms, namely the so-called 'type-identity', the claim amounts to a reductionist theory, whose aim is to provide an analysis of mental states that allows their reduction to states of the nervous system. The reducing theory, namely neurophysiology, could then give a physicalist and extensionalist account of mind and intentional action, a law-based account inspired by the ideal of the unity of science. In order to succeed, it would need to discover bridge laws connecting types of mental states with types of neurophysiological states. These laws would assert the equivalence between the belief that p or the intention to q and, say, the firing of neurons r or the firing of neurons s. The prospects of finding these laws, however, are rather bleak. There is no a priori reason to expect that our system of intentional concepts, which has developed in complete independence of neurophysiology and of any scientific purposes, will manageably match up a neurophysiological classification of nervous states and processes. Are we really prepared to believe that my intention to go to the cinema and a Chinese boy's intention to do so involve a common state in our respective nervous systems? Attribution of mental predicates is brought about according to standards that have nothing to do with attribution of neurophysiological properties. As one physicalist has come to acknowledge, it would be close to a miracle if our classification of intentional states were to match up a scientific classification of neurological states.[3]

A non-reductionist form of the identity claim is the so-called 'token-identity theory'. This position assumes that the difficulties in finding psychophysical laws are insurmountable, while still accepting physicalism. Token-identity theory rejects identity between types of mental states and types of neurophysiological states. Its claim is the much weaker one that each particular mental state is identical to a particular neurological state. For example, the belief that p is not identical to the firing of neurons r, but John's belief that p at time t would be identical to the firing of a certain set of neurons in John's nervous system at time t. Even if it turned out to be true, token-identity theory does not allow for a social science based on physical laws or shaped on the model of physics. Identity of tokens is too weak to allow for the statement of those psychophysical laws that are needed if intentional concepts are to be reduced to concepts of physical sciences. In fact, token-identity theories are compatible with a positive attitude towards the autonomy and specificity of social sciences. I doubt, however, whether they are also compatible, when combined with a deterministic view of the physical world, with free agency. That human intentional actions are not predictable in terms of laws, as this position assumes, does not immediately imply that they are free. This question will be partly discussed in the last chapter of this book.

Lack of confidence in reductionist analyses of intentional states, when combined with a strong commitment to a physicalist ontology, an extensionalist semantics and an empiricist view of knowledge, can also lead to eliminative proposals concerning mental states and properties. According to W. O. Quine, there is no definite answer, determined by physical facts, to questions about what someone believes, hopes, intends or desires. The holistic character of mental concepts allows for a variety of interpretative hypotheses about someone's mental states, all of them compatible with the same set of behavioural or otherwise physical facts about him or her. Mental properties cannot be given a definite extension, fixed by physical facts, and this should raise suspicions concerning their ontological respectability. Intentional concepts remit to one another in a circle with no way out to a possible fixation by facts, being irreducible to and independent of physical concepts. This was the basis on which the German psychologist Franz Brentano wanted to build the autonomy of psychology and other social sciences from natural sciences. The conclusion of the eliminative materialist, however, is not the autonomy of those sciences that deal with intentionality, but the denial of their possibility and of the ontological respectability of intentional states. As Quine writes, 'one may accept the Brentano thesis either as showing the indispensability of intentional idioms and the importance of an autonomous science of intention, or as showing the baselessness of intentional idioms and the emptiness of a science of intention. My attitude, unlike Brentano's, is the second.'[4] Even if intentional idioms are useful, even indispensable for practical purposes, they would find no place in an ultimate, true description of the world. A discussion of Quine's position would exceed the limits of this book. Let us just say the following. Quine holds that intentional contents and propositional attitudes are hardly justified by the fact that they are required by 'the vernacular of semantics or intention'. The proper reply is that the elimination of mental properties is hardly justified by the fact that it might be required by a tough scientistic view of knowledge.[5]

Let us finally refer to a position that has gained wide acceptance in recent times, namely functionalism. Functionalism shares with identity theory the willingness to avoid both a behaviourist or eliminative rejection of inner mental life and a dualist commitment to a sort of non-physical stuff that those states would consist of. It tries to avoid the former by viewing mental states as internal states that explain overt behaviour. And it tries to avoid the latter by viewing those internal states as having a particular physical realization in each case. Functionalism, however, shares with token-identity theories and with eliminative materialism a mistrust of physical or neurophysiological reduction of intentional concepts, departing from type-identity theories with respect to this. Even if it were to be possible, this reduction would have quite unwelcome consequences, for it would commit us to deny mental states to any being whose physical constitution was fairly different from ours.

Functionalism intends to fulfil all these requirements by conceiving mental states as functional states, characterized by their causal role in prompting, and being prompted by, other such states and behaviour. To be in a functional state is to be such that, given certain inputs, and given other functional states, certain outputs are causally ensured. Two different systems can share the same set of functional states even if their physical structure is different. For example, to believe that p or q is to be such that, given that not-p, and given certain dispositions, one goes to the belief-state that q. So, two persons may be said to believe that p or q on the condition that both of them show these causal tendencies, even if their brains or nervous systems do not share a common state. The intention to go to the cinema may be attributed both to me and to a Chinese boy with no need of a common neuro-physiological state in our respective brains, provided that both of us display certain dispositions to act. In each case, however, that functional state will have a particular physical realization in each brain. In fact, a type of mental functional state may be instantiated not just by human brains, but also by computers or, say, silicon-based Martians. Physicalism is preserved, for functional states cannot exist without being physically realized, but not in its tough version, for a type of functional state does not require a specific type of physical state.

The notion of functional state can be applied to a wide range of devices. Two cars, for instance, have several functional states in common, even if their respective engines are differently designed. This means, however, that not every functional state is a mental state, true as the converse might be. Note that a functional state is classified in terms of its role in causal patterns. We should ask, then, whether the notion of functional state can be specified so as to meet the constitutive features of the intentionality of mind, or, in other words, whether a functional state deserves to be called 'mental'. I propose to focus on two features of intentionality, namely normativity and content, as we referred to them in the preceding chapter.

Can the notion of functional state account for that normativity which constitutes possession and attribution of mental states? No functional state failing to satisfy certain minimal normative requirements could count as a mental state. This is one of the features that distinguish those functional states that are candidates to be considered as mental from those that, as happens with the functional states of a car, are not. A functionalist frame should represent minds as complex causal networks of states that happen to satisfy, at the same time, those normative constraints we assume human minds should minimally meet. This is why computers are taken to be good models of human minds in some functionalist approaches. Computers are physical systems designed in such a way that their causal functioning matches certain normative rules. However, if normativity is not to appear as an inexplicable standard, external to the theory, it has to be accounted for in terms of causal dispositions or tendencies of certain systems to go through certain stages. But then the specific normative aspect of human mind is misrepresented as a merely factual trait: the essential tension between the way we ought to reason or act and the way we do in fact reason or act, a tension which characterizes human thought and action, collapses in the functionalist view. The counterpart of normativity in functionalist views of mind is but a poor surrogate for the real thing.

On the other hand, in conceiving of mental states as functional states that satisfy certain normative constraints, functionalism seems to commit itself to the claim that any device that shows similar functional states has mental states. Computers, therefore, have mental states, according to this view. In what sense, however, may functional states of a computer be said to be similar to human mental states? Suppose that I believe that my friend Peter is either in a certain restaurant or in the cinema. Suppose that I get to the restaurant and find that he is not there. I can be said to have acquired the information that my friend is not in the restaurant. This information, together with the first state of belief, causes me to go to a new state, namely the belief-state that my friend is in the cinema. This train of thought can be conceived, in a functionalistic manner, as a case of information processing, whose states relate causally to one another. Now compare an apparently similar situation in a computer. Suppose that the computer is said to be in the state EITHER P OR Q. If it receives the input NOT P and if it is appropriately programmed, it will go to the state Q. Let P be interpreted as the sentence 'My friend Peter is in the restaurant' and Q as 'My friend Peter is in the cinema.' Now both I and the computer may be said to share certain functional states, according to the causal relations they show. But consider that this functional perspective on my mental states brings about a literal reduction of them: an impoverishment of their content. For the content of the computer's states is purely formal. A computer is a syntactic device. It processes signs according to their form. My states, however, seem to have a semantic content, not only a syntactic one. In believing that my friend is in the cinema I am *referring to* my friend and to the cinema. This intentional directedness to reality is absent from the computer's states. The computer can give as output the string of signs MY FRIEND IS IN THE CINEMA, but surely it is not referring either to my friend or to the cinema. It is simply transforming signs into other signs, not dealing with meaningful expressions. Now, in viewing mental states as functional ones, functionalism blurs all their semantic aspects. There are reasons for asking whether *functionalist* analyses of mind are really analyses of *mind*. They depict the content of mental states as a purely formal scheme, with no projection on to the world. This picture is hardly recognizable as the content of human mental states. We could say, once again, that the counterpart of intentional content in functionalist accounts of mind is just a poor surrogate for the real thing.

A functionalist might reply that in so far as he is trying to build an explanatory frame for human mind and behaviour, the semantic properties of mental states are not relevant, for the effects of my belief-state would remain the same even if my friend or the cinema had never existed. The important thing, that is, would be the mental scheme as such, not its projection on to the real world.[6] I am sceptical about the virtues of this split between causal role and semantic content. For even if it turned out to be true that my friend and the cinema were just creatures of my feverish imagination, they would still act on my other states and behaviour as representations *of* real things, not as meaningless, merely formal signs. Besides that, there are ways of thinking that are both essentially referential and especially important in prompting and causing behaviour, namely those thoughts that involve demonstratives or indexical expressions, such as 'this', 'now', 'here' or 'I'. I may intend to attend a meeting at eleven o'clock, but I start moving as soon as I realize that *now* it is eleven o'clock.[7] Conceiving the content of such thoughts in terms of a formal scheme seems to be particularly improper. For what concerns demonstratives, for instance, we plausibly assume that their content is the real object in the world referred to by them.

A detailed discussion of functionalism, however, would take us far beyond the reasonable limits of this introductory book on the philosophy of action. I propose, then, to restrict the general problems we have dealt with in this chapter to the specific question of whether action explanations in a scientistic vein can plausibly be given. Let us pay attention to it. Our first target will be P. M. Churchland's contention that the tension we assumed to exist between our everyday explanatory account of human actions and a scientific explanation of them is a mere appearance, the former showing the same logical structure as the latter.

8

Laws and Explanation of Actions:
P. M. Churchland

The deductive-nomological model of explanation, considered as an ideal reconstruction of scientific explanation, is at least as old as J. S. Mill, though K. R. Popper and C. G. Hempel have offered more accurate and refined expositions of it. A scientific explanation, so this account claims, has the form of a deductive argument whose premises contain general laws and descriptions of singular events as causes and whose conclusion is a suitable description of the explanandum. The general idea behind the model is that nothing but a general law of nature, conceived as a universally quantified conditional, whose truth is neither necessary nor a priori, can allow us to justifiably explain why some particular event happened by citing another event as its cause. So, the model is quite in line with the Humean view of causation, according to which a causal relation is ultimately a case or instance of a general regularity of nature.

The model has been widely held to represent the general form of every scientific explanation, or, perhaps better, the form that any explanation should have in order to count as a scientifically respectable one. The idea that any explanation must be backed by a law is central to this line of thought.

At least as old as the first formulations of the model is the idea that everyday and social-scientific explanations of intentional actions in terms of their reasons, beliefs, desires, etc., have a different structure from that of explanations of events in natural sciences, by which the model was originally inspired, and, in particular, that they are not backed by laws. Schleiermacher, Droysen, Dilthey, Collingwood and Dray would surely favour this contention. The defenders of the deductive-nomological model and especially Carl G. Hempel have claimed, on the contrary, that ordinary and social-scientific (particularly historical) explanations of intentional actions conform essentially to the model, their main contention being that only a general law can support the 'because' of any of those explanations. The polemic that developed from the forties to the sixties between Carl G. Hempel and William Dray contains perhaps the most detailed exposition of the arguments of both parties.[1]

An important argument in favour of the opponents to the model used to be that its defenders were not able to offer a clear example of a law covering any of those explanations of intentional actions. I will be concerned here with a more recent attempt to provide a law backing those explanations. The attempt was made by Paul M. Churchland in his paper 'The Logical Character of Action Explanations', dating back to 1970.[2] 'My immediate aim', Churchland says, 'is to make a prima-facie case in favor of the view that action-explanations are indeed of the familiar D-N [deductive-nomological, C.M.] mold . . . I shall try to make out that . . . there are some fairly sophisticated nomic principles or "laws" *specifically* presupposed by our ordinary action-explanations, and that a variety of interesting features of action-explanations can be clearly understood when this background structure is brought to light.'[3] Churchland speaks of the explanandum as being a 'full-blooded action', but from his remarks we can deduce that he understands that expression as meaning 'intentional action', and this is the term we shall be using from now on.

Churchland's strategy is to uncover, starting from current objections to an explanation of the kind 'X A-ed because he wanted ϕ', the explanatory conditions we are supposing in such explanations, so that he can construct a universal conditional having as its antecedent this set of explanatory conditions and 'X A-s', that is, the action so explained, as its consequent.

Here is the universal conditional or 'law' which backs our explanations of intentional actions and gives its force to the 'because':

Let X range over agents, ϕ over things wanted by him and A over actions. So we have:

L_1: (X) (ϕ) (A) (If [1] X wants ϕ, and [2] X believes that A-ing is a way for him to bring about ϕ under those circumstances, and [3] there is no action believed by X to be a way for him to bring about ϕ, under the circumstances, which X judges to be as preferable to him as, or more preferable to him than, A-ing, and [4] X has no other want (or set of them) which, under the circumstances, overrides his want ϕ, and [5] X knows how to A, and [6] X is able to A,
then [7] X A-s.).[4]

The first two premises state that appropriate wants and beliefs are positive causal factors of an intentional action; they contain, that is, the familiar belief–desire model that is defended by most causal theorists of action, such as Donald Davidson and Alvin I. Goldman. Premises [3] to [6] state negative conditions or *ceteris paribus* clauses excluding the influence of other factors in undermining the causal efficacy of the first two factors. These features suggest the first natural objection to the nomological character of L_1, namely that laws are unrestricted universal conditionals, containing no *ceteris paribus* clauses.

Churchland meets the objection by pointing out that *ceteris paribus* clauses enter into many respectable law sketches in the field of natural knowledge. Certainly, L_1 is a law sketch, but this does not undermine its nomic character. Here are two examples of law sketches: '(a) If a bar magnet is placed under a flat surface on which iron filings are evenly spread, then, if there are no other significant forces on the filings, they will shift into a pattern of whorls oriented on the line of the bar. (b) If a sulphur-phosphorus match is struck, then, barring vitiating factors, it will burn.' And, as Churchland says, 'gaps and fuzzy areas in our knowledge of nomic connections are standardly filled with such *ceteris paribus* clauses.'[5] The objection, however, is not so easily met. For there are differences, and very important ones, between (a) and (b), on the one hand, and L_1, on the other. The nomic character of (a) and (b) – I would prefer to call them true generalizations rather than law sketches – derives in part from the fact that they can be related to, and supported by, *unrestricted* universal conditionals – proper laws – using no terms such as 'bar', 'filings', 'iron', 'match', and whose truth does not presuppose the truth of (a) and (b), say the laws of electromagnetism, combustion, etc. Nothing parallel happens in the case of L_1. If L_1 is to be supported by, and related to, other 'laws', these will be statements or principles using such terms as 'wants', 'actions', 'beliefs', etc., and whose truth will not only support, but will also be supported by the truth of L_1, thus failing to be unrestricted conditionals. One such principle could be, for instance, the following, cited by Donald Davidson: 'If an agent wants to do x more than he wants to do y and he believes himself free to do either x or y, then he will intentionally do x if he does either x or y intentionally.'[6] This shows that L_1 cannot be placed at the same level as *ceteris paribus* law sketches in the field of natural sciences. It seems to have a much more basic role. It seems to belong somehow, properly corrected, as Churchland suggests it could be, to our basic understanding of what it is to act intentionally or to want or to act because of a want. This leads to the second natural objection, namely that L_1 is not an empirical law, but a sort of analytic statement, 'analytic' being understood as something like 'true by definition'. So, L_1 could not be held as having a nomic character. C. H. Whiteley refers to a related view by pointing out that to say that a person wants x is to say that if he or she has the opportunity of achieving or bringing about x he or she will do so, *ceteris paribus*, so that it is a necessary truth that people do what they want to do.[7] Whiteley does not have in mind Churchland's paper, which appeared later. It is worth noticing the close connection of Whiteley's claim with Churchland's L_1 *and* the fact that Whiteley presents his claim as a sort of *definition* of 'wanting': this shows that the objection of analyticity has something in its favour.

I do not subscribe to it, however, if not for other reasons, at least because I think that L_1 is false and an analytic statement is supposed to be true. But, leaving this aside for the moment, what interests me is to point to Churchland's *answer* to this objection:

> After all, the suggestion is that L_1 is a deeply entrenched theoretical nomological central to our understanding both of human behaviour and of such states as wanting, believing and preferring – a basic principle of the conceptual framework in terms of which we conceive ourselves. It *is* difficult, perhaps impossible, to deny L_1 without undermining the conceptual machinery which makes such understanding possible or, better, *constitutes* it, but none of this entails that L_1 is 'analytic' in any sense inconsistent with its being nomological in character. One could not deny the principle of mass-energy conservation without threatening similar havoc in the conceptual framework of modern physical theory, and one would encounter similar difficulties in trying to describe a noncontroversial case which would falsify that principle. If there are any relevant differences between these two cases, they are differences only in degree.[8]

Churchland's answer to the analyticity objection looks all right. After Quine's criticism we are nowadays less prepared to accept a clear-cut distinction between analytic and synthetic statements and better prepared to accept that the fact that a statement belongs to the centre of a theory does nothing to undermine its empirical character, if it has that character.

What is not all right, however, is the *conjunction* of this answer and the answer to the first objection. You simply cannot answer the objection that L_1 is not nomological given that it contains *ceteris paribus* clauses by saying that L_1 could be placed at the same level as other low-level, *ceteris paribus* generalizations such as (a) and (b), which nobody would dream of placing at the centre of physical theory, *and* answer the objection of analyticity by saying that L_1 could be placed at the same level as the principle of mass-energy conservation, an unrestricted universal law belonging to the very core of physical theory. Quite simply, both statements are inconsistent with one another. We can conclude, then, that Churchland has not succeeded, so far, in defending his claim that L_1 has a nomic character and is similar to the laws of natural sciences. L_1 cannot be comparable to the principle of mass-energy conservation, for it contains *ceteris paribus* clauses, but it cannot be comparable to low-level generalizations such as (a) and (b) either, for it clearly has a much more basic character in our understanding of human actions. And, if the nomic character of L_1 has not been established, explanations of intentional actions have not been shown to be deductive-nomological in character, either.

We can now move a step further. I said that, in my opinion, L_1 was false. To justify this I propose a sort of 'do-it-yourself' refutation. Here it is: wait until there is something, call it D, you really want; make sure you know an action, call it A, by means of which you can get D and that there is no other action you judge preferable to A in order to get D; make sure there is not anything else you want more than D; make sure you know how to A and that you are able to do it. Given all that, to refute Churchland's law, simply do not do A. Therefore, L_1 is false, Q.E.D.

A defender of L_1 could argue that, after all, L_1's conditions were not satisfied, for there *was* something you wanted more than D, namely to refute Churchland's law, call it R. But then he is linking the antecedent and the consequent so strongly that *nothing* could falsify L_1, so that its empirical character begins to fade away. Churchland's 'law' rests crucially on the notion of strength of deires and on the possibility of comparing the relative strength of different desires. We act upon our strongest or 'overriding' desire if nothing prevents us, etc. The empirical content of this notion is dubious, to say the least. This is shown by this possible and natural answer to our objection, for how does our opponent *know* that there was something we wanted more than D, that we had a stronger or overriding desire? Simply because we acted upon it. That is, we explain an action by appealing to the overriding desire of the agent, and we establish this overriding desire by appealing to the action he performs. We have, then, no other independent criterion to establish which is the overriding desire than the action itself, so that an explanation of the action in terms of that desire looks like a platitude, lacking empirical content. However, since very often explanations of actions in terms of desires are *not* platitudes, something must be missing in Churchland's model.

Now, what does my 'refutation' show, if anything? Churchland suggests that we could, starting from L_1, state a *criterion* for 'full-blooded actions', or, in our terms, for intentional ones. The criterion is this: 'To say that an event-description of the general form "X A-ed" is a description of a full-blooded action is to say that the event under that description *takes a certain kind of explanation* – specifically, one in terms of L_1 and the corresponding singular conditions . . . *simpliciter*.'[9] Now, I think that this conception of intentional action is misguided. The situation in our counterexample could be described as follows: I had a want D (say, drinking a cup of coffee), and an aim or purpose R (namely, to refute Churchland's law); we can also call R a want, if we wish; anyway, I do not see any compelling reason to accept that R overrode D; in the situation, as described, D was very strong and could in fact be stronger than R; but we can also say that R and D are just not homogeneous enough to be compared in strength, R being, say, a 'cold' want, or a mischievous purpose, and D being a 'hot' want, a need for bodily pleasure; then what happened was that I *decided* or *intended* to act so as to favour R and conceived a *plan* to achieve it, namely not to act so as to get D; and I *fulfilled* my decision by *following* my plan and following it *correctly*. So, what I wanted to point at with my 'refutation' is something that is missing in Churchland's model, namely that human agents show *reflexivity* in their intentional actions, that is, they can make their desires objects of further reflection and that, as a result of this, they can, at a higher level, decide or intend to act on this or that desire, and even on no desire at all. My example is far from uncommon: often we act against what we would most like to do. Churchland's 'law' does not include this, and so it cannot account for quite simple cases of intentional actions except in the empty way we pointed out above. To make our point in other terms: human agents have not only desires, but also a 'rational will'.[10] The conclusion, then, is that L_1 needs completion, and that something like intentions, decisions or plans should enter into it and, on the other hand, that these and other *normative* notions, such as rationality, coherence, good reasons, etc., should somehow be included in the criterion of intentional action, on the lines suggested in chapter 5. It is simply not enough to state causal conditions factually linked to an action as their effect. But, so completed, L_1 loses its apperance as a kind of law or nomic statement.

We can say, now, that L_1, corrected in the normative sense suggested above, guides our explanations of actions, excluding certain explanatory hypotheses and prompting others, and, in extreme cases, if its constraints are not met at all, even favouring the conclusion that we are not dealing with rational agents nor intentional actions. However, it is not a law, since it does not state a mere factual relation, but a normative one, by using uneliminably normative concepts.

It would be unfair, however, to deny that Churchland gives normativity a place in the explanation of actions. I think that it is the wrong place, but it will be very instructive to see why this is so. Churchland concedes that explanations of intentional actions on the lines suggested by L_1 include, *besides* a causal-explanatory relation, a 'reasonable-in-the-light-of' relation between explanandum and explanans, so that the action, so explained, appears also as reasonable in the light of the agent's beliefs and desires.[11] But this 'reasonable-in-the-light-of' relation comes, according to him, from another source than the causal-explanatory relation, so that the two relations remain somehow separate. The normative, 'reasonable-in-the-light-of' relation comes from and holds between the *propositional contents* of the psychological states. The causal-explanatory relations comes from and holds between the psychological *states* themselves, considered as something separable from their contents and, presumably, according to some remarks, as bodily or physiological states. According to Churchland,

> L_1 . . . and a large variety of other law sketches appropriate to persons presuppose a logical theory: that of propositions and the logical relations between them. Wants, beliefs, and a variety of other psychological states and episodes are identified by reference to a specific proposition (hence the referential opacity in such contexts). We should not find it odd therefore that certain of the laws describing our operations should embody or reflect certain extra-nomic logical relations, relations such as 'reasonable-in-the-light-of'. In what else might our status as 'rational agents' consist?[12]

What I want to question is the legitimacy of such a separation in the frame – which is Churchland's – of accounting for 'full-blooded' or intentional actions. We cannot separate states and propositional contents, nor causal-explanatory and logical relations and still be dealing with explanations of 'full-blooded' or intentional actions. Think of the activity of drawing conclusions from premises. I concede that logical, abstract relations between premises and conclusion are not the same as the relations between my considering the premises and my drawing the conclusion. The former relations hold, we want to say, even if nobody sees or accepts them, whereas the latter involve concrete, particular acts and persons. This, I think, is what makes that separation plausible, and what prompts the view that the second relation is a mere causal, factual relation between particular and discrete events, so that normativity concerns only the logical relations between propositions. As Whiteley points out, the logical explanation or validation of an inference in terms of relationships of implication or probability does not exclude or conflict with a causal explanation of the fact that a person has come from the acceptance of the premises to the acceptance of the conclusion.[13] But if by 'causal explanation' we understand an explanation relating mere facts, with no reference to norms, we will face problems. In order for a description of someone's act as 'drawing a conclusion' to be true, as a description of a 'full-blooded' or intentional action, his drawing the conclusion has to be a result of his *considering the content of the premises*, and this involves being guided, in drawing the conclusion, by the logical relationships between it and the premises. That is, the relationship between his act of considering the premises and his act of drawing the conclusion cannot be kept apart from the normative relationship between the premises and the conclusion itself, if 'drawing a conclusion' is to be true of that agent as a description of an intentional action. Normativity concerns the relationships between intentional action and the states by means of which we explain it, and not just the abstract relations between the propositional contents of the states. If my drawing the conclusion is not caused and explained precisely by my considering *what the premises say*, but, say, by a sort of causal chain between states deprived of content, so that the logical relationships between the contents do not play any explanatory role, my action, if it is one, cannot be truly explained under the description 'drawing a conclusion'.

Churchland, however, denies any explanatory power to the logical relations in every case, including intentional action explanations: 'Such extranomic logical relations between explanans/explanandum pairs are neither unique nor explanatory.'[14] These logical relations are not unique, we suppose, in the sense that we find them in cases other than action explanations. This is undeniably true. After all, according to the orthodox Deductive-Nomological Model, the explanandum must be logically deduced from the explanans. Besides that, there are logical relations between the statements of a scientific theory. So far, so good. Moreover, they are not explanatory, we suppose Churchland to think, because the explanatory power lies in the laws that link some particular facts as causes and another particular fact as effect, the logical relations being here, so to speak, a means by which the explanatory ability of the law is transmitted to those particular facts as causes.

But now, this seems to challenge our previous criticism of the nomic character of L_1, according to which L_1 – corrected in the sense indicated – is not a law since it does not state a mere factual relation, but a normative one. So formulated, our criticism would have very unwelcome consequences, for it would imply that most scientific theories are not nomic. Think, for instance, of the fact that physical theory incorporates very sophisticated mathematical models. These can be said to be normative in character, since their theorems are linked by strict logical relations with one another and with axioms and other parts of the theory. Even more, we can say that the fields of reality explained by means of those models *instantiate* those normative relations. But then, Churchland could reply to our previous criticism, what is the supposedly *essential* difference between scientific theories and everyday explanation of actions? After all, the normative, 'reasonable-in-the-light-of' relation between explanans and explanandum, which Dray stressed as characteristic of action explanations, seems to be common to all scientific forms of explanation, but this does not undermine the nomic status of scientific laws. So, in Churchland's view, 'the particular view of action-explanations being defended is but one aspect of the more general view that the common-sense conceptual framework in terms of which we conceive ourselves, *qua* persons, has all the relevant structural and logical features of those lesser conceptual frameworks we call scientific theories (for example, molecular theory).'[15]

So far, then, our discussion has not taken us too far. Our criticism of Churchland's claim that action-explanations are deductive-nomological arguments and that something like L_1 backs them rested on two main contentions: first, that L_1's status as a law was unclear, for it was too basic to be comparable to a low-level scientific generalization and contained too many *ceteris paribus* clauses to be comparable to a central physical law such as the principle of mass-energy conservation; and, second, that L_1 should be corrected in a normative sense in order to account for obvious cases of intentional actions. Now, this second objection seems to have been met by pointing to the normative character of most scientific theories, on the lines suggested above. And, as for the first, Churchland should concede that L_1 cannot be compared with the principle of mass-energy conservation, for it contains too many *ceteris paribus* clauses, but, after all, this is not an *essential* difference. As he points out, 'if there are any relevant differences between these two cases, they are differences only in degree.'[16]

To block this way out we need to point to a *crucial* difference in the role played by normativity in scientific theories and explanation, on the one hand, and in principles like L_1 and action-explanation, on the other. Churchland's point is that there is no such crucial difference. I think his view could be stated by saying that *in the same sense* in which we can say that a magnetic field *instantiates* a mathematical model (a normative device), we can also say that intentional actions and their explanatory states *instantiate* L_1 (a normative device, too). What I contend is that those senses are *crucially* different. We say that a magnetic field instantiates a mathematical model in the sense that its unfolding *accords* to the model, so that it can be described and predicted by means of it; normativity belongs to the model; it would be absurd to say that it belongs to the magnetic field itself in the sense that the field *adjusts* its unfolding to the model, for this would imply attributing to the field, for instance, the possibility of literally making *mistakes* in following the model. That this is absurd is, of course, a presupposition of scientific theories and of the existence of unrestricted laws. But *this* is precisely the sense in which we can say that intentional actions, states and agents instantiate normativity and normative principles: normativity belongs to the actions we explain and to the states by means of which we explain them. That is why normative relations cannot be kept apart from explanatory relations, but must be essentially linked to them, and that is why we are not allowed to keep the psychological states apart from their propositional contents in explaining intentional, or 'full-blooded' actions. A belief, a desire, a decision, etc., cannot explain why someone performed an intentional action if we deprive them of their content. My action of signalling for a turn while driving can be explained, under that description, only by referring to a *belief that* a turn is coming, not, say, by a belief that it is cold outside. And, moreover, there are normative relations not only between, say, p & q and p, but also between *believing* that p & q and *believing* that p. I can make the mistake of believing the first and not believing the second, but just the fact that my beliefs can be mistaken shows that they are subject to norms.

But now our previous objections again take on all their force. We can understand now the strange status of L_1 as at the same time central to our conception of human actions and full of *ceteris paribus* clauses. Certainly, the laws of electromagnetism would also contain *ceteris paribus* clauses if magnetic fields *followed* the normative principles embedded and involved in those laws in the sense in which human beings follow the normative principles embedded and involved in L_1, corrected on the lines suggested above.

I think we can conclude, then, that Churchland has not succeeded in defending his claim that explanations of intentional actions are on a par with deductive-nomological explanations.

In providing a supposedly nomological statement, couched in terms of our everyday psychological concepts, that backs ordinary explanations of actions, Churchland is not trying to defend the truth and correctness of that conceptual frame. He thinks, on the contrary, that what is now called 'folk-psychology' is a false and radically misleading theory about the causes of human behaviour.[17] Rather, he is aiming to show that this ordinary conceptual frame is an *empirical theory* among others, having no special privilege or respectability, a theory which, given its explanatory weakness and lack of accuracy, should be abandoned in favour of better theories, especially neurology and neurophysiology. Churchland is, in fact, an eliminative materialist. Against all this, my contention has been that L_1 is not an empirical law; the concepts it employs, namely those of 'folk-psychology', are related not by factual but by normative relationships which are, and this is the essential point, not merely instantiated but followed by human agents in a reflexive way. It is the fact that human beings reflexively follow normative constraints that gives their doings the character of intentional actions. If I am right about all this, replacing this ordinary conceptual frame with a neuroscientific one would not be just the replacement of a bad empirical theory about human action with a better one. The new theory would have no chance of explaining and predicting human actions, for these are such in the context of that normative conceptual network, and would not survive as objects of a descriptive, empirical theory, as neuroscience is supposed to be.

9

Laws and Prediction of Actions: Decision Theory

The essential idea behind Churchland's law is that what we intentionally do is a function of two factors, namely the strength of our desires (what we most want) and appropriate beliefs about how to satisfy them. No doubt, the idea has some plausibility. If we face two alternatives, not equally desirable, and we think we can bring about the first as easily as the second, who would doubt that (unless we decide to falsify Churchland's law) we will favour the one we feel more attracted by? Furthermore, is not that just the *reasonable* thing to do under the circumstances? In this case, what we will be doing coincides with what is reasonable for us to do. But then, why not use norms we find it reasonable to follow so as to build upon them a nomological theory concerning what we will be doing as a matter of lawlike necessity? A theory which respected certain standards of what a reasonable action is could then be the basis on which a nomological theory of human action could be built. And it seems we have the former: Bayesian decision theory, a fairly sophisticated mathematical construction, highly developed in recent times, provides an initially plausible model of rational decision and action.

We often face decision problems. We deliberate about what is best for us to do under certain circumstances. According to decision theory, the relevant factors to take into account in order to answer this question are certain specific beliefs and desires of the agent. Rational decision will be determined by a conjunction of these factors. Decision theory provides a function that takes these factors as arguments and yields rational decision as result.

In order to see how rational decision is conceived from the standpoint of this theory, let us start with an idealized construct: the

Rational Decision Maker (RDM, for short). RDM is equipped with a complete and consistent pattern of preferences. That the pattern is complete means the following: given any two consequences, X and Y, of RDM's possible ways of acting, either RDM prefers X to Y, or Y to X, or it (let us use this non-personal pronoun to refer to RDM) is indifferent between X and Y, where the conjunction 'or' is understood in its exclusive sense, so that the holding of one of those three possible preference relations excludes the holding of the other two. That the pattern is consistent means, at least, the following: given that RDM prefers X to Y, and Y to Z, then it prefers X to Z. In other words, the preference relation is transitive. RDM is not allowed to prefer X to Y, Y to Z, and Z to X. Decision theory does not ask about the moral or any other justification of this pattern. Its only constraints are completeness and consistency. So, an acceptable part of the pattern would be to prefer the world's destruction to a small cut in one's finger, to use a Humean example.

Secondly, the theory assumes that RDM's pattern of preferences is determined by RDM's subjective expected utilities for those consequences or outcomes of its acts. Subjective expected utilities, in turn, are a function of two factors, the first being the probabilities that RDM assigns to those outcomes of its possible acts, or, more exactly, to the obtaining of certain conditions that, according to its subjective judgement, will determine the final outcomes of several incompatible ways of acting it can engage in, and the second being the subjective values or desirabilities it assigns to those outcomes. The theory does not assume that RDM's probability assignments are objective, that is, it does not assume that RDM assigns to the outcomes their true objective frequencies. RDM's probability assignments are subjective in that they reflect its idiosyncratic beliefs, whether these are true or not. Subjective probability and desirability of each outcome combine to yield its subjective expected utility.

Let us see how RDM proceeds in order to arrive at a rational decision. Imagine our RDM undecided between two possible and incompatible acts that it envisages, say A1 and A2. Suppose that, from its point of view, A1 has two possible outcomes, depending on which of two conditions hold, and so has A2. What will RDM do? First of all it goes through the possible outcomes it envisages. The number of envisaged outcomes equals the product of possible acts and conditions. Four outcomes, then, are present in our case in RDM's deliberative landscape. Now RDM goes on to assign probabilities and desirabilities to each of those outcomes. It does it, let us suppose, by giving numerical values, separately, to those probabilities and desirabilities, say from 0 (no probability, no desirability) to 1 (highest probability and desirability). After doing that, each outcome has been associated with two numbers, corresponding, respectively, to its subjective probability and desirability. RDM proceeds now to obtain the expected utility of each outcome by getting the product of those two numbers. Suppose that RDM has assigned a probability of 0.5 and a desirability of 1 to a possible outcome of A1. That outcome, then, has, from RDM's point of view, an expected utility of 0.5. Having done this for all the outcomes, RDM obtains the expected utility of each act by adding the numbers that represent the expected utilities of its possible outcomes. These additions will yield a ranking of those acts in terms of their respective expected utilities. RDM now has all it needs to make a rational decision. It decides to perform the act which has the higher expected utility in the ranking. If both acts have the same expected utility, then RDM is indifferent between them. It will be performing the rational act in either case.

Decision theory contends that RDM's proceeding provides a model of human rational deliberation and decision making. This claim may sound strange. Few of us, if any, would recognize ourselves, as decision makers, in RDM's way of proceeding. For example, we are not conscious, in most cases of deliberation, of our assigning probabilities to outcomes. In fact, most of us simply do not know which probability to give to the obtaining of certain conditions. Often we simply do not care. As for desirabilities, we seem to restrict ourselves to comparing the lure of several alternatives we sometimes face. So, there are reasons to ask what the relationships are between this abstract and formal model and our actual decision making.

First of all, let us give some initial plausibility to decision theory's claim to model human rational decision by giving some flesh and blood to our RDM. Notice that in our actual decision making we simply see no point in acting so as to bring about something we highly desire unless we also believe that there is some chance of bringing it about. If we believe that a desired end is impossible for us to obtain, we would find it irrational to decide to act in order to reach it. We would not make that decision. Now that is precisely what the theory yields as a result, for, according to it, even if an outcome has the highest desirability for RDM, it will contribute nothing to the final expected utility of an act if RDM assigns to it no probability at all: the product of any positive number and zero is zero.

As a further step towards giving initial plausibility to decision theory, think of the following decision problem, that I borrow from R. C. Jeffrey:[1] John is the dinner guest of some friends of his and is expected to provide the wine; he has forgotten whether chicken or beef will be served; he has a bottle of white and a bottle of red, but cannot bring both, for he is going by bicycle; moreover, he has no telephone, so he cannot find out what will be served. Which bottle of wine should he bring? Suppose that, as far as he knows, chicken is as likely as beef. Suppose, moreover, that, plausibly enough, he does not like white wine with beef at all, whereas red wine with chicken, though a bit odd, is still acceptable. It seems, then, that bringing red wine is better after all, for it will be fine with beef and just acceptable with chicken, whereas white wine, though fine with chicken, will be unacceptable with beef. Now, if we translate this problem into the formal mould sketched above, distinguishing between acts (bringing white wine, bringing red wine), conditions (beef, chicken) and outcomes (white with beef, white with chicken, red with beef, red with chicken), and assigning numerical values to the probabilities and desirabilities of the outcomes, according to the information provided above, the act of bringing red wine will be ranked higher than the alternative. So, what seems to be the rational decision, according to ordinary, non-formal criteria, is also yielded as the rational decision according to the formal procedures of decision theory.

Decision theory's claim to be providing a model of human rational decision might not be misguided after all. And its rationale should by now be clearer. In E. Eells's words, the model says that 'a course of action has merit to the extent that it makes good consequences probable and that a rational person pursues a course of action that makes the best consequences the most probable, where the goodness and probabilities of the consequences are the agent's subjective assessments thereof'.[2] In more technical terms, rational decision making is to be understood, in terms of the model, as a process of maximizing subjective expected utility (SEU, for short).

Let us go on to discuss in more detail the relationships between the SEU maximization model and the real processes of human decision making. The model can be interpreted as a normative proposal concerning how we should proceed in order to make rational decisions. It can also be interpreted as a descriptive-explanatory theory concerning how we do in fact make decisions, as an empirical theory of human decision and action.

On any of those readings, decision theory makes quite strong assumptions about such things as the nature of deliberation, decision, practical reason, agency and mental states. Philosophically, it can be seen as siding with naturalistic and empiricist views of human beings on all those matters. It is worth pursuing an examination of these assumptions, which are implicit in the formal model sketched above.

To begin with, deliberation is conceived as a sort of information processing. The processed data are subjective probabilities and desirabilities of several possible outcomes and conditions. The theory claims that those data are to be interpreted as corresponding to degrees of belief and desire in a human subject. Data are processed by being treated and ordered so as to obtain a unique ranking of acts according to their SEU. This being so, a necessary assumption of the theory is that degrees of belief and desire are fixed before deliberation starts and are independent of it in that deliberation does not change them, its only function being to register, combine and order them in the ways prescribed by the model.

These are very strong theses indeed about deliberation. Bear in mind that, according to the SEU maximization model, degrees of belief, and especially of desire, are not evaluated. On the contrary, they are the fixed standards by which courses of action are evaluated and ranked. But I do not see any reason for this restriction. While deliberating we can and do evaluate desires according to other standards that cannot be assimilated to desires. We do not simply ask which way of acting is better to promote a desired end. We can and do sometimes ask whether that desired end is worth promoting after all, given certain principles. Reflexive evaluation of desires is surely part of what we take deliberation to be. The fact that we sometimes do not question our desires does not justify raising this case to a general paradigm of human deliberation. On the contrary, reflexive distancing from desires seems to me to be a specific mark of human deliberation. If this is right, it threatens to undermine another assumption of the theory, namely that degrees of belief and desire are fixed before deliberation and are independent of it. Reflexive thinking can *give* relevance and weight to these desires and beliefs, instead of merely registering a previously established ranking. A strongly felt desire may not retain a determining role in decision after reflection, whether its felt strength were to remain unchanged or not.

Decision, the output of deliberation, is viewed by the theory as a dependent variable, a function of pre-existing degrees of belief and desire. Decision is not autonomous from these factors. Decision theory connects at this point with classical causal thinking about human action, on the lines drawn by David Hume and John Stuart Mill, who see human action as the upshot of given causes, especially desires and volitions. Deciding to do something, in terms of the theory, is not different from passively acknowledging the higher expected utility of a certain course of action, as determined by subjective assignments of likelihood and desirability to outcomes. However, once the decision-theoretic picture of deliberation has been questioned, there is not much left in favour of this view of decision. If beliefs and desires can be reflexively evaluated and do not necessarily keep a determining role in decision after reflection, a gap opens between beliefs and desires, on the one hand, and decision, on the other, that prevents the latter from being a mere function of the former. Decision must be given an active and relatively autonomous character. This book allows for this requirement by conceiving of decision, and future intention, as commitments to actions.

Practical reason, in turn, is viewed by this theory as instrumental reason, as an ability to select optimal means to certain ends, not as having the power to establish those ends or to choose between them. Ends are taken as given by the subject's pattern of preferences. This view of practical reason is also Humean in spirit: reason is seen as an instrument at the service of desires, or, in Humean terms, as the slave of passions. This is why cases of moral conflict do not seem to be solvable in this frame. One form of moral conflict, in effect, is characterized by the fact that any alternative way of acting we can engage in honours one important principle while, at the same time, violating another, no less important one. The theory's advice is to deal with this problem in terms of the SEU of those acts. This, however, would not amount to dealing with *this* problem, but to changing its terms and shifting to a different question. The SEU of those several actions does not seem to be what matters here, for it is not, or not only, their consequences, but their intrinsic relation to principles we are committed to, and so our self-respect, that is at stake. Moreover, if at least some of our actions conform to a Kantian picture of practical reason, that is, if we can act against our desires, no matter what the consequences are to our subjective utility, then the decision so to act does not seem to be the result of measuring and ranking expected utilities.[3]

This instrumental view of practical reason severely restricts the scope and use of decision theory. It is time to discuss the theory's basic assumption that a subject's set of preferences is complete and consistent. Equating rationality of preferences to their completeness and consistency clearly shows the theory's indifference towards ends. A defender of SEU theory might retort that this is a conscious and legitimate restriction.[4] But these uncared-for ends might take revenge by undermining certain central concepts and assumptions of the theory, namely the concept of utility and the assumptions of completeness and consistency of a subject's pattern of preferences. In the context of the theory, utility is a formidable abstraction, in terms of which any outcomes can be uniquely ordered. But if we shift to real cases of deliberation and decision making we may find that the theory's advice to choose the action with the highest subjective expected utility often cannot be obeyed, for utility is relative to certain ends, so that one and the same action can come first according to one criterion and last according to another. So, going out for a drink tonight, for example, may be ranked high from the standpoint of promoting friendship and low from the standpoint of promoting work tomorrow. There is no reason for thinking that these and several other ends can be measured in terms of a supernotion of utility-to-nothing-in-particular. Decision, then, is not fixed in terms of the theory. As Martin Hollis puts it: 'Radical pluralism implies radical indeterminacy.'[5] There is no reason for thinking that ends can be commensurable and so become the object of a quantitative calculation.

Now, incommensurability threatens the assumptions or axioms of completeness and consistency of a subject's pattern of preferences. Recall that the completeness assumption holds that, given two outcomes, X and Y, either the subject prefers X to Y, or Y to X, or he is indifferent between them. It is possible, however, that there be many pairs of outcomes to which this does not apply, due to the lack of a single criterion of comparison. To be indifferent between two outcomes would mean roughly, in the frame of the completeness axiom, to like the one as much as the other. This may be the case, for example, with drinking coffee and drinking tea. Someone can like the first alternative as much as the second one. Quite another thing might be, for example, the choice between being healthy and being loved. One may not be able to say whether one prefers one thing to the other, nor even whether one is indifferent between them, because, unlike coffee and tea, they are not homogeneous enough to be compared for preference. As for consistency, it is a necessary condition of the truth of decision-theoretic axioms that a subject's set of preferences be such that if the subject prefers X to Y, and Y to Z, then he prefers X to Z. Given incommensurability of ends, however, this seemingly plausible claim becomes rather dubious. A subject may prefer X to Y and Y to Z according to one criterion, and Z to X according to another. This is not to say that the agent is inconsistent in his preferences. He would be so if the preference relation were stated from the same point of view, but not when two criteria play a role in it. What this means is rather that the theory's concept of consistency is simply too narrow to account for the complexity of human preference. Instead of this nice unique and transitive set of preferences, allowing for a ranking of outcomes and acts, there seems to be a rather complicated network of different and heterogeneous rankings that change with the individual's development and are sensitive to more factors than change of belief and shifting of desirabilities. There is room for agency to play a more distinguished role than registering expected utilities. There is room for it to choose between ends and rankings. So it seems that human decision making cannot be a formal calculation.

This is not to imply that decision theory is not an impressive and interesting intellectual achievement, nor that it is not useful for certain purposes. My contention is just that it does not model human deliberation, decision and preference. Decision theory is appropriate where the goodness of a certain end and its role as criterion are taken for granted, as happens with making profit in a capitalist economy, so that the utilities and probabilities of several outcomes are commensurable and so measured, with a bit of willingness, in terms of their contribution to that end. This is one of the reasons why the theory arose in the context of economics and has been developed mainly in relation to economic behaviour, both as an approach to rational economic decision making and, as we shall see, as a step towards a nomological theory of human behaviour in a scientistic vein.

Finally, let us see, before going further, how the theory conceives of mental states, especially beliefs and desires. Decision theory treats subjective probabilities and desirabilities as more or less theoretical entities that lie behind and explain the observable phenomena of preference and choice. The theory takes these theoretical entities to be degrees of belief and desire; it interprets them as being so, and it must do this if it is to be a theory of rational choice. Rational choice needs some relation to such mental states. One problem with interpreting the theoretical variables as beliefs and desires is that, as we suggested above, we do not introspectively find, in most cases of decision making, beliefs and desires that take the form of subjective probabilities and degrees of desirability. Nor does the theory assume that we should. However, when certain subjective probabilities are correctly attributed to someone in terms of the theory, then there is the assumption that the subject has in fact such a degree of belief, even though he is not conscious of it. So, in order to reconcile all these requirements, decision theory has to commit itself to a particular view of beliefs and desires, namely a dispositional one. According to a dispositional theory, beliefs and desires are just dispositions to action. To believe that p is simply to be disposed to act as if p were true. To desire that q is to be disposed to act so that q becomes true. This view explains the fact that we do not find the postulated entities by introspection. One can have several dispositions, say, to get hay fever or to eat fast, without 'finding' them introspectively or, for that matter, without even being conscious of having them. Dispositional accounts of belief and desire, however, are far from uncontentious. So, if decision theory needs such an account as a conceptual foundation, the eventual implausibility of this latter might mean the ruin of the former. Conceiving beliefs and desires as being just dispositions to action implies a strong commitment to a behaviouristic reduction of mental states. We referred to the bleak prospects of this reduction in chapter 7. Moreover, if 'A believes that p' has the logical form of 'glass is fragile', I do not see what entitles a dispositional theory to be a theory of mind: dispositions do not show what we were calling, in chapter 6, the constitutive features of mental states. Finally, I do believe that hundreds of birds are flying up there, but I do not know what sort of action I am disposed to perform in believing that. We shall come to this later, when dealing with the descriptive-explanatory interpretation of the theory.

So far, we have discussed and criticized decision theory's view of deliberation, decision, practical reason, preference and mental states. Let us go on now to see the implications of our discussion to decision theory, both in its normative and in its descriptive-explanatory reading.

On its normative reading, decision theory provides some rules concerning the way one should proceed in order to reach the best decision available to one. It dictates how our beliefs, desires and decisions should be related in order to be rationally related. As R. C. Jeffrey points out, decision theory's framework 'is normative in much the same way that deductive logic is: it is not put forth as a descriptive psychological theory of belief or value or behaviour, but as a useful representation of some very general norms for the formulation and critique of belief and decision'.[6] In the example of the dinner guest, if he had chosen to bring white wine, we could have criticized this decision by showing him that, given his taste, bringing red wine would have been a better decision for him to make, for it would have maximized his subjective expected utility, making better results more probable. In this example, however, several problems have been solved in advance: both options, for instance, have been made comparable in terms of a unified criterion, and the rightness of this criterion has been taken for granted. As soon as we introduce several criteria that yield different rankings of the same set of possible acts or start reflecting on the rightness of those crieria, decision-theoretic norms cease to have a clear application and decision-theoretic criticism begins to look rather baseless. In cases where several ends yield several rankings of acts, the advice would be: reduce those rankings to a single one, either by eliminating the others or by embracing a new end that yields a unified ranking out of the initial plurality. But why should we? The only justification for this procedure would be to make our problem capable of decision-theoretic treatment. But the question was precisely whether decision-theoretic norms ought to be adopted, and this advice begs the question by assuming that they ought.

Notice that, as we suggested, adopting decision-theoretic norms in cases where plural and incommensurable values define the terms of the problem would not mean solving *that* problem but shifting to a different, much simpler one. But what we want is to solve our decision problems, not to dodge them. If, for example, my problem is one of choosing which of two moral principles to honour by acting, I am not dealing with it if I stop thinking of moral principles and start to think of consequences of two possible acts, ranked according to their contribution to some utilitarian end. In sum, decision-theoretic norms can be useful where the terms of the problem meet certain constraints, such as commensurability of alternatives in a unified ranking. Extending those norms to cover other problems, however, implies a radical and arbitrary narrowing of deliberation and a sweeping away of the problems themselves. Shifting to a decision-theoretic deliberation and problem setting is an act for which reasons should still be provided. I cannot see any, though I do see causes that would account for such an only too explicable impulse towards simplifying and impoverishing human life.

There are reasons for doubting whether decision theory can claim, as a normative representation of practical reasoning, the high credit logic has achieved as a normative representation of theoretical deductive reasoning. A somehow paradoxical consequence of adopting a decision-theoretic frame is that you have to be told what your real beliefs and desires are. Recall, in effect, that preference and choice are taken to reflect an underlying pattern of theoretical entities, called subjective probabilities and desirabilities, which are supposed to correspond to degrees of belief and desire. Beliefs and desires, in turn, are taken to be latent dispositions to action. But if they are, you are not going to find them by introspection nor will you know what they really are. Decision theory, then, has to provide some method of fixing and measuring subjective probabilities and desirabilities. Taking them to be dispositions to behaviour, behaviour will be the best evidence. Several methods have been proposed.[7] Their objective is to fix the pattern of an agent's subjective desirabilities and probabilities. Once the pattern is fixed, the agent's behaviour would reflect, according to the theory, this underlying pattern, that is, the agent would in fact behave as if he were assigning values to outcomes, probabilities to conditions and choosing the act with the highest expected utility.

This leads to the descriptive-explanatory reading of decision theory. On the normative reading, the theory does not assume a deterministic picture of human action as a process governed and predictable by laws. On the descriptive-explanatory reading, it does. On this interpretation, what decision theory would yield as the rational thing to do, given our *real* degrees of belief and desire, is what we will be doing after all, as a matter of nomological necessity. That is, our actions would unfold according to the SEU maximization model of decision theory. Our subjective desirabilities and probabilities determine the action we perform. We need, then, a nomological statement to relate those antecedents to actions. And here it is: people act so as to maximize their subjective expected utility. In other words, people will always perform those acts having the highest associated subjective expected utility. Our putative empirical theory contends that, given a subject's pattern of subjective desirabilities and probabilities and given a decision-making situation as initial conditions, the output, namely the subject's action, can be predicted by means of the SEU maximization model and the law according to which the subject will perform the action with the highest SEU, computed in terms of that model.

Not every pattern will do, however. The subject's pattern of preferences has to be complete and consistent if the theory is to work at all. As we suggested above, there are no reasons for thinking that our potentially or actually conscious values meet those requirements. What we find, instead, are several conflicting and sometimes incommensurable values, giving rise to different orderings of the same sets of acts. The theory retorts that our conscious pattern of values does not coincide with the pattern of preferences in the sense it gives to this expression. We are not conscious of this latter, which is rather a set of latent dispositions. These, and not our conscious values, are what accounts for our choosing behaviour. A similar answer would be given to the objection that our conscious deliberation does not show the form of a unique ordering of acts according to estimated probabilities and utilities, and that, given incommensurability of crieria, it could not show it afterwards. The answer would be that the real process of deliberation would develop behind the superficial appearance and beyond our consciousness. As Eells puts it: 'Just as unconscious, intuitive grasp of the laws of mechanics underlies the skill of a cyclist or a tight-rope walker, so, in the same way an unconscious, intuitive grasp of some principles of decision theory may underlie human decision making.'[8] The cases, however, are not parallel, for riding bicycles or walking on a tight-rope are not norm-following processes. Some well-trained animals can be quite good at those activities. So, according to what Eells says, they would be unconsciously grasping the laws of mechanics too. But this is absurd. They are not grasping any laws, either consciously or unconsciously. Neither is a cyclist, for that matter. The question reduces to skill and training. Decision making, however, is a norm-following process. We cannot follow the laws of mechanics, for we cannot violate them. But we can follow and violate the principles of decision theory. A decision theorist would deny that we can violate them. But it seems to me obvious that we can, if we know them. One way of doing it is to perform the second or third act in our ranking, instead of the first. If he were to say that the fact that we perform the second one shows that it comes in fact first in the ranking, he would be guilty of the same empirical emptiness we found in the concept of the 'overriding desire' when dealing with Churchland's law. But in fact his answer would be subtler: he would contend that the real ranking is beyond our conscious reach, so that we could only be under the illusion of violating the principles, but we would not be doing it actually. Well, how does he know? Where does his insight into the real nature of decision come from? The answer would be: from an a priori scientistic conviction, totally unsupported by evidence. He does not have a better grasp of anyone's 'real' ranking than I do. My contrary attitude also has a priori roots, but it is at least supported by evidence, namely by the evidence provided by our conscious practice of deliberating and making decisions. For it seems that in this practice we follow norms and sometimes violate them.

It could be contended that the decision-theoretical model guides in fact our deliberation and practical reasoning in roughly the same way as grammatical rules guide our speech. On this view, we would be following decision-theoretical norms even if these were not consciously represented, just as we can speak correctly without even being able to state the grammatical rules. There are reasons for thinking that this view is not true. Our discussion of deliberation and related notions speaks strongly against it. But even if, despite our arguments, this view turned out to be true, this would not favour the possibility of a law-based prediction and explanation of human action. On this view, our practical reasoning and intentional actions are still norm-following processes, as I think they actually are. But, as we said in dealing with Churchland's law, the idea that an empirical field does not follow, in a potentially or actually reflexive way, a theoretical model is a presupposition of scientific theories and of the existence of strict predictive laws. The view we are considering implies precisely that and therefore cannot support the possibility of decision theory as an empirical nomological theory of human action. On that view, we would have to accept that agents can literally make mistakes in following the norms and can, reflexively, violate them, just as we can violate grammatical rules for several purposes, say to make jokes or for aesthetic effect.

If decision theory principles cannot be violated, then they must be more similar to the laws of mechanics than to linguistic rules or to the norms we follow in deliberating. So, the only plausible position is to hold that our actual conscious processes of deliberating and acting simply *accord with* the model, in much the same way as a mechanical system functions according to a successful model of it. And in fact a mechanical analogy seems to underlie this explanatory reading of decision theory. The amount of expected utility would be rather like the weight of an object, moving irresistibly the invisible plates of invisible psychic scales. Only someone who is seduced by this or other analogous sorts of metaphor can dare to state a deterministic law on the above lines. On this view, the real process would lie, for the most part, behind our consciousness, though it could be reflected there in the illusory form of reflection and agency.

On the view we are now examining, decision theory is a purely empirical theory of human behaviour, on a par with empirical theories in the field of natural sciences. It draws a mathematical model and contends that the unfolding of a certain field of reality accords with it. What I want to ask is whether the variables of this theory may still be considered, in this context, as mental states and processes, as sorts of ordinary beliefs, desires and decisions. The question is pertinent, for the model as such is a highly abstract and purely formal mathematical construction, whose variables are still open to several interpretations.

The comparison between the principles of decision theory and the laws of mechanics is not a mere accident, nor is the retreat to an unconscious mechanism as a reply to any counterexample or objection. And the two moves are connected. Think also of the view of beliefs and desires as dispositions and the explicit comparison between them and physical dispositions such as fragility or solubility.[9] When we join these scattered pieces the picture that starts to emerge is that of a formal model, on a par with physico-mathematical ones, having no special relation to human deliberation, decision and action. The possibility that the theory is not a theory of human choice and decision should be taken seriously. For the uninterpreted model is a formal device, whose variables could range over any entities whose relations were to satisfy at least the axioms of completeness and transitivity. Human values and preferences, as we suggested above, do not seem to satisfy those axioms, owing to the incommensurability and plurality of our ends. Paradoxically, then, the model could be closer, in the end, to the behaviour of some physical system than to human intentional action.

If the theory is to work as a predictive one, it must hold that we are wildly mistaken about the true explanations of our actions, for we explain them in terms of actually or potentially conscious mental states. And conscious mental states are subject to several normative constraints, quite different from decision-theoretic principles. Conscious mental life is subject to norms that can be followed and violated. So, our conscious mental states are not going to behave as the theory dictates. Then, it is essential to the predictive purposes of the theory that the true explanatory factors lie behind our consciousness. These factors are, according to the theory, subjective probabilities and desirabilities, or so they are called, and are interpreted as degrees of belief and desire, and so as mental states. But we can now see very strong reasons for raising doubts about this interpretation and for wondering whether items that neither are conscious, nor cannot be brought to consciousness, deserve to be called 'mental' at all. A real mental state is such that its relationships to other mental states can be reflexively brought to light by the agent that has it. To say that mental states are subject to constraints of coherence means that the agent to whom they are attributed has to be sensitive to those constraints and react appropriately. Mental states, then, can exist only as part of the life of an agent who can follow normative rules. Our putative empirical theory of human mind and action cannot allow the values of its variables to have these features, on pain of losing any hope of law-based explanation and prediction. So, subjective probabilities and desirabilities may well be theoretical entities, but they are certainly not types of mental states. They are not beliefs, desires or decisions, and cannot take particular mental states as values. Moreover, the variable maximized by the model, namely expected utility, is not a desire, nor is it 'expected' by anybody either. Finally, what the theory can explain and predict cannot be human intentional behaviour, for behaviour is intentional only in the context of and in relation to mental states, which are no longer present. The theory, however, gets its initial data out of preference or choosing behaviour, which is a good example of intentional acting, and in doing so it has to attribute to the subject a large set of mental states and abilities: so, it has to accept, in order to get itself started, what it will be obliged to deny later.

So, I do not think, to conclude, that decision theory can be turned into a strict predictive nomological theory of human action. None the less, so far as we allow of its normative reading, it could well be a useful instrument for some purposes, in artificially purified frames.

Let us go on now to examine a less extreme attempt to reconcile intentional actions and their explanations with some scientistic assumptions, namely Davidson's causal theory of intentional action.

10

Davidson's Causal Theory of Intentional Action

The starting-point of Davidson's causal theory of intentional action is his well-known 1963 paper 'Actions, Reasons, and Causes'.[1] He reacts here, like Churchland seven years later, against the view that explanations of actions by reasons are not causal explanations and that reasons are not causes of actions. This view has one important source in some remarks by Wittgenstein in *The Blue and Brown Books*, even though its anti-scientistic roots are much older. We can find connected views in R. G. Collingwood as well as in the hermeneutic tradition of the nineteenth century. Wittgenstein's philosophy has been developed in the direction of an anti-scientistic philosophy of the social sciences and of human action by such philosophers as G. E. M. Anscombe, S. N. Hampshire, Peter Winch and A. I. Melden. William Dray, on the other hand, shows more prominently the influence of Collingwood. This is the background against which Davidson reacts. His general position is stated clearly:

> What is the relation between a reason and an action when the reason explains the action by giving the agent's reason for doing what he did? We may call such explanations *rationalizations*, and say that the reason *rationalizes* the action. In this paper I want to defend the ancient – and commonsense – position that rationalization is a species of causal explanation. The defence no doubt requires some redeployment, but it does not seem necessary to abandon the position.[2]

Underlying the view that rationalizations were not causal explanations and that reasons were not causes of actions was the Humean view of causation, according to which cause and effect are discrete, separate 'objects', so that their relation as cause and effect derives merely from the fact that they instantiate a regularity or law of nature. As we saw in the case of Churchland, this conception was also basically shared by the defenders of the deductive-nomological model of scientific explanation, including Churchland himself. Causal explanations require laws. So, one of the main objections to the view of rationalizations as causal explanations was that there seemed to be no laws backing them. In order to follow a parallel treatment, we can approach Davidson's view with this objection as a guideline. Another objection was connected with the Humean contention that cause and effect, being separate 'objects', had independent existence, so that causal relations were to be sharply distinguished from logical or conceptual ones ('relations of ideas'), whose relata had no such independent existence. Rationalizations – so the objection ran – are not causal explanations for there seems to be a 'conceptual' or 'logical' relation between the reason and the explained action, so that the action appears in some way as a logical or at least reasonable consequence of that reason.

We know Churchland's answers to both objections. The second one is related to what Churchland called the 'reasonable-in-the-light-of' relation.

Davidson's response is quite different from Churchland's and, in my opinion, much more sophisticated. Its ramifications touch upon many issues in ontology and in the philosophy of psychology. In fact, I think that extensive parts of Davidson's metaphysics and philosophy of mind can be considered as an attempt to cope with all the consequences and side-problems raised by his early thesis that rationalizations are a species of causal explanation. This attempt will give rise to what I consider to be one of the most challenging and interesting philosophical views in these fields in the last twenty or twenty-five years. In fact, the discussion of Davidson's views constitutes a substantial part of this book.

The structure of rationalizations, as conceived in 'Actions, Reasons, and Causes', is quite simple. It was to be revised and completed in other papers, as Davidson realized that in this simple form it cannot account for very common situations. The revision is important, but, for our purposes, we can restrict ourselves, for the moment, to the simple, initial Davidsonian model. We shall also see that, as in Churchland's case, Davidson conceives the notion of intentional action in terms of the structure of its typical explanation.

Typically, according to the simple model, a rationalization contains a desire or other pro-attitude, a belief and an action. Here is an example of rationalization: 'John left Peter's birthday party because he wanted to offend Peter, and believed that leaving the party was a good way of doing that.' Typically, a rationalization states a desire or other pro-attitude and a belief under which the action appears as *reasonable* and says that the action was performed *because of* that desire and that belief. A rationalization, then, shows two aspects: it *justifies or rationalizes* the action and it says *why* the action took place. The first aspect, according to Davidson, is characteristic and distinctive of rationalizations, marking them off from other explanations of non-actional events. Concerning the second aspect, Davidson's thesis is that the 'because' is causal. This thesis is the distinctive Davidsonian claim that rationalizations are causal explanations. In Davidson's more technical terms, a rationalization explains an action by giving a *primary reason* why the agent performed it. And a primary reason has to satisfy two requiremets. The first is a necessary condition: 'R is a primary reason why an agent performed the action A under the description d only if R consists of a pro-attitude of the agent towards actions with a certain property, and a belief of the agent that A, under the description d, has that property.'[3] This condition states the justifying aspect a reason must have: the reason must state something that, from the agent's point of view – whence the clause 'under the description d' – was desirable, agreeable or worthwhile in his action. So, this justifying aspect introduces an *intensional* element into rationalizations: one and the same action can be justified when described in a certain way and fail to be so when described in another. For instance, I want to have some fun and I believe that firing my gun will give me some; I fire my gun and, involuntarily, I injure someone; so, my want and my belief justify my action under the description 'firing my gun', but not under the description 'injuring someone'. Now, this justifying aspect does not by itself say why the action took place: in the example above, imagine that I invent a reason to justify my injuring that person and say, for instance, that I thought he was in turn aiming his gun at me. This reason justifies what I did but is not the reason why I did it. Something has to be added to a primary reason in order to distinguish this case of mere rationalization or justification *ex post facto* from a true explanation of an action and this is precisely that the reason must be the reason why the action was performed. This connection between reason and action is, according to Davidson, causal. Hence the second requirement for a primary reason: 'A primary reason for an action is its cause.'[4] Holders of the view that reasons are not causes rely upon the element of justification that reasons provide, but they cannot account for the difference between merely inventing or having a reason and acting for that reason. The simplest way of accounting for it is just to say that in the second case, but not in the first, the reason caused the action. And, according to Davidson, there are no compelling arguments for denying the causal character of reasons when someone acts on them. We can go on now to Davidson's defence of this claim against the main objections to it.

Davidson's answer to the objection that there are no laws covering the relation between reasons and actions does not take, unlike Churchland's, the form of providing some example of a rough, *ceteris paribus* generalization. According to Davidson, 'generalizations connecting reasons and actions are not – and cannot be sharpened into – the kind of law on the basis of which accurate predictions can reliably be made.'[5] That is, Davidson begins by conceding the main point to the opponent in order to show that this point need not undermine the causal character of rationalizations. If every true singular causal statement had to be covered by the statement of a law, few such statements could be made. When we see that a window broke because it was struck by a stone we can formulate a true singular causal statement, but we do not have a law connecting the breaking of windows with the impact of stones. So, the lack of strict laws is not to be found only in the case of rationalizations, but in most cases of ordinary causal explanations. This, however, shows only that the vocabulary we employ in making such causal statements is simply too rough, too vague for that causal statement to be deduced from a law and initial conditions in a deductive-nomological argument. To be so deduced, the causal statement would have to be formulated in a suitable vocabulary: it is simply hopeless to try to deduce a statement in such terms as 'the window broke' from a law plus initial conditions *described* in terms of the impact of stones. This does not show that there is no law backing this causal statement. If the statement is true, it must be backed by a law, if we accept Hume's view of causation. But to be 'backed by a law' can be understood in two different senses:

It may mean that 'A caused B' entails some particular laws involving the predicates used in the descriptions 'A' and 'B', or it may mean that 'A caused B' entails that there exists a causal law instantiated by some true descriptions of A and B. Obviously, both versions of Hume's doctrine give a sense to the claim that singular causal statements entail laws, and both sustain the view that causal explanations 'involve laws' . . . Only the second version of Hume's doctrine can be made to fit most causal explanations; it suits rationalizations equally well.[6]

We should notice that from this argument against the law-objection there follows no positive conclusion in the sense that rationalizations *are* causal explanations, but only a negative one, according to which the fact that we have no laws connecting reasons with actions does *not* prevent rationalizations from being causal explanations. It is also worth noticing that Hume's view of causality does not receive a positive defence by means of arguments showing its correctness, but it is simply *supposed* as basically true. In fact, we will not be able to find a proper defence of the nomological view of causation in any of Davidson's papers. Throughout his work, Davidson simply assumes or starts from its basic correctness.

Underlying this preliminary answer to the law-objection there is a view of causation that Davidson makes more explicit in a 1967 paper called 'Causal Relations'.[7] According to Davidson, some philosophical analyses of causality, such as Mill's, have failed to distinguish two different levels implied in causality: the ontological level of causal *relations*, which hold between particular *events*, and the linguistic level of causal *explanations*, which deals with *statements* or descriptions of events and their relations. A causal relation is a relation between particular events. A causal relation is expressed in a singular causal statement by means of two expressions referring to events and related by the term 'caused'. Singular causal statements are, for instance, 'the impact of a stone caused the window's break', 'the short-circuit caused the fire' or 'Smith's fall caused his death.' 'Caused', according to Davidson, has to be understood as an ordinary diadic relation or predicate that is true of ordered pairs of events. A singular causal statement, such as 'the short-circuit caused the fire', says that there are two events, e and e', such that e is a short-circuit, e' is a fire, and e caused e'. 'Caused' does not relate sentences, but particular events referred to by those expressions. Causal relations between events can be expressed in an extensional language: if 'e caused e' ' is true, it is so independently of how the events are described. If, for instance, the fire referred to was the event reported in the second column of *The Times* of 2 February 1982, it is true that the short-circuit caused the event reported in the second column of *The Times* of 2 February 1982.

Now, we should distinguish the causal relation from the relation of causal *explanation* in the sense of the deductive-nomological model. According to this model, to explain an event is to deduce it as a logical consequence of laws and singular statements describing particular facts. What we can deduce, of course, is not the event, but a *statement describing* the event, and we can deduce it from other statements. So, this relation of causal explanation holds between statements. And here much depends on how the events are *described*. One and the same event can be explained under one description but not under another. It would be hopeless, for instance, to try to deduce from physical laws an event described in terms of reports in *The Times*. In a sense, then, causal explanation is intensional. If physical laws are stated in terms of, say, molecules or atoms, we will have to describe an event in those same terms if we are to deduce it from laws. The relations of causal explanation are expressed, not by predicates, but by sentential connectives: they hold between statements.

We can now try to formulate the relationship between the two levels in the following terms: if 'a caused b' is true, then there are descriptions of a and b such that the result of substituting those descriptions for 'a' and 'b' in 'a caused b' is implied by true premises among which there are laws.

Note that from this general view of causation, Davidson can also meet the other objection against the conception of reasons as causes of actions, namely that reasons cannot be causes of actions because there are 'logical' or 'conceptual' relations between them, so that they are not 'separate objects', in Hume's terminology. In the case of rationalizations, the 'logical' or 'conceptual' relations are supposed to be those in virtue of which the action appears as a reasonable consequence of the reason. As we saw, Davidson considered this justification relation as distinctive of rationalizations. The objection is met again by distinguishing between the level of events and the level of descriptions of those events. A causal relation between events holds independently of how they are described. 'Logical' or 'conceptual' relations hold at the level of descriptions and statements. Now, we can describe two causally related events so as to have a 'logical' relationship between those descriptions, with no consequence to the causal character of the relation between the events. To see this, imagine an extreme case. Think of a singular causal statement, such as 'the short-circuit caused the fire'. Suppose this statement is true. Then, we can refer to the short-circuit in terms of the description 'the cause of the fire'. 'The short-circuit' and 'the cause of the fire' refer to the same particular event. Substituting the second description for the first we obtain the statement 'the cause of the fire caused the fire.' This is not very illuminating as an explanation, for the *descriptions* of the cause and the effect are conceptually related, but this does not prevent the first event from being the cause of the second one. Certainly, the case of rationalizations is not so platitudinous. Rationalizations are more illuminating than that. But this works in favour of Davidson's answer: if the answer is right in the extreme case mentioned, it will be so in less extreme cases. As applied to rationalizations, the answer would run, obviously, along the following lines: in rationalizations we describe the reason and the action so as to have a 'reasonable-in-the-light-of' relation, but this does not prevent what we describe from being related as cause and effect.

We should notice, again, that this answer does not constitute a positive argument in favour of the causal character of rationalizations. It simply says that the fact of the special relations of coherence holding in them is no obstacle to their being causal in character.

We are now in a position to see how Davidson tries to reconcile intentionality and science in the case of intentional actions and their explanations by reasons. He does so by means of a distinction of levels parallel to the distinction he draws in causation relations. The main features of intentionality, such as normativity, subjectivity, etc., are placed at the level of the *descriptions* we make of reasons and actions; we describe them – and the agent sees them – in such a way that the action appears as coherent and appropriate, given those reasons. As Davidson says, 'in the light of a primary reason, an action is revealed as coherent with certain traits, long- or short-termed, characteristic or not, of the agent, and the agent is shown in his role of Rational Animal.'[8] According to Davidson's first model, the action can be considered as the conclusion of a practical syllogism whose premises are the reasons, or at least as corresponding to a conclusion stating that the action is desirable. This conception will be revised in later papers. The requirements of a scientific point of view, on the other hand, are placed at the level of the *events* referred to by those descriptions. Beyond their justifying role, shown in the logical relationships the descriptions of reasons and action hold with one another, these descriptions must also refer to events holding causal relationships with one another, if rationalizations are true causal explanations and not merely justifications *ex post facto*. The explanatory aspect of rationalizations points to beliefs and desires as events that cause another event, namely the action. Under this aspect, rationalizations correspond to singular causal statements: they say that (at least) such and such a belief and such and such a desire caused such and such an action. Under this aspect they are *extensional*: we can refer to those events in different descriptions with no change in the truth value of the initial statement. If, to use the example we construed above, my action of firing the gun was identical to my action of injuring someone, this last action was caused by my desire to have some fun and my belief that shooting the gun was a way of having fun. Of course, the justification aspect gets lost, but we still have the causal relation. We can also refer to the desire in other terms, say, as 'that stupid desire I had that morning', and still have a true causal statement.

But what does it mean to say that the belief and the desire *caused* the action? Recall the relationship between singular causal statements and deductive-nomological explanations. As applied to rationalizations, understood as singular causal statements, this relationship yields: if 'that desire and that belief caused that action' is true, then there are descriptions of the desire, the belief and the action such that the result of substituting those descriptions for 'that desire', 'that belief' and 'that action' in the initial statement is implied by true premises among which there are laws. Roughly stated: if the reason caused the action, then, under some description, they instantiate a strict law. And this is the way *physicalism*, the second aspect we distinguished in scientism, enters into the picture: in order to instantiate a strict law, beliefs, desires and actions must have true physical descriptions, since only physical (chemical, neurophysiological) laws are strict laws, and so they must be physical events. Physicalism takes the form of a theory of identity between mental events and physical events. This identity theory, which Davidson was to develop in other papers, especially in 'Mental Events', is only suggested in 'Actions, Reasons, and Causes', but it is clear that Davidson's way of justifying the claim that rationalizations are causal explanations commits him to such a theory. Here is the suggestion in the latter paper:

> The laws whose existence is required if reasons are causes of actions do not, we may be sure, deal in the concepts in which rationalizations must deal. If the causes of a class of events (actions) fall in a certain class (reasons) and there is a law to back each singular causal statement, it does not follow that there is any law connecting events classified as reasons with events classified as actions – the classifications may even be neurological, chemical or physical.[9]

We shall not go into the problems of psychophysical identity here. We shall restrict ourselves to the specific problems raised by the framework in terms of which Davidson deals with rationalizations. First of all, we should notice that Davidson's view of rationalizations involves and gives rise to a conception of intentional action. According to this view, intentional action is conceived in terms of its typical explanation in rationalizations, as a doing that is caused by those attitudes of an agent that rationalize his doing, namely appropriate beliefs and desires.[10] An intentional action is conceived in terms of its typical causes. But what we called the 'justifying aspect' must also enter into the picture: those causes must at the same time rationalize the action in order for this to be intentional, for otherwise, in our example, injuring someone would be intentional; it is not intentional because it is not rationalized, under that description, by the desire and belief the agent had. So, both aspects, causality and rationality, have to get into a causal conception of intentional action. But in Davidson's view, as we have seen, the two aspects are *kept apart* from one another. There is a *split* between causality and rationality: reasons do not cause actions in virtue of their justifying or rationalizing them, but in virtue of their instantiating a strict law; and reasons rationalize actions in a way sharply separated from their causal aspect, namely by virtue of having descriptions which cohere appropriately with the description or descriptions under which the agent saw his action. This is coherent with a scientistic point of view about causality. Causal theories of action claim, in effect, that beliefs and desires cause the action in the same sense in which a physical event causes another physical event. And they must make this claim, for if the word 'cause' had not the same sense in both cases, these theories would be led to a position which is only negligibly different from the one they wanted to oppose to, namely that the general, scientific concept of cause does not apply to human actions. This thesis lies behind the anti-scientistic claim that reasons are not causes. But if causal theories were to hold that, though reasons are causes, they cause actions in a special way, different from the way in which one physical event causes another, they would be making no substantial point against their opponents, the difference being then reduced to one of spelling. This is why causal theories of action must keep causality and rationality strictly separated: if normative, rational aspects were allowed to take part in causal chains, this would amount to acknowledging a non-scientific sense of the word 'cause' as applied to actions, for science cannot allow normative aspects to interfere in causal relations between physical events. That is why we find the same split in other causal, scientistic theories of action, such as Churchland's or Goldman's. In fact, it is a structural feature of this kind of approach.

Now, I think that the relation between reasons and action resists assimilation to causal relations between physical events. In Davidson's frame, the problem I have in mind could be stated as follows. According to Davidson, causal relations are extensional. They hold no matter how we describe the related events. This should apply to the relation between reasons and actions if the Davidsonian thesis is correct that reasons (beliefs and desires) are causes of actions and rationalizations are singular causal statements. Now, the claim that causal relations are extensional does not seem to hold true as applied to the relationship between reasons and actions. Apparently, a belief and a desire *cause* the action *as described in a certain way*, namely as the belief that so-and-so and as the desire that so-and-so. My action of turning is caused by my belief that a junction is coming, not by my belief that, say, birds are flying. The content of beliefs and desires looks essential to their prompting actions. This causal relation, if it is one, is intensional. In acting on a belief and a desire we concede causal relevance to the propositional content of these attitudes. This intensional aspect is absent from causal relations between physical events. Science does not conceive of propositional contents as possible terms or aspects of causal relations, and it has good reasons for not doing so. Now, it is surely part of what we ordinarily understand by 'acting out of reasons' that we act because of the specific content of our reasons. In Davidson's view, however, the idea that reasons cause actions seems to amount to something like: reasons and actions have descriptions that are subsumed by laws. These descriptions, being physical or neurophysiological, are not, we can be sure, the ones to which we concede causal weight in acting out of reasons. So, there is something to be said for the view that reasons are not ordinary scientific causes and against Davidson's claim to be providing a correct analysis of rationalizations by conceiving reasons as ordinary causes.

Neither Davidson nor other causal theorists of action allow rationality to have causal efficacy. They are forced to this position by the very nature of the view they endorse. Rationality and causality must be kept apart in causal theories of intentional action. This split does violence to our everyday understanding of the role of reasons in intentional action, as I have just suggested. And, in my opinion, the real structure of human intentional action takes its revenge by giving rise to a major obstacle in the way of causal conceptions of intentional action: the problem of wayward causal chains. In Davidson's framework the problem lies in the fact that even if an item of behaviour is caused by rationalizing attitudes, namely appropriate beliefs and desires, it can still not be an intentional action. The problem will concern us in the next chapter.

But before going on to that, let me sketch out a preliminary etiology: the problem of wayward causal chains arises from the fact that 'intentional action' is a normative notion, as I have been trying to show, and, being so, it cannot receive an appropriate analysis in purely factual, that is, Humean-causal terms. The problem of wayward causal chains manifests the resistance of the normative structure of intentional action to being captured in terms of mere facts.

11

Wayward Causal Chains

The problem of wayward causal chains arose first in connection with the austere causal theory of intentional action according to which the only elements we need to give a causal analysis of intentional action are beliefs and desires. The motivations for this austere model that we can find in such authors as Davidson, Goldman and Churchland are related to the problems classical causal theories of action had to face. These theories (for example those of Locke, Hume and Mill) appealed typically to mental events called 'volitions' or 'willings', saying that an intentional or a voluntary action is that which is caused by them. Then the following dilemma arises: if volitions are themselves actions, say 'acts of will', a regress-problem threatens, for it seems that we need volitions to cause them, and again new volitions to cause these second-order ones, and so on. (It is worth pointing out that what we called New Volitional Theories avoid the problem by considering volitions as their basic actions, concerning which it makes no sense to ask if another volition caused them, as it makes no sense to ask if an act of will is itself voluntary. For the New Volitional Theory, actions are not events *caused* by volitions; they *are* volitions.) On the other hand, if they are not actions, but mere happenings, the problem is then to give an account of their nature, for they seem to be quite mysterious events, whose causal connection with the action remains in the dark. As D. F. Gustafson points out: 'Pure conative attitudes, volitions or acts of will can appear mysterious in themselves; as part of the supposed etiology of intentional action and rational action, they can appear to require notions of causation "foreign to science".'[1] The austere, familiar belief–desire model seems to avoid both horns of the dilemma. Beliefs and desires are not themselves actions, but states people happen to be in. And, on the other hand, they do not appear as mysterious in themselves, or at least not more so than other ordinary mental states. Davidson himself points to these advantages of the belief–desire model:

> The only hope for the causal analysis is to find states or events which are causal conditions of intentional actions, but which are not themselves actions or events about which the question whether the agent can peform them can intelligibly be raised. The most eligible such states or events are the beliefs and desires of an agent that *rationalize* an action, in the sense that their propositional expressions put the action in a favourable light, provide an account of the reasons the agent had in acting, and allow us to reconstruct the intention with which he acted.[2]

On the other hand, this model 'does not require that there be any mysterious act of the will or special attitude or episode of willing. For the account needs only desires (or other pro-attitudes), beliefs, and the actions themselves.'[3] So, beliefs and desires cause actions, and if we perform an action under a description connected in an appropriate way with the content of the belief and desire, that action, under such a description, should be intentional.

A second aspect of causal theories of action, and certainly an aspect of Davidson's, Churchland's and Goldman's theories, is that the way in which beliefs and desires cause actions and the way in which they rationalize them are independent of each other. We referred to this aspect both in Churchland's and in Davidson's conceptions of intentional action. Churchland distinguished between nomic relations holding between an action and its antecedents understood as events or states, and extranomic relations holding between the propositional contents of the states. Davidson distinguished between the causal relation holding between beliefs, desires and actions as particular events (which, under certain physical descriptions, instantiate laws), and the logical relations holding between certain mental descriptions of those same events. Now, *both* relations have to hold if an action is to be intentional. But, since they are independent, the fact that both of them hold should be sufficient in order for the action to be intentional. The particular form that each relation takes should not affect the final result, namely the performing of an intentional action. If, on the one hand, someone has beliefs and desires that rationalize an action and performs that action *and*, on the other hand, those beliefs and desires cause him to perform that action, then the action should be intentional.

The examples of wayward causal chains seem to show that something is wrong with one or other aspect of the causal theory, or with both of them, that is, these examples can be taken as showing that the causal element of the model is too simple, so that new elements, besides beliefs and desires, should be added, or as showing that the way in which causality operates has to be specified or restricted, for not just any causal relation will do, or as showing both.

Chisholm was the first to point to the problem that wayward causal chains represent to causal analyses of intentional action in terms of beliefs and desires. It is worth pointing out that in 'Actions, Reasons, and Causes' Davidson took intentions to be analysable in terms of beliefs and desires: 'To know a primary reason why someone acted as he did is to know an intention with which the action was done . . . The expression "the intention with which . . ." has the outward form of a description, but in fact is syncategorematic and cannot be taken to refer to an entity, state, disposition, or event.'[4] In fact, Chisholm's example is directed against such a conception of intention, but it equally affects the notion of intentional action linked with it. This is Chisholm's criticism:

> Some philosophers . . . have attempted to define purpose, or endeavor, in terms of belief, causation, and desire. It has been suggested, for example, that a man might be said to bring about something X *for the purpose of* bringing about something Y, provided that the following three conditions hold: (i) he desires Y; (ii) he believes that, if he brings about X, then he will bring about Y; and (iii) this belief and desire jointly cause him to bring about X. But this type of definition is too broad and does not in fact capture the concept of purpose. Suppose, for example: (i) a certain man desires to inherit a fortune; (ii) he believes that, if he kills his uncle, then he will inherit a fortune; and (iii) this belief and this desire agitate him so severely that he drives excessively fast, with the result that he accidentally runs over and kills a pedestrian who, unknown to the nephew, was none other than the uncle. The proposed definition of purpose would require us to say, incorrectly, that the nephew killed the uncle in order to inherit the fortune.[5]

And the causal conception of intentional action presented above, we could add, would require us to say, incorrectly, that killing his uncle was, under that description, an intentional action of the nephew.

This example challenges both aspects of causal theories of intentional action mentioned above: first, it suggests that beliefs and desires alone are too narrow to account for intentional action; for note that if, having in mind that belief and desire, and seeing his uncle crossing the road, he had *decided* or *intended* to kill him by running him over, his action would have been intentional, and would have been rationalized by that belief and desire; secondly, it shows that the relations of causality and rationality cannot be conceived as so independent of one another, for when the action is caused in certain ways, as the example shows, the rationality relation is not preserved: even if the nephew's belief and desire caused him to do what he did, they were not his *reasons* for doing it, nor could his action be rationalized by appealing to them. 'The point', as Davidson makes it, 'is that not just any causal connection between rationalizing attitudes and a wanted effect suffices to guarantee that producing the wanted effect was intentional. The causal chain must follow the right sort of route.'[6]

The challenge, then, can be met by causal theories of action in two ways: either by introducing intentions, or something similar, into the picture of intentional actions, or by adding restrictions to the causal relation so that it matches the rationality relation. What I shall be contending is that each step taken in those directions will be depriving causal theories of action of their distinctive features and bringing to light the normative structure of intentional action.

Concerning the second way of mending the theory, namely putting restrictions on the way the causal chain must work, there is a clause which has gained wide acceptance, namely that the causal chain must operate 'in the right way'. But of course this simply labels or points to the difficulty; it does not solve it, unless that 'right way' is specified.

A natural move to be made is to suggest that the causal chain must operate in such a way that it corresponds, at least roughly, to the pattern of the subject's practical reasoning. In Chisholm's example, for instance, there is no such correspondence, for running over his uncle was not the way in which the nephew planned to kill his uncle, it was not among the means the agent had considered to attain what he desired. The action could have been intentional if the nephew had planned to kill his uncle by running him over, that is, if running him over had been the means the agent thought of in order to cause his uncle's death, in order to inherit the fortune.

This move is a reasonable one, but it is not sufficient to ensure the intentionality of the action. For we can produce examples which satisfy this condition without the result being an intentional action. These examples involve, in Davidson's terms, not external causal chains, but internal ones. Here is a Davidsonian example:

> A climber might want to rid himself of the weight and danger of holding another man on a rope, and he might know that by loosening his hold on the rope he could rid himself of the weight and danger. This belief and want might so unnerve him as to cause him to loosen his hold, and yet it might be the case that he never *chose* to loosen his hold, nor did he do it intentionally.[7]

The example fits the suggested condition because loosening his hold was precisely the means the climber thought of in order to get what he wanted. The causal chain corresponds to the practical reasoning of the agent, but the action still fails to be intentional.

The prospects of specifying 'the right way' in which the causal chain has to operate without appealing to the notion of intentional action seem far from rosy. Think of the fact that the causal chain is a chain of physical – internal to the body and external – events. Faced with this problem, Goldman refers to the sciences in order to obtain a specification of the right way in which beliefs and desires must cause actions for these to be intentional: 'To this question, I confess, I do not have a fully detailed answer. But neither do I think it is incumbent on me, *qua* philosopher, to give an answer to this question. A complete explanation of how wants and beliefs lead to intentional acts would require extensive neurophysiological information, and I do not think it is fair to demand of a *philosophical* analysis that it provides this information.'[8] What we should ask, instead, is whether it is fair to demand of science this kind of answer. We do not need only neurophysiological information, since the causal chain also involves the external world: think for instance of Chisholm's example. And now think of the indefinite multiplicity of intentional actions people can perform and of the even more extensive ways in which the causal chains can operate, externally and internally, in each of those actions. Can we seriously expect that the sciences will be able to provide a manageable specification of the right sort of causal chains involved in intentional actions? We do not have any a priori reasons to expect that the task can be fulfilled, since our criteria of classification of actions as intentional might not correspond to a finitely specifiable disjunction of kinds of causal chains described in physical terms.

Davidson is much less optimistic than Goldman concerning this problem. He could have had in mind some of the last-mentioned considerations when he wrote: 'What I despair of spelling out is the way in which attitudes must cause actions if they are to rationalize the action.'[9]

We were saying that causal theories of action could cope with the problem of wayward causal chains in two different ways. One of them has not shown itself as very promising. In fact, it seems to be hopeless. So, more recent attempts to solve this problem have tried the other way, namely that of widening the range of the causes of actions by adding new, more plausible candidates, especially intentions. As a matter of fact, the belief–desire model seems to have some strongly implausible and counter intuitive consequences. It seems that as soon as I have some desire and some belief about how to satisfy it, that should cause me to act accordingly. But the human world would be a chaotic place, much more than it already is, if that were so. Certainly, I have many desires and beliefs about how to satisfy them, but very few of them end in actions.[10] It seems that something other than beliefs and desires is needed in order to give rise to an action. This has some bearing on the problem of wayward causal chains: beliefs and desires are, so to speak, too remote causes of actions and this distance between them and the action allows the unwelcome interference of disturbing factors in the causal chain. As Myles Brand points out: 'Wanting plus believing . . . is not a good candidate for the proximate cause of action. Although wanting and believing appear to play some role in the initiation of action, they are not the kinds of events that directly cause action.'[11] The same dissatisfaction with belief and desire as causes of actions is shown by Irving Thalberg. Both Brand and Thalberg agree that Davidson's and Goldman's causal theories of action fail in their specification of the proper causes of intentional action, so that this failure would make them powerless against the problem of wayward causal chains.

Thalberg's and Brand's proposals show important similarities. We shall begin by examining the former.

Thalberg's contention is that, in order to avoid the problem of wayward causal chains, we should begin by pointing out that the proper causes of intentional action are intentions, not desires. The first condition to be met by an adequate causal analysis of intentional action is that intentions be considered as the proper causes of actions: it is not enough that the agent desires to get Y, he has actually to *intend* to get Y by doing X.[12] But further conditions should be added. The second condition is to specify in detail the content of the intention. *What* the agent intends to do has to be specified, as well as *how* and *when* he intends to do it, for if the way or the time are not those intended by the agent, his action will not be caused by his intention, but by something different from it. It is clear, for instance, that in Chisholm's example the way and the time the nephew killed his uncle were not those intended by him. Thirdly, our intention must genuinely cause our behaviour: we are not allowed to suppose that when our intention to do X causes us to get nervous, and this state in turn makes us do X, our intention is *ipso facto* the cause of our doing X. This condition alone seems to exclude cases such as Davidson's climber. Thalberg's contention seems to be that intentions should cause our actions *directly*, not by means of causing any other state. We shall find this idea in Brand's proposal as well. Fourthly and finally, the agent's behaviour has to be an action, which excludes other counterexamples in which there seems to be a mere happening.[13] Think, for instance, of this case: a chemist wants to kill his colleague and believes that by dropping cyanide into his colleague's cup of coffee he will kill him; this want and desire make him nervous, so that his hands tremble and, as a result of this, he drops some cyanide into his colleague's cup of coffee. In such a case, what happened seems to be better described as the poison's falling from his trembling hands. There was not an intentional action there because there was not even an action. It is worth noticing that the case of Davidson's climber is not clearly excluded by this last condition, for, as Davidson describes it, it could well be that the climber loosened his hold on the rope, and not simply that his hold loosened.

Note that the case of Davidson's climber is quite recalcitrant. It seems to be excluded only by the third condition. It is not excluded simply by the first, general condition that the action's cause should be an intention, because we could easily add an intention to the causes of the climber's action and the action could still not be intentional. To see this, think of this modified example: a climber wants to get rid of the weight and danger of holding another man on a rope and believes that by loosening his hold on the rope he could rid himself of the weight and danger. In accordance with this want and belief, he forms an intention to loosen his hold in, say, two minutes' time. This want, belief and intention unnerve him during the next two minutes so as to cause him to loosen his hold. This action could still not be intentional, even if there was an intention causing it. Consider that the second condition is also met by this example, for he did *what* he intended to do and he did it *how* and *when* he intended to. So, the only condition that excludes it is the third one, namely the requirement of genuine (say, direct) causation. We shall also find it in Brand's proposal, and we shall discuss it then.

After stating these four conditions, Thalberg adds a new proviso concerning the way in which intentions should cause actions: this causation has to be sustained or continuous. The intention, that is, has to remain operative while the action unfolds, if this is to be intentional. The idea Thalberg wants to capture is one of Harry Frankfurt's to the effect that as long as a person is performing an action he or she is necessarily in touch with his or her body's movements.[14] The idea is that of monitoring or controlling our movements and Thalberg conjectures that we are in touch with, we are monitoring or controlling these movements if our intention causes them in a sustained way.

Thalberg's conditions seem to me essentially sound. My only objection is that what he is trying to capture of the idea of intentional action by means of them cannot be captured without introducing normative restrictions incompatible with the intended causal character of this theory. I shall try to defend this idea by means of a counterexample meeting all conditions that Thalberg states and, nevertheless, not giving rise to an intentional action. Corresponding to the detailed restrictions of Thalberg, the example will be quite complicated, but still possible. This example is a modified version of Chisholm's case. We have again a man who wants to inherit a fortune and believes that by killing his uncle he will be able to inherit a fortune. Accordingly, he forms the intention of killing his uncle by running him over at about

7.30 in the evening. He knows that his uncle crosses Broad Street every evening at that time, while having his habitual evening walk. So, at 7.15 the man gets into his car and drives towards Broad Street (which, we can suppose, is quite narrow). At 7.29 he is in Broad Street when, suddenly, an old pedestrian starts crossing the street at a despairingly slow speed (the poor man had broken his leg the day before). The nephew thinks, in a completely cold manner, that if he waits for this man to cross the street he will not be able to run over his uncle at 7.30, and who knows if tomorrow he will dare to go ahead. So, he decides to run over the old pedestrian and does it at 7.30. Of course, the old pedestrian was his uncle. All conditions Thalberg requires are met, even the proviso concerning the 'sustained causation' by his intention. And, nevertheless, the man did not kill his uncle intentionally.

What happened? Well, he made a *mistake*. He did not recognize (explicably enough) his uncle, and so he thought he was running over an old pedestrian while in fact he was running over his uncle. Even if what he objectively did *coincided* with his intention he was not *following* his intention in doing it. But this means that his intention is not merely something that caused his action, but also a normative standard by which he was guiding and measuring his action. And the nephew's own explanation ('I made a mistake. I did not know . . . etc.') would show that he was in fact trying to follow normative standards reaching far beyond his intention, since this was related to his beliefs, plans, expectations, and so on. Intentional actions refer then, essentially, to a *subjective* point of view about the world, constituted by a network of intentional states having normative claims on the subject. Intentional action refers then, if it is to receive an adequate analysis, to the whole intentionality of mind. We could express what is missing in Thalberg's proposal by saying that the agent has to be conscious of fulfilling his intention; it is not enough that he in fact fulfils it, as the example shows. Or, in terms which connect with Brand's proposal, he has to be *following* his intention while acting, and not simply to act in such a way that his action *accords* with his intention.

In fact an important aspect of Brand's proposal is that an intentional action is an action that *follows* a plan. His proposal has two parts, which correspond to the two kinds of causal waywardness Brand distinguishes, namely 'antecedential waywardness' and 'consequential waywardness'. The first kind of waywardness is represented, according to Brand, by Davidson's climber example. It concerns the causal antecedents of action and, according to Brand, it affects the notion of action, in that 'the antecedent mental event can cause the overt behaviour without there being an action.'[15] In fact, according to Brand, Davidson's climber did not perform the action of loosening his hold on the rope. The second kind of waywardness is represented by Chisholm's nephew example. It concerns the effects of the bodily action and, according to Brand, it raises the issue of intentional action and not merely of action. The nephew in Chisholm's example did something, unlike Davidson's climber, namely killing his uncle, but he 'did not kill his uncle intentionally.'[16]

Brand's strategy to solve the two types of waywardness he distinguishes is to treat separately the question of action and that of intentional action. He tries to cope with such examples as that of Davidson's climber by stating a criterion to distinguish between actions and non-actional events, according to which, an action is characterized by its having as its cause an 'immediate intention': 'The forcefulness of the . . . nervous climber case derived in part from the identification of the antecedent to action with wanting plus believing. Rather the best candidate for the proximate cause of action . . . is intending. The version of the Causal Theory I will be advocating, then, differs from Davidson's and Goldman's in regard to the mental antecedent to action . . . I will follow Sellars in taking the proximate cause of action to be an intending to do something here and now.'[17] On the other hand, he tries to cope with such examples as that of Chisholm's nephew by stating a criterion for intentional actions according to which 'an intentional action is an action performed following a plan.'[18] Accordingly, 'intentional action falls within the pattern of a plan; nonintentional action does not . . . Intentional action is partially caused by large-chunked representations in memory . . . Nonintentional action is preceded (or accompanied) only by immediate intention.'[19]

Let us focus now on the first contention. How does it work against Davidson's climber example? Brand's argument seems to be that, since the climber did not have an 'immediate action' to loosen his hold on the rope, that was not an action, and, *a fortiori*, not an intentional action. None the less, the force of this argument against Davidson's example is dubious, for Brand considers certain reflex acts as nonintentional *actions*: 'An example of a nonintentional action is putting one's hands forward to break a fall. A person is normally moved to do this, not because of some plan, but rather because it is a "natural" response to the circumstances. The "naturalness" of this action seems to derive from its innateness. It is plausible to think that breaking a fall by putting one's hands forward is "hardwired" into persons.'[20] But from this point of view, I do not see any compelling reason to deny that what Davidson's climber did was an action, for a 'natural' response to nervousness is moving one's body and limbs, and this could be something the climber did and which, under those circumstances, was identical to loosening his grip on the rope.

I suppose that Brand would meet this objection by denying the claim about identity, so that loosening his hold was not an action but perhaps moving the limbs was, because there was no immediate intention to loosen his hold. In fact, Brand rejects Davidson and Anscombe's claim that every action is intentional under some description.[21] Not being intentional (under some description) but being caused by an immediate intention is, according to Brand, the criterion of an action. Intentional actions are a subclass of actions, namely those which, besides being so caused, are performed following a plan. But this has quite unwelcome consequences. For think of this Davidsonian example: I switch on the light, illuminate the room and (unknowingly) alert a burglar. According to Anscombe and Davidson's view (and according to mine), alerting a burglar was an (unintentional) action of mine, in that it was intentional under other descriptions. But Brand would have to say, implausibly, that alerting the burglar was not something I did, for no 'immediate intention' caused that action. Many unintentional actions we perform would then cease to be actions. Brand could adopt a Goldman-like concept of causal generation, so that alerting the burglar was causally generated by switching on the light, and so it was an action itself, but then he would have to accept that loosening his hold was something the climber did, for it was causally generated by moving his limbs. Moreover, it is counterintuitive to think that many actions we perform without following a plan are unintentional. Think for instance of picking a flower while we are walking along a path, or of sitting well back when we feel uncomfortable. I think that these actions are intentional, although in the minimal sense we pointed at in chapter 6.

I do not think, then, that the first part of Brand's proposal takes us very far. Its effects on 'antecedential waywardness' are not impressive, and, besides that, it faces difficulties of its own. Much more interesting is the second part, designed to cope with 'consequential waywardness'. If the first part corresponds roughly to the third and fourth conditions in Thalberg's proposal, the second part corresponds to the others. According to the second part, an intentional action should be conceived as 'an action performed following a plan. Carl's [the nephew in Chisholm's example, C.M.] killing his uncle was not intentional because his plan was [say] to shoot him at home, not run him down in the street.'[22] But Brand's proposal has important advantages over Thalberg's, because Brand insists on the fact that following a plan must be distinguished sharply from acting according to a plan, appealing to a similar distinction in L. Wittgenstein: 'Following a plan is to be contrasted with acting according to a plan. This distinction derives from one made by Wittgenstein (1953) between acting according to a rule and following one.'[23]

The advantages of Brand's proposal over Thalberg's can be seen clearly in that the former, but not the latter, can avoid our counterexample, because in it what the nephew did simply *accorded* with his plan, but he was not *following* it. That is, even if the nephew, in our example, did what he intended to do (namely, killing his uncle) and did it how and when he intended to, he did not kill his uncle intentionally because he was following an intention of, say, killing that old pedestrian, not an intention of killing his uncle, although this last intention was sustainedly operative in making him form the intention of killing the pedestrian. So, his killing his uncle simply *accorded with* his intention of killing his uncle, but was not performed *following* that intention. Moreover, Brand's proposal is also efficacious against such cases as Davidson's climber, with the only condition that those cases be considered as affecting the analysis of *intentional action*, which is the frame where the problem of wayward causal chains originally arose. So, Davidson's climber did not loosen his grip intentionally because he was not *following* his plan to get rid of the weight and danger of his fellow by loosening it; his loosening his grip simply *accorded* with his plan. In other words, this would allow Brand to cope with causal waywardness in a unified, elegant way, avoiding by so doing the problems we raised concerning the first part of his proposal.

None the less, Brand's proposal faces problems of its own. For Brand's notion of following a plan, but not Wittgenstein's related notion, is intended to fall within a *causal* frame, to remain as a causal theory of intentional action. So, he has to conceive of a plan in merely factual terms, say as a complex functional structure of neural states. But then, if a plan is so conceived, the possibility of its causing the action through a deviating or wayward causal path cannot be excluded. So, to avoid this possibility Brand needs to add a clause specifying that the plan has to play 'the appropriate causal role in the action . . . It is crucial . . . to specify the appropriate causal role of plans.'[24] But then 'the appropriate causal role' of plans parallels exactly 'the right way' in which, in the old theory, beliefs and desires should cause the action and faces all the insurmountable difficulties we found in this kind of clause.

I think that Brand's notion of following a plan cannot be given a merely causal interpretation, for it goes naturally beyond a causal frame. To see this, let me produce a quite simple counterexample in which an action is performed following a plan but this following a plan acts causally on behaviour so that the resulting action is not intentional. John is working out a fairly complicated and long addition problem. His plan is to get the correct result by adding the first pair of digits, and then adding the result of this addition to the next digit, and so on to the end. He is following his plan, but due to, say, fatigue, he makes ten mistakes in adding, in such a way that they compensate for one another so as to give rise to the correct answer by mere chance. I contend that even if he thought he got the correct answer intentionally, he would abandon this belief when told about his mistakes by saying that, after all, it was simply by luck or accident that he got the right answer. The notion of mistake is essential to the notion of following a plan, and this suggests that following a plan is subject to normative constraints. Its merely causing the action is not sufficient for this to be intentional.

What should then be added to Brand's condition? The answer is: the clause 'correctly', that is, an intentional action should be considered as an action performed following a plan correctly. Of course there are causal and functional factors involved, but it is irrevelant which way they go provided that the agent follows his plan and follows it correctly. The advantages of Brand's proposal come at a high price, since the normative character of his notion of following a plan is much more easily uncovered and the way in which this proposal leads beyond the limits of a causal theory of intentional action is brought to\ light. Brand's notion of following a plan overcomes the independence of causality and rationality which was in the very essence of a causal theory of intentional action from the beginning and shows the notion of intentional action as an irreducibly normative one. If our counterexample to Thalberg's proposal tried to uncover the *subjective* aspect of the subject's commitment to norms, our present counterexample tries to uncover the *objective* aspect of that commitment: it is not enough that the agent be aware of following a plan or an intention of his; he has to follow them correctly, if his action is to be intentional.

There was, after all, a point in the clause 'in the right way'. But the place of this clause was wrong. It is not the causal chain that has to operate in the right way: it is the way the agent follows his plan or intention that has to be right. But this is the natural place for this clause, since in this place we do not find the insurmountable difficulties involved in its first location. Following a plan or fulfilling an intention are subject to normative constraints, and the requirement of correctness is perfectly adequate here, whereas a causal chain is not subject to those constraints, and it is odd to require it to be right. The initial appeal of this clause derives in fact from the normative structure of intentional action.

In a recent paper, A. R. Mele has claimed that the problem of antecedential and consequential waywardness has been solved by Thalberg and Brand.[25] I hope to have shown that it is not so and that, if the problem is to be solved along these lines, it is only at the price of abandoning the causal frame, with its essential independence of rationality and causality. Besides that, Mele claims to have discovered a type of waywardness that challenges Brand's causal analysis of intentional action. Mele's example can be assimilated to the counter-example we construed against Brand's proposal. So, we will not quote it. The case is one of making a mistake while following a plan, but in such a way that one gets what one intended by mere luck. Mistakes are turned into successes by accident, so that succeeding cannot be taken to be intentional in this context. So far, Mele's example can be used, against his own intentions, to bring to light, once again, the normative, non-causal structure of Brand's notion of following a plan. When the following of a plan causally prompts an unintended mistake, the result is not an intentional action, even though the subject gets what he was after. The plan or intention, so our conclusion ran, have to be correctly followed for the action to be an intentional one.

However, Mele's example suggests the existence of another normative aspect in intentional action. In the context of a discussion of his case Mele points to the non-intentional character of obtaining a correct result when the plan leading to it is a mad one. Think, for instance, of a student having a plan to provide correct answers to a multiple choice test by throwing dice. In this context, providing some correct answers is not an intentional action, for its relationship to the planned means is too accidental. This suggests a further normative requirement of intentional action. Besides *following* a plan or intention, and following it *correctly*, the plan or intention have to be rational themselves. They have to include an intelligible representation of means–ends adequacy. A mad plan or intention do not give rise to an intentional action, even if the agent follows them and gets what he or she intended.

Mele thinks that causal theories of intentional action have overcome the problem of antecedential and consequential waywardness and hopes that the kind he has discovered 'will be resolved more expeditiously'.[26] Far from this, what I have been contending is that an adequate solution to the problem of wayward causal chains involves the overcoming of the basic features of causal theories of intentional action. Mele's case reinforces this conclusion by suggesting, against his own intentions, another normative feature in the structure of intentional action.

To conclude this chapter, let me refer to a suggestion we find in a recent book by Alan Donagan.[27] According to this author, who on this point is indebted to J. R. Searle,[28] the problem of wayward causal chains can be avoided by conceiving the relation between intention or choice and action as being one of self-referential explanation.[29] A choice or intention must explain the action in a self-referential way, if the action is to be intentional. His idea seems to be the following. When I choose to act in a certain way, I choose it on the basis that those beliefs I took into account in making that choice are true, and I choose that my action will be explained by that very choice as I made it, including those beliefs. So, what I choose in choosing to act in a certain way is that this very choice will explain my action, whence the talk about self-referentiality. Cases of waywardness, according to Donagan, are those in which action is explained by a choice, but not in a self-referential way. My feeling is that this view about the structure of choice or future intention as containing itself as its object is rather artificial, unnecessarily intricate and not clearly consistent. I will be saying, on the contrary, that the content of an intention is typically a first-person, future-tensed action verb. I am not sure that self-referential explanation can cope with all cases of waywardness. But leaving this aside, my contention is, for what concerns us in this chapter, that self-referential explanation largely overruns the general, scientific concept of causality with which causal theories want to account for human intentional action. An event, as conceived by physics, cannot explain another in this way, unless we attribute to it the magical quality of referring to itself. Only agents seem to be able to refer to themselves by being self-conscious. And in fact we do find that self-reference in the context of an intention: my intention is that *I* will do X. This is not, however, a reference of intention to itself, but a reference of the agent to himself or herself as the one who is to act as he or she intends to do. I do not imply that self-consciousness is an easily explicable phenomenon. Quite the reverse. But I do not think that we gain much advantage by adding to this puzzle a new one concerning the self-reference of intentions and other mental attitudes.

12

Intention and Intentional Action

In chapter 6 I was proposing a normative and holistic picture of intentional action. My discussion of waywardness has offered me the opportunity, not only of criticizing alternative, causal conceptions of intentional action, but also of defending my own conception. I consider Thalberg's and Brand's proposals as basically sound, and so I have tried to incorporate them into my view, but at the same time I think that only by being reinterpreted in a normative sense are they able to cope with counterexamples. The reason is that intentions and plans are intentional states, sharing the normative features of intentionality, and that the notion of intentional action, being defined by reference to those states, cannot be captured by merely stating a purely factual relation to them, as they involve essentially normative constraints. These constraints must be incorporated to their causal efficacy in actions if they are to be successfully proposed as necessary and sufficient conditions of intentional actions, but, by so doing, we abandon a constitutive feature of causal theories of intentional action, namely the independence of the rational and the causal relations between mental states and behaviour. This independence is essential if human actions are to be understood in terms of a general, scientific concept of cause, as scientism requires. What the problem of wayward causal chains appears to show is that this cannot be done.

I am now trying to summarize the discussion so far by formulating more accurately my own definition of intentional action. I will include in this formulation.Anscombe and Davidson's conception of actions as particulars capable of being variously described, for, as we saw in chapters 3 and 4, there are good reasons in favour of this conception. Here is my proposal: a particular activity or piece of behaviour of A is an intentional action (under the description D), if, and only if, in performing that activity or behaviour, under that description, A follows correctly a rational intention of his or hers. I take it that this definition includes Brand's contention about plans: not every intention incorporates a plan, especially if the intended action is fairly simple, but following plans in acting presupposes following intentions. In our definition, 'intention' should be understood in the sense of future and generic intention, that is, in the sense in which one has now an intention to do something later and the content of that intention includes generic concepts. My intention to visit a friend next week is of that type. But we should provide room for what we were calling intentional actions in the minimal sense, that is, for actions such as sitting well back when one feels uncomfortable or picking a flower while walking along a path. These actions express only immediate and indexical intentions, with no need of generic concepts or temporal concepts concerning the future. Future and generic intentions can only be had by rational beings that master certain abstract concepts, whereas immediate and indexical intentions are shown by many animal organisms. Both kinds of intentions interact in fully intentional actions. Future and generic intentions need to be made specific in immediate and indexical intentions if we are to act at all. For instance, I have the intention to attend a meeting at 12 o'clock, but I am sitting comfortably in my room until I realize that *now* it is 12 o'clock; at that moment I begin to move.[1] Or I am walking with the intention of going to my friend's house; my walk goes on until I realize that *that* is my friend's house; at that moment my behaviour changes and I go into the house. Immediate intentions, then, seem to act on behaviour causally. Moreover, they can be caused by desires. But it would be a mistake to think that fully intentional actions can be accounted for only in terms of these immediate intentions. My belief that *now* it is 12 o'clock or my intention to go to the meeting *now* explain my beginning to move only because I had the future intention of attending the meeting. Similarly, my intention to go into *that* house explains my behaviour only as a specification of my future intention to go to my friend's house. We do not need future intentions to account for minimal intentional actions, and these include much animal behaviour.

Future and immediate intentions do not exhaust the senses of the word 'intention'. We should at least distinguish also the notions of 'intention with which' and 'intention in acting'.[2] The first notion would be roughly replaceable by that of 'purpose' or 'aim'. When we ask what someone's intention was when he did or said such and such we normally want to know the 'intention with which' he acted, what his purpose was. The 'intention in acting' in turn is a content we can 'read' in someone's action, even if this content is not a fully conscious one for him. Actions may exhibit certain characteristic traits of the agent by showing 'directedness' towards some ends, with no need for the agent to act 'with' that intention. As Gustafson points out: 'A person's action may exhibit the intention, say, to avoid controversy, but he is not acting with the intention to avoid controversy.'[3] Intentions in acting are used as clues to someone's character or inclinations in our understanding of persons. These different senses of the word 'intention' are not unrelated: one's character and inclinations are partially reflected in one's purposes; these in turn lead us to form future intentions to act in certain ways later; and the content of a future intention to do something sometimes provides the intention with which one acts later. For instance, my future intention of visiting my friend provides the intention with which I am walking along a street, namely to visit my friend.

None the less, I take it that future intentions are crucial in an account of human intentional action. As I said, this is the sense in which 'intention' is to be understood in my definition of intentional action. Although animals can be said to have 'intentions with which' and 'intentions in acting', in that they act purposively and they show their inclinations and character in their actions, they do not have future intentions. And the reason why they do not have them, it seems, is that in order to have future intentions one has to master the *concept* of time – and not only its 'intuition' – and, moreover, one has to possess the means to represent and refer to what is not present to the senses, so to master 'abstract' thinking. The variety of actions that can be performed by beings having those abilities cannot be accounted for purely in terms of intentions with which or purposes.

I am aware that my proposal concerning intentional action clashes with widely accepted views, especially after the attacks of Ryle and some Wittgensteinians against mental acts and episodes. Such views can be represented in the following text by Gustafson: 'Much of what we do intentionally we do without having *had* future intentions to do it. Hence, it would be a mistake to claim that intentional actions are realized future intentions.'[4] Now, my definition seems to imply precisely this, namely that in each of one's intentional actions one is following a future intention, an intention formed in advance. It seems to picture human agents as constantly planning their future, as calculating beings. And this is implausible. My answer is the following. First of all, we should recall the distinction I drew between minimal intentional actions and fully intentional actions. My definition concerns only the second ones. Minimal intentional actions do not require future intentions. However, when Gustafson talks about 'what we do intentionally', he is including minimal intentional actions (he calls them 'primary intentional actions'). But even if we exclude these, it can still seem implausible to suppose that all fully intentional actions require future intentions. So, my answer goes on to say that future intentions are not necessarily conscious mental episodes, even if they sometimes are. If, as I arrive at the University as I do every day, someone asks me whether I had the intention to come to the University that day, I will answer yes, and it is *true* that I had that intention, although I may not remember having gone through a process of forming that intention. It is equally true that I have the intention of coming to the University tomorrow and the day after tomorrow, but again that does not necessarily mean that I have gone through a conscious process of forming that intention or entertaining it, though I could have gone through one: that intention is simply part of my ordinary obligations as a teacher. But it is true that I have it and that if I follow that intention and come to the University, this is an intentional action of mine. Future intentions acquire typically a conscious form in the process of deliberation. For instance, I have to go to the doctor on a weekday, so that that is incompatible with my going to the University that day. I can form the intention to go to the doctor tomorrow. But to do that I give up my intention to go to the University tomorrow, because I *had* this intention before, even if no similar process of deliberation, ending with that intention, had taken place. Future intentions take conscious form, typically, when we break habitual patterns of behaviour, but there *are* future intentions in these patterns too, for we cancel these patterns in coming to form a different intention.

However, my view of fully intentional action as the correct following of a rational future intention can be challenged by other, more powerful arguments. Everybody would agree, I hope, that if I have a future intention and I correctly follow it in behaving, this behaviour is an intentional action of mine. That is, correctly following a future, rational intention is a sufficient condition of intentional action. But, according to my proposal, the entailment should also hold the other way round, that is, if I can be said to be performing an intentional action, I must be following a future intention. A future intention, then, is also a necessary condition of intentional action, or, to put it in the terminology of the authors we are going to discuss, namely Michael Bratman and Gilbert Harman, an intentional action has to be intended in order to be so. Both Bratman and Harman would resist this thesis. According to them, there are intentional actions that are not intended.[5] Their point, however, is different from Gustafson's. Gustafson's criticism seems to be based on the idea that we do not plan all our intentional actions in advance. That is why we answered that not every future intention has to be a conscious mental episode. Harman and Bratman hold, on the contrary, that there are intentional actions that are consciously foreseen in forming a future intention without being intended themselves, that is, without being the object of any future intention. These non-intended intentional actions would include, especially, the foreseen consequences of one's intended actions.

The point is subtle and interesting, and it will be worth examining in some detail.

Harman proposes the following example: an army commander (whom we shall call Commander I) forms the intention to kill the enemy soldiers hidden in a village by bombing that village, though he foresees that this bombing will have as a consequence the death of many civilians. We can suppose that, after careful deliberation, he concludes that there is no better way to kill the enemy soldiers and that he regrets the death of non-combatants. So, he bombs the village, kills the enemy soldiers and kills many civilians. Now, Harman's (and Bratman's) point would be, in our terms, that, though his action is intentional under those three descriptions, it is only intended under the first two. Killing the civilians is an intentional action of his, but he has no future intention to kill the civilians. He did not intend that. The object of his intention is only to bomb the village and to kill the enemy soldiers, the death of the civilians being a merely expected, but not intended, consequence of what he intended to do. It is an intentional, but not an intended, action.

It seems that, if we accept that killing the civilians is an intentional action, we are forced to say, according to our definition, that Commander I's future intention included killing the civilians, that he intended to kill them. This conclusion is not obviously false. Our intuitions can diverge at this point, and later we will try to see why it is so. But it can have some unwelcome consequences. In particular, it threatens to blur a difference that can be important. To see this, imagine that another army commander (Commander II) forms the intention to kill both the enemy soldiers and the civilians by bombing a village. In this case, killing the civilians is not merely an expected side-effect, but something he envisages as the object of his intention. We feel that there is a difference between the two cases, and one that can be morally relevant. Now, if my concept of intentional action forces me to say that killing the civilians was intended in both the first and the second case, am I not failing to preserve this difference? If I am, this seems to speak strongly against my view. Let me try to meet this objection. In order to succeed, I will have to show both that killing the civilians was intended in the two cases and that, none the less, there is still a difference between them.

Let us start by raising doubts about the premise that foreseen consequences of one's intentional actions are intentional actions themselves. First of all, we would not be inclined to say of every foreseen consequence of our actions that it was intentional. Suppose, for example, that I form the intention to study and that I occasionally think of the neural activity my studying will generate. I do not think we have any inclination to say either that the neural activity is something we intentionally did, or that we had the intention to produce it. In order to feel any inclination to consider foreseen consequences as intentional actions they must play some role in the practical reasoning that leads one to form an intention. In fact, this is what happens with our Commander I: he intended to bomb the village despite the fact that it would cause the death of civilians. Secondly, I contend that, even in this case, the premise is not indisputably true. We might not be clearly inclined to say that Commander I killed the civilians intentionally, that is, the same intuition that leads us to deny that the commander had the intention to kill the civilians can also lead us to deny that he killed them intentionally. The mere fact that we hesitate about the presence both of intention and of intentional action in cases like this speaks in favour of the link between intention and intentional action as conceived in my definition: we judge these dubious cases according to the standard provided by those intentional actions that are intended.

However, let us grant, for the sake of the argument, that the premise is true, and that Commander I killed the civilians intentionally. This granted, our task is to show that he intended to kill them as well, that is, that he had a future intention to kill them and, moreover, that the difference between him and Commander II still holds. Showing this will also explain, or so I hope, why our intuitions concerning these cases may diverge. In my opinion, what accounts for Harman's reluctance to attribute to Commander I an intention to kill the civilians is the fact that two different, though related, senses of the term 'intention' have been conflated in his treatment of this case, as they have been in our pre-theoretical intuitions as well, namely intention understood as 'intention with which' and as 'future intention'. This semantic ambiguity is, I contend, what accounts for our wavering intuitions concerning these cases. The 'intention with which' one acts is roughly equivalent to the purpose, desire or end one wants to fulfil through one's action. Referring to it often gives the reason why one acts and we express it with such locutions as 'my purpose was . . .', 'what I wanted was . . .', 'I was aiming at . . .', and so on. Now, our future intentions do not always coincide with our purposes, desires or ends. Rather, they are, as we shall argue, commitments to act in the future. Suppose that I desire to visit a friend and that I form the future intention to visit her and to go to her house on foot, because of possible traffic jams. I do not desire to go on foot, but I have the (future) intention to do so. This future intention, in turn, depends on my future intention (which shares its intentional object with my desire) to visit my friend, in the sense that I would not have formed the former unless I had formed the latter. A future intention is expressed, usually, by means of a first-person, future-tensed action verb: 'I will do A.' Now, my contention is, to put it briefly, that both Commander I and Commander II had the future intention (intended) to kill the civilians, though only Commander II, but not Commander I, bombed the village with the intention (purpose, desire, aim) to kill them. Killing the civilians was a reason Commander II had for bombing the village, whereas it was a reason Commander I had for *not* bombing the village, though it was outweighed by the importance he gave to his desire to kill the enemy soldiers. This is what accounts for the difference that we feel there is between them and for our hesitations in attributing certain intentions and intentional actions to Commander I. Both of them, however, had the future intention to kill the civilians. To see this, remember the way a future intention is typically expressed, namely by saying 'I will do A.' Now, this is what Commander I could say to express his intention: 'I will bomb the village in order to kill the enemy soldiers, though I know this will cause the death of many civilians.' His purpose was to kill the enemy soldiers, not the civilians. But what if he were to add: 'And I won't kill the civilians'? This is surely unacceptable and it shows that his future intention included killing the civilians, though it is true that he did not bomb the village with the intention of killing the civilians. If our Commander I were to say: 'I have no intention to kill the civilians' we could reply: 'So, don't kill them.' And he would certainly answer: 'I have to, given the circumstances.' In this 'I have to' lies his future intention. He does not want to do that, but he intends to do it, anyway. In saying he had no intention to kill the civilians, Commander I was using 'intention' in the sense of 'intention with which', 'purpose' or 'desire'. What this meant was: 'I don't want to, but I cannot help doing it.' If only the civilians were not in the village! Our Commander I would not need to apologize in that case. But, unfortunately, they were. He cannot change that. He can only abandon his intention to bomb the village. And if he does not, he is responsible for the civilians' death. True, his main future intention, whose object was also the object of his purpose, was to kill the enemy soldiers. He would not have had his future intention to kill the civilians unless he had had the other one. But having the latter, he could not help having the former. Some intentions, paradoxically, are imposed upon us by our forming other intentions. This shows the intricate relation between agency and nature: we form and execute intentions and we act intentionally in circumstances that we have not produced; we, as agents, depend none the less on nature. And this is a way in which moral ambiguity gets into and permeates our life. It belongs with our human condition. It is a natural condition of human life and we cannot escape it.

Before concluding the discussion of Harman's and Bratman's objection let me make a further, related point in defence of my view.

We can say that a future intention is closer to a decision than to a desire. 'I will do A' can express an intention and a decision as well. The advantage of the term 'decision', however, is that it does not show the semantic ambivalence of 'intention'. So, instead of saying that Commander I intends to bomb the village, let us say he has decided to do it. Listen to our commander talking about his plans: 'I have decided to bomb the village in order to kill the enemy soldiers, and I know this will kill many civilians too, but I have not decided to kill the civilians.' This is surely unacceptable. In fact, if I cannot do A without producing its foreseen consequences, I cannot decide to do A without deciding to produce those consequences I take into account in arriving at that decision. And the same holds for future intention. So, Commander I intended to kill the civilians after all. As we said, this does not mean that there are no differences between our two commanders, nor that the moral judgement should be the same in both cases. But it does mean that Commander I cannot avoid moral conflict and ambiguity. What consequences my actions will have does not depend on me. That is why I ought to consider those consequences in doing what does depend on me, namely exercising my agency and forming my intentions: because I am responsible for the former in following the latter. This bears some relationship to what Thomas Nagel has called 'moral luck'.[6]

What is a future intention then? In order to answer this question, it may be sensible to start by disentangling the main features of our pre-theoretical conception, comparing future intentions with other kinds of mental states, especially desires. Any adequate theory of intentions should, at least, accommodate these features.

First of all, whereas desire has a genuine contrary, namely aversion, there is no genuine contrary for intention;[7] one can adopt contrary attitudes, namely desire and aversion, towards the same thing, person, state of affairs or action, because of their different aspects, but nothing similar happens with intention: it is incoherent to have and not to have the intention to do one and the same action. In connection with this, an intention takes an action as its object, not a thing, person or state of affairs, whereas we have desires and other pro-attitudes towards things, persons and states of affairs, besides actions. Of course, we can intend to act so as to get an object or to bring about a state of affairs, but the 'direct' object of the intention is the action. Secondly, whereas I can feel a strong, weak or slight desire or aversion towards something, I cannot have a strong, weak or slight intention; that is, intentions do not have degrees; although we can speak about a strong or weak intention, meaning by that that we are not easily prepared to change our mind concerning the first but we are concerning the second, this is a different sense of 'strength'. So, intentions are not comparative. If I have the intention to do A, and not B or C, I do not

intend to do A 'more' than I intend to do B or C: I do not intend to do
B or C at all. But it is perfectly natural to speak about desiring to do
something more than to do something else. Thirdly, intentions and
desires show different logical features: I think, first, that one cannot
have the intention to do something one believes it is completely
impossible for one to do; in order to have an intention to do something
one has to believe there is some possibility of succeeding, even if a
minimal one; a corollary of this is that if I know two actions to be
incompatible, I cannot, without incoherence, knowingly and straightforwardly have the intention to perform both of them; and, equally, if I
know two actions to be compatible, I can have the intention to perform
both of them as well as separate intentions to perform each; also, if
someone has the intention to A and knows that B is the only means for
him to A, he ought, on pain of incoherence, to have the intention to B
(or to give up his intention to A), but this does not apply to desires and
other pro-attitudes. Finally, intentions are essentially first-person
directed: I can only have the intention to do something myself, but I
can desire that someone else do something; the only sense we can
attach to the intention that someone else do something is to do
something oneself in order to induce, persuade or force that person to
do that.

In the light of all this, I want to make my own proposal about what
future intentions are. Intentions have a content. We have said that the
object of an intention is an action and that intentions are first-person
directed. Moreover, we are talking about future intentions. This
suggests that their content is a propositon in the first person that
contains at least one verb of action in the future tense, although I am
aware that the content of intentions is a controversial issue.[8] Now, this
could also be the content of, say, a desire or a prediction. What
distinguishes intentions from desires or predictions may be, then, the
relationship of the subject to that content. If we reflect on certain of the
features listed above, like, for instance, the fact that intentions take
only actions as contents, and that they are essentially first-person
directed; if, moreover, we take into account certain logical requirements of intentions, such as the fact that I cannot intend what I think
it is impossible for me to do or that the intention to A involves the
intention to B if B is the only known means to A, we should be led to
think that intentions involve the agent in an especially strong way,
that they put the agent in an active relationship with their content. We
can try to capture this relationship with the content by saying that
what distinguishes an intention from a desire or a mere prediction is
that in having an intention I commit myself to make that content true.
However, this definition seems to be too strong. We said that in order
to have an intention to A, I have to think that A-ing is not completely
impossible for me. So, I can have the intention to hit a very difficult

target, although I believe that my chances are minimal. In fact, I do not believe that I will hit the target, but I still have the intention to hit it. So, believing that I will A is not a necessary condition of having the intention to A. This being so, if we define intention in terms of commitment, we cannot merely say that an intention is a commitment to make its content true, for in the above case I surely would not commit myself to hit the target, which is the content of that intention. So, to cover this kind of case, my proposal is that in having an intention I commit myself either to make (if I think I will be able) or to try to make (if I do not think I will be able) its content true. 'Trying' does not refer here to a mental act, but to an action in the ordinary sense, which is, and the agent thinks it is, a rational means to make the content of the intention true. In the above example trying would be aiming carefully at the target and the like. I have the intention to hit the target if, and only if, I commit myself to try to do it, that is, to aim carefully, and so on. In this case, then, the content of my future intention (to hit the target) provides the 'intention with which' I aim carefully at the target. Besides that, we should make room for the so called 'conditional intentions', that is, for intentions to do something if something else is the case. An example: 'I will go to the beach if it does not rain' or 'I will go to the theatre if there are some tickets left.' In having a conditional intention I commit myself to make the content true only if the condition holds.

Future intentions, roughly, are commitments to act. The converse, however, does not hold. Not every commitment to act is an intention. Think for instance of such other ways of committing oneself to act as taking a decision or making a promise. Decisions and promises show distinctive features, but they share with intentions the element of commitment. Intentions, decisions and promises are different ways of committing oneself to act. A decision seems to differ from an intention in that the necessary belief-condition is stronger, and includes, not only believing that the action is not completely impossible, but also believing that I will perform it. In the above example, we would not say that I have decided to hit the target. We can define, then, a decision as a commitment to make its content true, *tout court*. This suggests that at some points decisions and intentions may overlap. Finally, a (sincere) promise seems to include the same belief-condition as a decision, but it includes waiving our right to change our mind, as well as a promisee.

I am trying now to defend and elaborate further my proposal. The first, even if only negative, argument in favour of my conception is that it accommodates, in a natural way, the pre-theoretical features of intentions we listed above and accounts reasonably well for the logical requirements of intentions as well as for other features, such as the fact that intentions do not have degrees (one either commits oneself or does not commit oneself to do something; the sense in which commitments are strong or weak seems to be the same as that in which intentions are), or that it is incoherent to have the intention to do something one thinks impossible (it is incoherent to commit oneself to do something one thinks impossible), or that intentions are first-person directed (one commits oneself, properly speaking, even if one can commit others to do things indirectly).

Secondly, it could be argued that an intention commits one to act only when it is stated to others, so that it is the explicit *statement* of the intention, not the intention itself, that commits one to act. This objection seems to imply that only by becoming a kind of promise, involving an audience, is an intention a commitment to act. My answer is that I can explicitly state a desire, or an opinion, or a hope, etc., without committing myself to act, and that, this being so, what involves the commitment is not the fact that an intention is explicitly *stated* to others, but *what* is stated, namely the intention itself. Equally, it could be said that the idea of committing oneself is linked with the idea of a sanction if that commitment is broken, whereas we often do not fulfil our intentions and, none the less, do not suffer any sanction. A sanction is involved only, or so it seems, when the intention has been stated to others. Of course, if I state an intention and other people adjust their plans to my intended action, the sanction becomes patent and explicit when the action is not performed, so that I usually respond to the expected sanction by offering an explanation. But the sanction also exists when nobody except oneself is involved. One normally owes oneself an explanation (even of a weak kind like 'it was not so important', or 'I forgot', or 'I am not in the mood') when one does not do what one had the intention to do, although this explanation is in many cases implicitly provided by standard procedures of adjustment between our intentions and our actions. But if someone did not understand at all that *some* explanation is needed when an intention is not fulfilled, we would lose the basis for attributing intentions to him. So, there is a sanction, namely incoherence and meaninglessness, even though only oneself is involved. A systematic and inexplicable non-fulfilment of our intentions would make our behaviour unintelligible, not only to other people, but also to ourselves, and the minimal basis that is needed to attribute to ourselves intentions, and, in the end, rationality and mind, would blow up.

Thirdly, the claim that intentions are commitments to act becomes more plausible if we accept that decisions are too, because the borderline between intentions and decisions is not at all sharp. We speak of decisions when quite an important matter and quite a long process of deliberation are involved, and we speak of intentions when matters are less important and deliberation is slight or its result is settled in advance. There is, besides that, the difference we stated between the necessary belief-conditions. But in standard cases they can overlap without any problem, for decisions and intentions show a similar logical behaviour. If, after deliberating, I say to myself 'O.K., I shall do such and such', is that the expression of an intention or of a decision? Say what you like, I would answer.

Fourthly, it could be argued, against my claim, that intentions do not commit us to act because one can always change one's mind, whereas in promises changing one's mind is not allowed.[9] I agree that the difference between an intention and a promise is not a difference of degree. Promises are essentially public acts, while intentions are not. And, moreover, changing one's mind is allowed in the second case, but not in the first. We have already discussed the first difference. As for the second, if we settle the question by saying that, concerning intentions, one can always change one's mind, we are forgetting that intentions are part of a wider network of mental states and processes, and, especially, that in most cases they are supported by reasons. In such cases, simply changing one's mind will not do, unless there is a corresponding adjustment in the set of reasons, because of new information, changes in one's motives, or better reasoning. Intentions are not blind and compulsory forces. They are backed by reasons, and the more powerful the reasons, the deeper the justification we need to change our mind. Intentions are not idle thoughts and wishes we entertain and reject frivolously. If our behaviour is not going to fall into total obscurity, intentions must remain in touch with reasons. That is why the unrestricted possibility of changing one's mind would destroy, in the end, the notion of intention itself, and the basis for attributing intentions: the basis for distinguishing between the unfulfilment of an intention and a change of mind would blow up. On the other hand, intentions are conceptually prior to promises: we can conceive of someone's having intentions and acting intentionally without ever making any promise, but no one could make a promise without being able to form and have intentions. The commitment we acquire through a promise presupposes the simpler ability to commit oneself by simply intending now to do something later.

But what is it about intentions that commits us to act? The reason why unrestricted change of mind is not admissible gives us the clue to this question too. Intentions commit us to act by virtue of the force of those reasons we take into account in forming them. These reasons, in turn, express previous commitments we acquired in the past, the way we are, the story of our lives. Could we not then dispose of intentions and account for intentional action in terms of reasons and actions only? Reasons are not weights which prompt actions according to the force they exercise on invisible psychic plates. Even if past circumstances and mistakes narrow down and cast a shadow over our lives, we simply cannot let ourselves drift like jetsam in the river: we have, at least, to throw ourselves into the river. That is why we cannot dispose of intentions in accounting for intentional action. Reasons can be states and attitudes. Intentions, together with decisions and promises, are commitments to future actions, they express what in chapter 5 we called the core of agency. Reasons are not, *by themselves*, causes of actions. Our reasons do not give rise to our actions as heat gives rise to the boiling of water. Only when we intend or decide to act on those reasons do these become efficacious. This is the difference between merely having reasons to act and acting because of those reasons: not that in the second case reasons are causes of actions, while in the first they are mere considerations, but rather that in the second case we intend or decide to act on them. Agency is what makes reasons efficacious, and not conversely. It belongs to the human condition that we have to commit ourselves to act and to engage in acting in a concrete and definite way because desires, beliefs and drives are never decisive for us, rational and reflective beings, as, on the contrary, they are for most animals. Even the action we most desire has its dark and negative aspects. Intentions manifest our reflective nature, by virtue of which we can take our own needs and desires as objects of judgement, and commit ourselves to act with the sheer force of reason, even when intentions are prompted by irrational factors. Intentions are situated at a higher level than desires, inclinations and other states we happen to be in. The normative character of intentional action comes from the normativity of rational reflection as the source of the intentions we follow in acting intentionally. Finally, it is a mistake to suppose that reasons are formed by beliefs and desires alone. Reasons include intentions we formed in the past: that I had once the intention to write this essay is a reason for writing this chapter now and for many other actions. That intention, moreover, has since modified many of my wants and beliefs. It has prompted, for instance, my desire to finish the essay and following it has affected my beliefs concerning human action.

I am aware, again, that this view of intentions is not widely accepted. I could mention here, in favour of my view, such authors as M. A. Robins and A. C. Danto,[10] although I do not share many other points of their views, and some indications in other authors.[11] None the less, it is worth pointing out that the view according to which intentions involve some sort of commitment to action is currently finding increasing support. Michael Bratman's and Gilbert Harman's recent books are good examples of this presently growing tendency in the philosophy of action.[12] However, I would like to stress some important differences between Bratman's view of the committing role of intentions and the view that I defend. Bratman's theory of intention is part of a functionalist account, according to which intentions are seen as functional states, characterized by their typical causal roles in practical reasoning and action. This is also the perspective that Harman seems to favour.[13] These causal roles, however, are left unexplained. They are ultimate categories in a functionalist theory. Intentions, then, are considered as causal dispositions to act and to reason in certain ways. These causal roles are what Bratman calls the 'descriptive aspect' of commitment. Besides that, however, intentions are also subject to normative constraints, so that the commitment they introduce shows a 'normative aspect' as well. Now, the problem is how we are to conceive of the relationship between these two aspects. If they are seen as independent, we face the split between causality and rationality that gives rise to the problem of wayward causal chains. If, on the contrary, we are prone, in a functionalist vein, to ground normativity on factual, causal dispositions to act and reason in some characteristic ways, this tends to misrepresent normative relations, to blur the distinction between them and factual ones, and to deprive them of a significant efficacy of their own. In the end, it is not clear that this approach can avoid the problem of waywardness. To see this, let us quote Bratman's specification of sufficient conditions of intentional action:

S intentionally A's if:
(1) S wants to A and for that reason intends to try to A; and
(2) S A's in the course of executing his intention to try to A; and
(3) S A's in the way he was trying to A; and
(4) Conditions (2) and (3) depend, in an appropriate way, on S's relevant skills.[14]

Now recall the example we construed, in the preceding chapter, against Thalberg's causal account of intentional action. According to Bratman's proposal, it seems that the nephew would be killing his uncle intentionally, which is false. What this suggests is that the relationship which holds between intention and intentional action cannot be conceived of as factual, but as normative. Neither viewing intentions as involving commitments nor granting them a normative aspect is enough to give an adequate account of human intentional action. Normativity has to be given an effective role in the way intentions lead us to act. This is what we have tried to convey by saying that an intention has to be correctly followed by the agent if his action is to be intentional. Functionalist accounts, such as Bratman's, do not seem to me to do justice to our experience of being guided by an intention in acting.

Finally, the predominance of causal theories of action might help to explain the fact that intentions have widely come to be seen as identifiable with, or somehow reducible to, desires, beliefs, or a combination of both, as well as the fact that future intentions have been usually forgotten in favour of 'intentions with which'. The belief–desire model of intention and intentional action is still a dominant perspective in contemporary philosophy of action. It is not difficult, however, to perceive, in some recent literature, an increasingly suspicious attitude towards that model. This attitude is noticeable even in authors who side with the causal tradition in action theory, such as Irving Thalberg, Myles Brand and, as we shall see in our next chapter, Donald Davidson himself. More recently, Michael Bratman has developed a resolute attack against the belief–desire model.[15] And Gilbert Harman explicitly denies 'that one's intentions are merely implicit in one's beliefs or desires'.[16] As for myself, in contending that future intentions are best viewed as commitments to act and in placing them together with decisions and promises I want to stress that I consider future intentions as essentially different from desires or other pro-attitudes towards actions.

As an example of the attempt to reduce future intentions to desire plus belief let us quote this text by Robert Audi, where he tries to understand intending in terms of wanting and believing:

(x) (A) [x intends to do A if and only if
(1') x believes that he will (or that he probably will) do A; &
(2') x wants, and has not temporarily forgotten that he wants, to do A; &
(3') either x has no equally strong or stronger incompatible want (or set of incompatible wants whose combined strength is at least as great), or, if x does have such a want or set of wants, he has temporarily forgotten that he wants the object(s) in question, or does not believe he wants the object(s), or has temporarily forgotten his belief that he cannot both realize the object(s) and do A].[17]

I think that this account of intention fails, for several reasons. I contend, first of all, that from premises (1')–(3') it does not follow that x has the intention to do A. Let us put aside the talk about the strength of desires and the problem of giving a non-circular account of the notion of comparison between the strength of different desires: what we said in dealing with Churchland's 'law' could equally be applied to this case. Even if we dismiss this problem, it is easy to construe a counterexample in which an agent fulfils all those conditions and still does not have the corresponding intention. We can adapt, for instance, the Davidsonian example of the climber. Davidson's climber can have the belief that he will loosen his hold on the rope, can want to loosen it, may not have a stronger want, etc., and still not have the intention to loosen his hold. Of course, the climber's belief that he will loosen his hold cannot have as its ground his *intention* to loosen it, for this would

144 Intention and Intentional Action

beg the question; it has to be based on inductive grounds, for instance on the way he has acted in other, similar circumstances. This being so, I think my conclusion follows: such a belief plus the rest of the conditions do not imply that the agent intends to A. Equally, cases of compulsory or pathological behaviour could be made to work against Audi's proposal: think of a drug-addict who believes, on the basis of his previous experience, that he will take the drug, who desires to take it, has no stronger desire, etc., but still forms the intention *not* to take the drug. In general, think that Audi's conditions can obtain *while deliberating about what to do*, that is, before any intention has been formed: the fulfilment of those conditions, then, cannot imply that the subject intends to do such and such. The conclusion seems to be, then, that future intentions are clearly different from beliefs plus desires and cannot be reduced to them.

13

Davidson's Theory of Intention

That future intentions cannot be understood in terms of beliefs and ordinary desires is something that Davidson came to acknowledge after realizing that this supposition gives rise to insurmountable difficulties. Davidson's theory of intention is the result of the revision of his first model of intentional action, the one he defended in 'Actions, Reasons, and Causes'. This theory is sophisticated and challenging, and it will be worth examining. Let us outline it and see how it developed from the first Davidsonian conception of intentional action. After that, we shall examine some objections and try to defend our own conception of intentions in terms of commitments.

According to Davidson's analysis of intentional action in 'Actions, Reasons, and Causes', an intentional action is conceived both as the effect of a desire (or other pro-attitude) and a belief *and* as the conclusion of two premises corresponding to those causes, namely a premise that states a certain kind of pro-attitude towards actions that have a certain property and a premise that states a belief to the effect that a certain action has that property. Leaving aside the causality aspect, an intentional action is conceived as the conclusion of a practical reasoning, and this in turn is conceived as deductive in character. Davidson himself refers to his own early theory in the following terms: 'I accepted the view that the propositional contents of the explanatory want and belief should provide premisses from which the desirability of the action could be deduced. Not that I thought of the agent as first deducing the consequence and then acting. Instead, I embraced Aristotle's idea that drawing the conclusion could be identified with the action.'[1] A rationalization such as 'I flipped the switch because I wanted to turn on the light' would be analysed, according to the first Davidsonian model, in the following way: 'I hold that any action of mine is desirable that has as a likely result that the light turns on and I believe that (the action of) flipping the switch has that as a likely result; therefore, I hold that flipping the switch is desirable.' This conclusion, as Davidson points out, is identical with the action itself. Actions correspond, in this conception, to all-out desirability judgements of the form 'flipping the switch is desirable'. An objection, however, prompts itself easily: if I flip the switch intentionally, my premise cannot be 'I hold that any action of mine is desirable that has as a likely result that the light turns on', because, for instance, to butt the switch with my head has that likely result, but I do not hold that this action of mine is desirable, for I surely do not want to hurt my head. Moreover, this conception gives rise to contradictions. Here is an example: I hold that any action of mine is desirable that has the property of keeping me healthy. Going to the dentist has that property. Therefore going to the dentist is desirable = I go to the dentist. I hold that any action of mine is desirable that has the property of sparing me being in pain. Not going to the dentist has that property. Therefore not going to the dentist is desirable = I do not go to the dentist. Now, if from two acceptable premises a contradiction is deduced, it seems that this analysis of intentional action and practical reasoning is wrong.

Davidson, however, was led to see the failures of his first conception through reflection on the problems of weakness of the will and incontinent actions.[2] To act incontinently is to act against one's best judgement. Incontinence involves a conflict of attitudes, for and against a certain course of action. And the problem is that the model of 'Actions, Reasons, and Causes' cannot account for incontinence or conflict. Cases of incontinence and conflict, viewed in the light of that model, give rise to contradictions, similar to that of our example, that is, to conclusions to the effect that I both perform and do not perform one and the same action.

Because of such considerations, Davidson was led to modify considerably his initial analysis of intentional action, changing the content of the premises corresponding to the belief and desire and, partly as a consequence of this, introducing intentions as a new factor in intentional action, besides beliefs and desires. This is the way Davidson himself considers his revision:

> In 'How is weakness of the will possible?' I gave up the deductive model, and changed what I took to be the logical character of the propositional content of a want or desire. The premiss someone has who wants to see what is on the next page is not 'Any act of mine that has a good chance of letting me see what is on the next page is

desirable' but something more like 'Any act of mine is desirable in so far as it has a good chance of letting me see what is on the next page'. This premiss does indeed combine with the contents of a belief to the effect that turning over a new leaf has the desirable characteristic, but what can be deduced is only 'Turning over a new leaf is desirable in so far as it has a good chance of letting me see what is on the next page'. Such a conclusion, I argued, could not correspond to or be identified with an action since it is compatible with the agent knowing that the action (because of other characteristics) is highly undesirable. Actions, I urged, correspond to 'all-out' judgements like 'Turning over the page is desirable', and such judgements do not follow by ordinary logic from the premisses provided by our desires and beliefs.[3]

The judgement we need in order to account for the action, namely 'action A is desirable', cannot be deduced from the premises provided by the desire and belief, for desires correspond simply to prima facie conditional desirability judgements (of the form 'any action of mine is desirable *in so far* as it has such and such properties') from which an unconditional judgement cannot be deduced. The idea behind this is simply that, for example, if John wants to inherit a fortune and believes that killing his uncle will allow him to inherit a fortune, this only amounts to saying that John has something in favour of killing his uncle, namely that this action would allow him to inherit a fortune, but of course he can also have many things against killing his uncle, so that we cannot deduce from that belief and desire that John judges the action of killing his uncle unconditionally, that is, all-out desirable. Now, as a result of weighing up pros and cons of killing his uncle, John can form what Davidson calls an 'all-things-considered judgement', a judgement to the effect that, in the light of all considerations he takes into account, killing his uncle is more desirable than any available alternative. This judgement, strangely enough, is still, according to Davidson, a conditional prima facie judgement, in that it is relativized to those considerations. But we still need to detach this desirability judgement from its conditions in order to get an all-out or unconditional desirability judgement, a judgement that, say, killing his uncle is all-out desirable. The idea behind this seems to be that in order to engage in acting, considerations pro and against the action must be left behind. We need, then, an all-out judgement.

Since beliefs and desires do not correspond to all-out judgements, they are not enough to account for actions. We need something else, something like intentions or decisions, to perform the action. And intentions, according to Davidson, are that which corresponds to all-out judgements: 'An all-out judgement that some action is desirable, or, better, an all-out judgement that some action is more desirable than any available alternative, is not distinct from the intention: it is identical with it.'[4]

In 'Actions, Reasons, and Causes' the all-out judgement was identical to the action, that is, one draws the conclusion from the premises by straightforwardly acting. Now, however, an intention, or all-out judgement, is not identical with the action; it stands between the belief-and-desire and the action. What led Davidson to this position was his realization that there are pure intentions, that is, intentions that are not followed by actions, or that are followed by them after a temporal gap. In 'Actions, Reasons, and Causes' intentions were considered as something lacking a reality of their own, not being 'an entity, state, disposition, or event' and as somehow reducible to beliefs and desires. But in his paper 'Intending' Davidson writes:

> If someone digs a pit with the intention of trapping a tiger, it is perhaps plausible that no entity at all, act, event, or disposition, corresponds to the noun phrase 'the intention of trapping a tiger' . . . But it is not likely that if a man has the intention of trapping a tiger, his intention is not a state, disposition, or attitude of some sort. Yet if it is so, it is quite incredible that this state or attitude (and the connected event or act of *forming an intention*) should play no role in acting with an intention.[5]

What is going on here, I think, is that in 'Actions, Reasons, and Causes' Davidson understood 'intention' in the sense of 'intention with which'. In this sense, it is credible that we can know the intention someone has from knowing the belief and desire on which he acts. In 'Intending', however, Davidson comes to appreciate the reality of future intentions and their difference from intentions-with-which, as well as from beliefs and desires.

So much for Davidson's revision of his first conception of intentional action. We can go on to discuss the resulting notion of intention. As we saw, Davidson conceives of intentions as 'all-out judgements'. He also says that these all-out judgements are dispositions and also pro-attitudes towards propositions. See, for instance, the following text: 'How far apart are Peacocke and I on the nature of intention? Not very far, it seems to me. We agree that to intend to do something is to have an attitude towards a proposition. He calls this a disposition and I call it a judgement; but what I call a judgement is a disposition, and I am happy to give up the word "judgement".'[6] Davidson also says that intentions are ' "all-out" positive evaluations of a way of acting' and that an intention is 'an unconditional evaluative attitude'.[7]

However, since I can all-out positively evaluate a way of acting that it is impossible for me to engage in, but I cannot have the intention so to act, this conception of intention needs to be supplemented with some provisos about beliefs as necessary conditions of intending. These conditions can be resumed in the sentence 'one can't intend what is inconsistent with one's beliefs.'[8] A specific form of this claim is that 'an agent cannot intend what he believes to be impossible.'[9] Another form of this last claim is that an agent 'must believe there is some chance he will act as he intends.'[10]

It is also worth noticing that this conception of intentions remains faithful to a causal account of intentional action. If in the model of 'Actions, Reasons, and Causes' an intentional action was caused by pro-attitudes and beliefs – having appropriate logical relations to the action –, the introduction of intentions does not alter this basic insight, for intentions are conceived, after all, as pro-attitudes towards a way of acting. Davidson's account, however, does not show the evident failures of a theory such as Audi's, for it distinguishes desires from intentions as different kinds of pro-attitudes towards actions: while desires are prima facie pro-attitudes, intentions are all-out pro-attitudes. The question still remains whether this difference is strong enough to cope with the problems raised by the differences between desires and intentions.

Let us see, first, in order to evaluate Davidson's proposal, if it meets what we called, in the preceding chapter, the pre-theoretical features of intentions.

Intentions, we said, do not have genuine contraries. But all-out pro-attitudes, as Davidson conceives of intentions, do have contraries. The genuine contrary of an all-out positive evaluation of a way of acting would be an all-out negative evaluation of it. However, the associated feature of intentions by virtue of which it is incoherent to have and not to have the intention to do one and the same action, is in some sense met by the 'all-out' qualification: even if it is not incoherent to have prima facie opposite attitudes towards one and the same action, because of different aspects of this, it seems to be somehow incoherent to judge all-out positively and to judge all-out negatively one and the same action, for in a certain sense the talk about the aspects of the action is left behind in getting from a prima facie to an all-things-considered judgement and from this to an all-out judgement. The different aspects, positive and negative, of an action have been taken into account in the all-things-considered judgement, and this judgement in turn – leaving aside cases of *akrasia* – is deprived of this relativization to pros and cons and expressed in an unconditional judgement, namely that action A is best *tout court*, or is better than any of its alternatives. The idea behind the 'all-out' feature is that in forming the intention we stop considering pros and cons, and judge that an action is simply the best of our alternatives.

We said, moreover, that an intention takes an action as its object.

All-out judgements do not take only actions as their objects, but Davidson would no doubt say that they are intentions when they take actions as objects. After all, Davidson does not hold that all all-out judgements are intentions. Besides, all-out judgements are no worse, in this respect, than commitments, for commitments can take as their objects not only actions but, for example, ideals as well.

Concerning the third feature we listed, however, things are worse for Davidson's view of intentions. Intentions are not comparative, but they are, so to speak, all-or-nothing. If I intend to do A, and not B or C, I do not intend to do A more than B and C. I do not intend to do B or C at all. But all-out judgements are at least implicitly comparative. If I make an all-out judgement that an action is desirable, I am making an implicit comparative judgement that this action is *more* desirable than any alternative I am considering. As Davidson himself points out: 'An all-out judgement that some action is desirable, or, better, an all-out judgement that some action is more desirable than any available alternative, is not distinct from the intention: it is identical with it.'[11] This comparative nature of all-out judgements will prove decisive for the final plausibility or implausibility of Davidson's view of intentions, as we shall see below, in connection with Bratman's criticism of that view. This comparative nature of Davidsonian intentions will affect their ability to allow for certain bona fide logical requirements of intentions. We shall refer later, in connection with Bratman's criticism, to the question concerning the logical behaviour of intentions.

So, provisionally leaving aside this question, we said, fourthly, that intentions are essentially first-person directed. All-out desirability judgements do not show this feature, since I can all-out judge that someone else's action is desirable. In this respect, commitments bring in more directly this pre-theoretical feature of intentions. But this is not a decisive argument against Davidson's view, for we should recall again that, for Davidson, not every all-out desirability judgement is an intention. He could say, to accommodate this feature, that only all-out judgements which are first-person directed are intentions.

Let us examine now Bratman's criticism of Davidson's view of intentions and see if my own conception can answer satisfactorily those of Bratman's requirements and objections that a Davidsonian perspective finds hard to handle.

According to Bratman, all-out positive evaluations of ways of acting show two important features: they are at least implicitly comparative and they are about particular acts, not types of acts (as prima facie evaluations are). In order to account for future intentions, Bratman writes,

> Davidson's strategy . . . is to *extend* his account of the role of all-out positive evaluations in intentional action to the future-directed case.

In just having reasons for acting in a certain way I only accept certain prima-facie evaluative propositions. When I actually act for those reasons – and so act intentionally – I accept an appropriate all-out evaluative proposition. Similarly, on Davidson's theory, when I come to intend to go to the concert tomorrow I come to accept a future-directed all-out evaluative proposition in favour of going to the concert then: my future intention is this all-out evaluation. By extending his theory of intentional action in this way, Davidson can ensure that future intentions, like intentional action, can be a conclusion of practical reasoning.[12]

Bratman is referring here to the revised version of Davidson's theory of intentional action that we have set forth in this chapter, not just to the simple model of 'Actions, Reasons, and Causes'. We referred above to the grounds for the revision, so we can be spared repetition of them now.

Bratman's criticism starts from a 'natural constraint' on intentions, namely agglomerativity: 'Rational intentions should be agglomerative. If at one and the same time I rationally intend to A and rationally intend to B then it should be both possible and rational for me, at the same time, to intend *to A and B*.'[13] This constraint corresponds, roughly, to certain logical requirements for intentions we placed among their pre-theoretical features, namely to our condition that if two actions are known by me to be compatible, I can have the intention to perform both of them, as well as separate intentions to perform each; it connects also with the related condition that if two actions are known by me to be incompatible, I cannot, without incoherence, straightforwardly have the intention to perform both of them. These conditions were, roughly, corollaries of the general point that one cannot have the intention to do something one believes it is completely impossible for one to do. We saw that Davidson accepts this general point by saying that one can't intend what is inconsistent with one's beliefs. Then, Davidson should accept that one cannot intend to perform two actions which are known to be incompatible, since this is inconsistent with one's beliefs and, moreover, it is natural to think that he should accept that one can intend to perform two actions which are known to be compatible. This last contention follows from Davidson's rejection of a stronger belief-condition for intentions, besides the general point that the intended action, A, must not be incompatible with one's beliefs, namely that in order to have the intention to A one must believe one will be able to A or will A. (I rejected this stronger condition too, by pointing out that one can have the intention to hit a difficult target even if one does not believe that one will be able to do it or that one will do it. But I qualified this point by saying that in this case intending to hit the target means committing oneself to trying to do it. The stronger condition is not strictly necessary to intend to A, but of course it can be present in many cases.)

Let us go on now to Bratman's objections to Davidson's theory. They start from the problem of future intention in the face of equally desirable future options (the so-called 'Buridan problem'): 'Suppose I know I can stop at one of two bookstores after work, Kepler's or Printer's Inc., but not both. And suppose I find both options equally attractive. I judge all-out that any act of my stopping at Kepler's would be just as desirable as any act of stopping at Printer's Inc., given my beliefs.'[14] Now, the question is what follows from Davidson's theory in this case. Do I have both intentions? Neither intention? Or what? Recall that intentions are being conceived as all-out judgements and that these judgements are implicitly comparative. 'But there are weak and strong comparisons. A *weak* comparison would see A-ing as at least as desirable as its alternatives; a *strong* comparison sees A-ing as strictly more desirable than its alternatives.'[15] Now, if what Davidson's theory requires is only a weak comparison, I have both the intention to go to Kepler's and the intention to go to Printer's Inc. But since going to Kepler's and going to Printer's Inc. are incompatible – since to do both is 'inconsistent with one's beliefs' – I cannot have the intention to go to both. And this violates agglomerativity. It seems, then, that what is required is a strong comparison. In this case I have neither intention. But then, if I decide to go to one of the two bookstores, as I should do, it seems that I have an intention which does not correspond to an all-out strong desirability judgement, which violates Davidson's theory of intention.

However, Bratman goes on to say that even in the case of a strong comparison, Davidson's theory does not ensure agglomerativity of intentions. To show this, he construes a second example: 'I have for a long time wanted to buy copies of *The White Hotel* and *The Fixer*, and know I will be at a bookstore this afternoon. Further, I know the bookstore will have one or the other of these novels in stock, but not both. Unfortunately, I do not know which one will be in stock.'[16] Now, I can all-out judge buying *The Fixer* more desirable than any of the alternatives which are consistent with my beliefs and with my act of buying *The Fixer* (so, buying no novel is one of these, but buying *The White Hotel* is not). Then, I can form in this way an intention to buy *The Fixer*. And following a similar route I can form an intention to buy *The White Hotel*. 'But recall that I believe I cannot buy both novels. So it is not possible for me to intend to buy both. We are led to the result that though I rationally intend to buy *The Fixer*, and rationally intend to buy *The White Hotel*, it is not even possible for me to intend to buy *The Fixer* and to buy *The White Hotel*. On Davidson's theory rational intentions may fail to be agglomerative. And that seems wrong.'[17]

Even if Bratman's problem can seem to be easily solvable, it has poison in it. The most obvious solutions from a Davidsonian perspective generate new problems for the theory. A solution that suggests itself is that my intention is neither to buy *The Fixer*, nor to buy *The White Hotel*, but simply to buy the available book. And this is what Davidson answers:

> The alternatives or options that matter to intention are those an agent believes available to him, not those actually available; since one can't intend what is inconsistent with one's beliefs, this means there are often if not always things an agent can do that he can't, given his beliefs, intend to do. If Bratman believes only one of the books he wants will be available, among the relevant options he can consider are: buy the available book, buy *The Fixer*, buy *The White Hotel*, buy *The Fixer* only, buy *The White Hotel* only, and buy neither. Under the circumstances, the first option is the one Bratman will rank highest, and it will determine his intention.[18]

This answer looks all right, and one could say that after all Bratman's problem was only apparently a difficult one. But consider the fact that buying the available book is not incompatible with buying *The Fixer*, or with buying *The White Hotel*, for *The Fixer* could be the available book, and so could *The White Hotel*. And then we see that Davidson has avoided the difficulty only at the price of violating the second, related requirement for intentions, namely that if two actions are known by me to be *compatible*, I can have the intention to perform both of them, as well as separate intentions to perform each. So, suppose I can both study and have a cup of tea and suppose that I all-out judge that studying is more desirable than having a cup of tea; an adequate theory of intention should allow for the fact that I can intend to study and intend to have a cup of tea; but, according to Davidson's conception, I intend to study, but not to have a cup of tea. One reply, and one that Davidson would surely favour, would be to say that the alternatives are: studying only, having a cup of tea only, and studying while having a cup of tea, and that what I intend in this case is the last. But I think that this answer fails, for it implies that I will intend to study while having a cup of tea without intending to study nor intending to have a cup of tea, that is, without being able to have separate intentions to do each.[19] And this seems to be wrong. This example can also show the relationship of Bratman's point to our contention that while intentions are not comparative, all-out judgements are. In the above example, I can, obviously, both intend to study and intend to have a cup of tea, and if I do, I have both intentions; I do not intend to do one thing more than to do the other, even if I all-out judge that studying is more desirable than having a cup of tea. It does not seem that Davidson's theory can easily account for the fact that I have both intentions while all-out judging that one thing is more desirable than the other. This strongly suggests that the concept of all-out desirability judgement does not capture the content of the concept of future intention.

Now, how can my view of intentions deal with these points? Let us restrict ourselves to the most difficult case of *The Fixer* and *The White Hotel*, for the other example will be solved if this is. First of all, I cannot commit myself to buy *The Fixer*, for it may not be available, so that if I have the intention to buy this book, this intention needs qualification. The same would hold for buying *The White Hotel*. One suggestion could be that this case could be assimilated to that of hitting a difficult target: I do not think I will be able to do it, and so I cannot commit myself to hit the target, but I can commit myself to try to hit it. We are acting in both cases without confidence in our attaining the result. According to this, if I have the intention to buy *The Fixer*, this means only that I commit myself to try to buy it. And the same would hold for *The White Hotel*. Moreover, both intentions are compatible, for trying to buy *The Fixer* is compatible with trying to buy *The White Hotel*, even if buying *The Fixer* is not compatible with buying *The White Hotel*. And agglomerativity is preserved, for I can have the intention both to try to buy *The Fixer* and to try to buy *The White Hotel*.

However, I am not completely happy with this suggestion, for I think that if I have the intention to buy *The Fixer* in this example, this intention is not faithfully captured by 'I commit myself to try to buy *The Fixer*.' The same holds for the other intention. After all, the case is different from that of hitting a very difficult target. In this latter case, even if I think that hitting the target is very unlikely, I do not think it is strictly *impossible* for me to hit the target. And the fact that I had the intention to hit the target shows itself in that I tried to do it, did my best, aimed carefully, etc., even if, after all, although it was possible, I did not hit the target. But the case of buying *The Fixer* (*The White Hotel*) is not like this. It is not that buying *The Fixer* (*The White Hotel*) is very difficult and unlikely, even if still possible, but that it is either the easiest thing to do or impossible, depending on whether it is in stock. If it is in stock, the probability of buying it is 1; if it is not, the probability is 0. And, moreover, the fact that I had the intention to buy *The Fixer* (*The White Hotel*) does not show itself in that I tried to do it, even if, although it was *possible*, I did *not* do it. It seems, then, that what we have here is a decisive condition for my performing what I intend and I have to form the intention before knowing about that condition's holding. The availability of one or the other book is a condition that I know as relevant for what I will be able to do and will do in the end. And this being so, a conception of intention in terms of commitment to action must necessarily take it into account. From my perspective on intentions, then, I think that the most plausible account of Bratman's example is the following: I have the intention to buy *The Fixer*, but this intention is a *conditional* one, and could be expressed in terms of my view as 'I commit myself to buy *The Fixer* if it is (the one which is) available'. The same would hold for *The White Hotel*. And both conditional intentions are compatible and fulfil the constraint of agglomerativity. Adding both intentions we would have something like: 'I commit myself to buy either *The Fixer* or *The White Hotel*, the one which is available.'

The simplicity and plausibility of this solution speaks strongly, I hope, in favour of my view of intentions as commitments to act, in the terms detailed above.

Bratman, however, does not think that this kind of case is solely a counterexample to a Davidsonian view of intention. He also thinks that it undermines a certain view of the relationship between future intention and fully intentional action, namely the view, defended in this book, according to which a future intention is not only a sufficient condition, but also a necessary condition of a fully intentional action.[20] In the preceding chapter we examined and overcame, so I hope, a challenge to this view. The challenge consisted, we may recall, in the supposed intentional, but not intended character of the foreseen consequences of our actions. Let us face now what Bratman presents in his book as a second argument against the view we defend. To construe this argument he uses an example that has the same structure as the one we have just considered.[21] The example is, roughly, the following: think of two video games that involve guiding a 'missile' to a certain target; I decide to play both games simultaneously; however, they are known to me to be linked in such a way that it is impossible to hit both targets; if both targets are about to be hit simultaneously the machines shut down and I hit neither target; I play both games simultaneously, giving each game a try. Now, if I hit target 1, I do it intentionally, and the same holds for target 2. But I had neither the intention to hit target 1 nor the intention to hit target 2, for, given what I know, they would fail to be consistent. Since hitting target 1 is not compatible with hitting target 2, then, if I give each game a try, I can neither intend to do the first thing nor intend to do the second. Bratman's point is that I have neither intention, despite the fact that if I hit target 1 (or target 2) I do it intentionally. So, there are intentional actions that are not intended. It is easy to see how Bratman could also use the example of *The Fixer* and *The White Hotel* in order to draw a similar conclusion. But I think the conclusion fails, for, on my view, I had two conditional future intentions in both examples. Concerning the videogames example, my answer to Bratman's objection would run on the following lines: if I hit either target, I do it intentionally *and* I had the intention to do it; I had two conditional intentions, roughly to hit target 1 unless I hit target 2 before and to hit target 2 unless I hit target 1 before. Bratman's argument is powerless against these conditional intentions. They are consistent with one another and with my beliefs. The same would apply to the example of the two novels. Such cases, then, do not threaten my view of the relationship between intention and intentional action.

We have contended that Bratman's examples do undermine Davidson's view of intentions as all-out desirability judgements. But do they? What prevents Davidson from adopting the same way out as we have? Could he not get around Bradman's objections by allowing for similar conditional intentions? The answer, I think, is that he could not. After all, he does not take this way out in his reply to Bratman, though he seems to be aware of it. The reason why Davidson's theory cannot provide this solution is that for him a future intention is an all-out judgement (now) about the desirability of a (future) action, and the action of buying *The Fixer* (*The White Hotel*) *is desirable now*, whether it is in stock or not (which I do not know). That is why he cannot add this condition to the intention, making it a conditional one. An *enabling* condition, known as relevant, for the performing of the action is decisive for my view of intentions as commitments to act, but it cannot be for Davidson's unless it affects the present desirability of the action, which is not the case in Bratman's example. For Davidson, a genuine conditional intention must include a condition which is now a reason for acting in one way or another, that is, which affects now the desirability of the action, not its mere possibility. And it must be so, given his view of intentions. As Davidson himself points out:

> Genuine conditional intentions are appropriate when we explicitly consider what to do in various contingencies; for example, someone may intend to go home early from a party if the music is too loud . . . Bona fide conditions are ones that are reasons for acting that are contemporary with the intention. Someone may not like loud music now, and that may be why he now intends to go home early from the party if the music is too loud. *His not being able to go home early is not a reason for or against his going home early* [my emphasis], and so it is not a relevant condition for an intention.[22]

That the music is too loud is relevant now for the judgement about the desirability of going home early, and so 'I will go home early if the music is too loud' is a genuine conditional intention. But 'I will buy *The Fixer* (*The White Hotel*) if it is available' is not a genuine conditional intention in a Davidsonian frame, for the availability of *The Fixer* (*The White Hotel*) is not relevant, in Bratman's example, for the all-out desirability, now, of buying *The Fixer* (*The White Hotel*), and so for the intention to buy it. This is why the easy way out that is open to our view is not so for Davidson's.[23]

Other possible ways out for Davidson's view seem also to be blocked, as Bratman's reply shows. But we will not pursue them further. The interested reader can examine Bratman's reply.[24] My purpose was to strengthen the plausibility of my view of intentions by confronting it with a controversial case like Bratman's. And I think that the simplicity and intuitiveness of the solution given by my view, compared with the difficulties faced by Davidson's, suggests that my view of intentions comes closer to capturing their nature than Davidson's.

The conclusion to draw from the discussion around Bratman's problem seems to be that intentions are different from all-out comparative judgements. To judge that an action is better than its alternatives is not an intention; it is perhaps a reason for forming the intention to perform it, and to form this intention is to commit oneself to perform the action or, at least, to try to perform it. That is why it is essential for intentions to take into account the chances of success, because we are not simply judging the desirability or undesirability of an action, but committing ourselves to perform it. An intention appears as something different from a pro-attitude towards an action, even if this pro-attitude is 'all-out'.

Finally, for what concerns the relationship between reasons and intentions, on the one hand, and intentions and actions, on the other, I think that the revised Davidsonian model is too closely linked to the model of 'Actions, Reasons, and Causes' not to face similar problems. The revised model remains faithful to a causal account of intentional action. Davidson conceives those relationships in the following terms: 'The reasons cause the intention "in the right way"'; concerning the relationship between intention and action, 'in some cases there is no relation because the intention is not acted on. If the intention exists first, and is followed by the action, the intention, along with further events (like noticing that the time has come), causes the action "in the right way".'[25] I do not see how this answer can avoid the problems we found concerning the clause 'in the right way' when we discussed the problem of waywardness. Only if reasons cause the intention as reasons, if the intention gives rise to the action as a commitment to act on those reasons, and if in acting the agent follows his commitment correctly can we avoid the problems of waywardness. But then we are also giving up the prospects of a causal account of intentional action.

14

Agency and Physical Determinism

Agency, in the strong sense of the word in which only rational beings are agents, has as its core, we said, the notion of commitment. By intending and deciding we commit ourselves to a certain course of action. The insufficiency of beliefs and desires to account for intentional action, as shown in the fact that even causal theorists of action have seen themselves forced to include intentions into the picture, seems to point to an essential difference between intentions and decisions, on the one hand, and desires, on the other. Intentions and decisions, however, would be idle and useless if we never faced alternatives of behaviour: to commit oneself to do something would be a pointless ornament if one could not, after all, help doing it.

Now, suppose that those alternatives are real, in the sense that not even a complete description of the universe could predict apodictically which one will be actualized, and suppose, moreover, that it is up to the agent himself, guided by rational reflection, to select one of them by exercising his agency, that is, his ability to commit himself to do something in the future. Is the acceptance of this supposition compatible with the acceptance of a scientific picture of the universe as a network of causally related events where no 'holes' or 'gaps' are permitted?

This question necessarily arises because agency does affect the physical world and manifests itself in the movements of human bodies; and these movements are physical events and interact causally with other physical events. We saw that the occurrence of certain physical events (the so-called 'results' of actions) was a necessary condition for the performance of certain actions.

This anchorage of agency in the physical world manifests itself in the very structure of agency: I cannot rationally have the intention to fly or decide to live eternally. The scope of our commitments is partly limited by what is physically possible for us, and we take this for granted in deliberating about what to do. On the other hand, however, we ordinarily suppose that several possibilities are open to us and that it is not up to the physical world, but to ourselves, as agents, which one will be actualized. Can we rationally suppose this while, at the same time, retaining our acceptance of science as a true description and explanation of the universe?

This problem is a version of an old philosophical question, namely whether freedom and determinism are compatible. According to the conception of agency I have been developing here, I cannot accept Humean-like versions of compatibilism.[1] These versions assert, roughly, that freedom is compatible with determinism in the following sense: our wants and desires, being part of ourselves, determine what we do, so that we are in this sense self-determined, not driven to act by external forces; we are free to act, moreover, in the sense that we could have done otherwise if we had had other wants; we are not free only when external forces prevent us from doing what we want; determinism, however, is also true for our wants are events that are caused by other antecedent events and cause in turn our actions. If we give a materialist reading of wants, as physiological states, this conception of human agency is clearly compatible with science, but only at the price of denying to the agent any power to choose: I *could* have done otherwise if my desires had been different, but since which desires I have is not up to me, it is not really true that *I* could have done otherwise. The alternatives were not open to *me*.

Now, if we take choice and alternatives seriously, if we accept that what agents will do is sometimes up to them, and not just up to their desires, by virtue of their ability to commit themselves to act, can we still make this compatible with the existence of no causal gaps in the network of the universe and with the truth of science?

I will answer in the following terms: if agency is a reality, as I think it is, science can still be a true description and explanation of the universe, but not a *complete* description of reality, since, I will contend, science is structurally unable to detect agency; moreover, the efficacy of agency in the physical world need not necessarily create causal gaps, but we should accept that different causal stories, with no gaps in them, are physically possible, that is, compatible with the actual natural laws and the actual state of the universe. In saying this I am implying the following: if by 'determinism' we understand that the state of the universe at t_2 can be logically deduced from the natural laws and the state of the universe at t_1, then agency is not compatible with determinism; if by 'determinism' we understand that, given the state of the universe at t_2, we could relate a complete description of this state to its state at t_1 by means of causal statements backed by natural laws, then agency is compatible with determinism.

To see what I have in mind, let us imagine an example. Suppose that I am attending a political meeting. I am in complete disagreement with the speech, and I think I ought to leave the room ostentatiously in order to show my disapproval. At the same time, the speaker happens to be my boss, and it is very likely that I will lose my job if I leave the room, so that this consideration inclines me to remain seated. This conflict makes me feel uneasy; I am about to stand up, but thinking of my job pushes me back on to my seat; I even feel the tension in my muscles. Let us call this situation S1. Now suppose that I think that my political convictions come first and that to hell with the job, so that I stand up and leave the room. Let us call this situation S2a. Suppose, on the contrary, that I think of how miserable I will be unemployed and, even though I feel guilty, I remain seated. Let us call this situation S2b. Proceed now to a complete physical description of my body at S1. Now, S2a includes, at least, certain muscles contracting and my body moving through the room, which are physical events. S2b, in turn, includes my body remaining at rest. My body moving through the room and my body remaining at rest are not compatible at t_2. Moreover, my body remaining at rest is incompatible with the carrying out of my decision to leave the room, just as my body moving through the room is incompatible with the carrying out of my decision to remain seated. Now, if from a complete physical description of my body at S1 plus natural laws we could always logically deduce, say, that my body will remain at rest at t_2, then the process of deliberating about leaving or staying would be completely idle, a mere epiphenomenon, since no real alternatives are open to me as an agent, and agency would be simply an illusion, as I would be following, necessarily, a path determined in advance. This shows that the problem of the relationship between agency and the physical world cannot be solved by merely appealing to different levels of description or different levels of discourse, each having its own 'logic' and truth conditions, for we said that the occurrence of certain physical events, namely my body's movement or my body's rest, was directly relevant to my power as an agent and to my ability to select an alternative.

I have deliberately construed the example so as to have a case of deciding between two physical, non-meaningful actions, namely standing up and remaining seated. It is clear, however, that in our particular case each of those particular actions, if performed, would be identical, in this context, to a particular meaningful action, namely showing my disapproval and pretending to acquiesce respectively. It is the meaning of these physical acts that introduces dramatism in our decision situation. Showing disapproval, however, is a type of meaningful, pure action, so that it does not involve specific kinds of happenings and could be performed in many other ways. Strictly speaking, that my body moves through the room is not logically necessary for my performing an act of showing disapproval. But a particular meaningful action is performed in a particular physical way, and I have supposed that in our case we have thought of leaving the room as the way of showing our disapproval. I have supposed this in order to block an all too easy way out, namely to appeal to the multiple physical realizability of meaningful actions and to the fact that no specific kind of happenings is logically involved in them. Appealing to this fact was justified in the context of trying to block the reduction of actions to happenings and to justify our ordinary distinction between them. Our present problem, however, is slightly different: we are not wondering whether there really are actions as distinct from happenings, nor whether we make decisions and commit ourselves to act. Rather, we are asking whether those actions, decisions and commitments are really of some use in order to change things, independently of the previous state of the world, or are they just useless accompaniments with no real influence on the final course of events. And what I contend is that they would be such useless accompaniments if strict determinism were true of the physical world.

Now suppose that it is up to me, as an agent, which one of the two alternatives, S2a and S2b, will be actualized. What conditions are to hold if this is to be true and how would things appear from a scientific perspective?

First of all, S1 and the natural laws are to be compatible both with S2a and S2b, for if one of these alternatives is logically necessitated by S1 and the natural laws, agency has no real role to play. Secondly, the influence of agency on the physical world would not create causal gaps and would be undetectable for science. Suppose, for instance, that S2a becomes actual at t_2 owing to my deliberation and decision. Then, I contend, we could construe a complete causal path leading from S1 to S2a, without appealing to anything other than physiological and neurophysiological events, so that even if it is my decision that accounts for the actuality of S2a, this 'fact' would be completely undetectable for a scientific description and explanation of the path leading to S2a. The same would be the case if S2b becomes actual. If S2a is the case, then, I suppose, a scientist would detect, at a certain moment, the activation of certain neural and muscular paths causing the movement of my body, but this activation would be connected, with no gaps, with the previous states of the organism. This activation would not take place if S2b is the case, but in this case, too, the neural and physiological states of the organism at t_2 would appear connected, with no gaps, with the previous states. In either case, agency would not be detected, even if it was really efficacious.

If we take agency and freedom seriously, then, if the movement of our bodies is directly relevant to them, and if, as seems plausible, this movement is controlled by the brain, I think we should accept that the structure of the human brain has to be adequate for agency and freedom, that is, it must not be possible, at least for the movements related to our intentional action, and before a decision has been made, to deduce logically from the brain's state at that time its general state at a later time. If agency is not a useless ornament, the human brain cannot be a strictly deterministic system, that is, a system such that we could logically deduce from its state at t_1 plus certain laws its state at t_2. Given its enormous complexity, there are no a priori reasons for thinking that we can explain and predict its operations in the same fashion as we might explain and predict, to use a famous example of Hempel's, the bursting of a radiator due to low temperature, namely by deducing the bursting from natural laws plus initial conditions previous to it. Several different neural and muscular routes must be compatible with the state of the brain at t, and we should be able to construe a true causal story leading from this state to the actual route. Only in this sense could the brain be said to be a deterministic system.

It is often held that the deterministic or indeterministic (probabilistic) character of physical laws has no direct bearing on the question of human freedom, for a human being would not enjoy more freedom if his or her actions were caused by random movements of elementary particles than if they were necessitated by their deterministic movements.[2] To this extent, I agree. But I think that the issue has an indirect bearing on the freewill problem. An indeterministic physical world is hospitable to agency. A strictly deterministic one is not. Physical indeterminism, of course, does not imply the existence of agency as an efficacious ability, but it does not exclude it, contrary to strict physical determinism. So, the fact that physics might not be, ultimately, strictly deterministic could have some bearing on the possibility of free agency.

Acceptance of agency and freedom is, I think, only incompatible with the acceptance of a strong version of determinism, namely a 'logical deducibility' version, but not with a version of it according to which there are no gaps in the causal network of the physical universe and each physical event has a complete causal explanation.

Nothing of what I have said so far amounts to a 'proof' of agency. My concern has been only to point to the physical conditions necessary for the possibility of agency and to stress that belief in the reality of agency does not require the rejection of belief in science, though it does require that we temper our confidence in it as a complete description and explanation of reality.

If the story I have told and the arguments I have developed so far are plausible, we can draw some corollaries concerning some traditional issues in the philosophy of mind that have been mentioned throughout this book, namely the question of eliminative materialism, the conflict between causal and rational explanations, and the question of identity between mental and neurophysiological states. I do not intend to settle these questions here, but only to provide some comments about them.

As for the first, if one commits oneself to science as the only true access to reality and the only criterion for ontology, that is, for what really exists, then eliminativism of the mental, including of course agency, which has an essential mental aspect, seems to be a perfectly – maybe the only – coherent position to adopt. Recall the example of the political meeting. Science would tell a complete causal story leading from S1 to S2a or S2b. Nothing but physical events, however, would appear in it – no trace of agency, of agents, or decisions. Science is structurally unable to detect and apprehend agency. Then, if science alone gives a complete account of reality, agency does not exist. The antecedent, however, has not much to recommend itself; it rests merely upon a subjective conviction, upon a choice that goes far beyond the limits of science itself. Eliminative materialism rests upon no compelling reasons.

As for the second question, bearing in mind our example, we can compare the causal explanation that physical sciences could give of, say, S2a with a rational explanation of it, that is, an explanation in terms of the reasons the agent had for leaving the meeting and for remaining in it, his deliberation, decision, etc. As for the former, leaving aside the question of the proper *object* of the explanation – whether science would be explaining an *action* or rather a physical movement –, I think that, if I am right, a true causal story, in terms of physical states and events, could be told leading from S1 to S2a, and in this sense S2a would be explained. However, since *ex hypothesi* S2b was also possible, this explanation would leave aside the crucial question of why S2a, and not S2b, became actual. Typically, in such a situation we want to know not only why the agent did what he did, but also why he did that instead of doing something different. This question is answered by a rational explanation, and in this sense this latter is superior in explanatory power to a purely causal one as far as human intentional action is concerned.

Finally, the reasons and considerations that led the agent to leave the meeting, as well as the reasons he had for remaining, would not be understandable without our knowing the relationships of the agent to his surroundings, to political and economic life, to his boss, etc. They show an essential semantic aspect, an essential relation to certain realities that reach far beyond the limits of the body or the brain. This semantic aspect of reasons is, however, completely absent from the states which might correspond to them at a neurophysiological level. This speaks strongly against a possible identity between those mental states and processes and these neurophysiological ones, whether in the sense of a type-identity theory (according to which, say, decisions are identical to a certain type of neurophysiological state) or in that of a token-identity theory (for which, say, each particular decision is identical to some particular neurophysiological state). The issue of identity is, of course, much more complex than this. I just wanted to point to some bearing our discussion of agency could have on it.

My contention that the brain cannot be a strictly deterministic system if agency is to be a real ability to change things according to our rational will may sound too strong. Some people might be more disposed to abandon the belief in agency than to accept the idea that the brain, a physical system among others, might not be deterministic. However, if freedom is a real property of human beings, nature must have provided the basis thereof. The increasing complexity of the human brain through evolution might have turned it into a qualitatively new system, able to meet the constraints that our everyday idea of free agency seems to include. Our fully intentional actions, so I have been urging throughout this book, are not just more complex than intentional behaviour in non-human animals: they show a different structure, that manifests itself in our ability to reflect on our desires and beliefs and to form future intentions as a result of reflection. This structure has taken human beings far from their natural roots, maybe too far to allow their survival in the long run.

Conclusion

The starting-point of our inquiry was our ordinary, twofold distinction between actions and happenings. This distinction, which many important aspects of human life hinge upon, reveals itself, on reflection, as slippery and elusive. So much so that it can even be held that the term 'action' is a mere convention to refer to what is in fact a special chain of happenings. These reductionist attitudes can be fostered by a scientific outlook on real processes of acting combined with the undeniable fact that the occurrence of specific happenings is involved, as a necessary condition, in the performing of several kinds of actions. This is the basis, we may recall, of the so-called 'regress-problem' in action theory. This involvement of happenings in actions prompts attempts to isolate the actional aspect of actions from the happenings involved, but these attempts run into the shocking discovery that, after subtracting happenings from a process of acting, nothing else seems to be left. And this surprising result favours the reductionist conclusion: actions are but sequences of happenings.

This conclusion can be resisted from a volitional perspective. According to the New Volitional Theories, there *is* something left after subtracting happenings from a process of acting. What is left is an act of will, a volition or a trying. This is the genuine actional element in actions, the rest being just causal consequences of this one act. Our criticism of this sort of theory rested on the contention that they face a dilemma: either volitions are the first steps of physical movements, and then they involve specific physical happenings and cannot stop the infinite regress, or they are purely mental acts, and then volitional theories are obliged to explain how purely mental acts can cause physical happenings.

We have joined the New Volitional Theories in their anti-reductionist attitude, but we have departed from them as far as their strategy and results are concerned. Our first substantial claim has been resolutely anti-reductionist: the distinction between actions and happenings is as sharp as our natural everyday attitude tends to assume and we cannot get actions out of a set of mere happenings, complex as this set may be. Our path towards this claim started from finding some kinds of ordinary, specifically human, meaningful actions (such as greeting people, marrying, bidding, and so on) that do not involve specific kinds of happenings as logically necessary conditions. No analysis in terms of happenings can possibly capture the concept of such actions. They are, then, a major obstacle in the way of reductionist analyses of actions. They can stop the infinite regress as they do not logically involve specific kinds of happenings; they are, so to speak, cases of pure acting. So, they can be used as a guide for identifying that elusive actional aspect that, if actions are not to be mere sequences of happenings, must be left in any other case of acting after subtracting any happenings involved.

The clue to identifying this actional aspect is to realize that those actions whose concept does logically involve specific kinds of happenings can be unintentionally performed, in that the happenings involved can be brought about by the agent unintentionally. On the contrary, those actions whose concept does not logically involve specific kinds of happenings must be intentionally performed if they are to be performed at all. Their being necessarily intentional is related to their being cases of pure acting, independent of specific happenings. And being intentional, so we have claimed, is somehow involved in any case of acting as the mark that distinguishes it from a mere happening.

Being intentional, however, is still in need of further analysis. If those actions that are necessarily intentional cannot possibly be analysed in terms of happenings, their being intentional must be related to an essentially active element. The clue to our identifying this element was provided by our realizing that meaningful, necessarily intentional actions cannot possibly be performed except by agents who have some sense of what sort of things are required in the future by what they are doing at present, or, in other words, some ability for committing themselves to certain future, more or less specific ways of behaving. Necessarily intentional, meaningful actions involve certain commitments on the part of the agent. Commitments, however, are essentially active performances, involving the agent as an active being. This is why those necessarily intentional, meaningful actions cannot be analysed in terms of happenings and can stop the infinite regress: because they involve commitments and these cannot simply occur. They cannot be mere happenings.

So, our inquiry led us from the distinction between actions and happenings to those actions which, in being logically independent of specific kinds of happenings, are necessarily intentional, and from these to commitments as being that which accounts both for their necessarily intentional and for their purely actional character. We generalized this relationship by holding that being intentional is the criterion of agency and that a fully intentional action is a piece of behaviour which follows a commitment on the part of its agent. This leads to our second substantial claim: human agency is an ability to commit oneself to do things in the future and it is this ability that justifies a sharp distinction between actions and happenings. Agents are beings who are able to commit themselves to act.

Now, we have further contended that the simplest way to commit oneself to act in a certain way is to form a future intention to do so. A future intention is an agent's commitment to make its content true by acting him or herself. Whereas Davidson classifies intentions among pro-attitudes, such as desires, we have placed them together with other forms of commitment, such as decisions and promises. An intentional action, then, can be conceived as the correct following of a rational future intention on the part of an agent. This includes the case in which the action is intentional by being the fulfilment of a decision, a vow or a promise, for decisions, vows and promises imply future intentions.

If intentions and intentional actions are to be understood in terms of commitments, the fact that certain living beings show teleological and purposive behaviour, as many animals do, is not enough to attribute to them intentions and intentional actions in this strong sense. We have distinguished between two related, but different levels implied in intentional action: a minimal or weak level, characterized by intentions that can be 'read' into purposive behaviour (immediate intentions and intentions with which), and a high or strong level, where we find future intentions. Our proposal concerning intentions is meant to apply only to this latter level. Although this rests on the former and develops out of it in human beings, it cannot be seen as a mere extension of it, but as constituting a qualitatively new ability. This ability to commit oneself to do things in the future is implied in the performing of meaningful actions. It is in this strong sense that (some of) these actions can be said to be necessarily intentional. That is the reason why they cannot be accomplished by those beings that show only intentional actions at the first level, such as the higher non-human animals. Failure to notice this distinction gives rise to misunderstandings and confusions in some current discussions of intentional action, for having an analysis of the first level is not to have an analysis of the second one. This latter, high level of intention and intentional action is what makes the notion of agency important and challenging and what forms the basis of our sharp intuitive distinction between actions and a causal order of happenings.

Human beings do not only desire and believe and act because of their desires and beliefs. Between these attitudes and overt behaviour we can find a normative structure which has its clearest and simplest expression in future intention as a commitment to act. Future intentions and other forms of commitment stand between the background of reasons and the action.

A further central thesis of this book has been that intentional action, in the strong or full sense referred to above, has an uneliminable normative character that permeates its whole structure, whence the requirement for correctness as applied to the following of intentions. This normative character, together with the human capacity for making primary attitudes objects of reflective thinking, which is implied in the concept of intentional action as the *following* of an intention, has formed the basis of our criticisms of naturalistic and scientistic approaches to human action.

On my own view intentions are not ordinary causes, nor are they factually linked with actions. Rather, they prompt actions as standards that the agent commits himself to meet and to do so correctly. Their relation to reasons is not merely factual, either. Intentions are backed by reasons in that reasons provide good arguments for forming them. That the relation between reasons, intentions and intentional actions is normative and that normativity itself has to be given genuine efficacy in prompting our intentional actions is strongly suggested by the fact that the opposite assumption cannot yield a correct and complete analysis of intentional action, as the problem of wayward causal chains seems to show. If we dig deep enough into this problem we are naturally led to the conclusion that a general, scientific concept of cause is not able to capture the structural relations involved in human intentional action, and an old thesis of the hermeneutic tradition, namely that the general method of natural sciences does not suit the study of intentional action, gains new and unexpected support against scientism.

If we give reasons as such genuine efficacy in intentional action, that is, if we grant the agent the power to appreciate them as arguments, we will have to admit the fact that they cannot be like forces whose intensity can be measured in advance and whose effects can therefore be accurately predicted. It is the agent who gives them their force by acknowledging their goodness and so committing him or herself to act on them by forming an intention. But no goodness of reasons can be appreciated unless reasons themselves can become objects of reflective thinking and evaluation. In order for reasons to be efficacious *qua* reasons, their content must be capable of being examined and found good by an agent. Our account of human intentional action includes the subjective point of view of a reflective agent. The ability to commit oneself to act goes hand in hand with the ability to make one's own desires and other sorts of reasons objects of reflection and evaluation. This reflective capacity allows human agents to place their own desires and urges at a distance and to judge them worth pursuing or not. This prevents human intentional action from being a dependent variable, whose value can be fixed by objectively measuring the value of some other, independent variables. This is one sense in which agents can be said to be the source of their own actions, independently of the past history of the world.

Scientistic attempts to bring human intentional action under the methods and explanatory forms of physical sciences run up against this reflective and normative structure, which has no analogue in the objects that these sciences deal with. If we want to find an analogue of intentional action in the field of physical sciences, the most appropriate candidate would be not their objects of study, but scientific practice itself, as an intentional and norm-following activity carried out by reflective human agents.

The level of reflection, norm following and commitment distinguishes human agents from the higher non-human animals. This level allows agents to filter the influence of desires on their actions and to act in a way that can be autonomous as to the relative strength of desires. I have made extensive use of these features in criticizing scientistic accounts of human action, especially Churchland's and decision theory. No analysis of human agency can be correct that does not provide room for future intentions. The intentional actions of those beings who can reflect on their desires and beliefs cannot be accounted for in terms of these attitudes. Future intentions are specifically different from beliefs and desires and irreducible to them. In viewing intentions as all-out pro-attitudes Davidson conceives of them as too similar to desires not to face problems before cases of intending which are not cases of judging the object of the intention as the most desirable alternative.

Are my criticisms of naturalism and scientism devastating? Well, not quite. First of all, my criticisms stand on condition that my interpretation of certain features of human agency, especially reflection, norm following and future intention, is accepted. But other interpretations of them, much closer to a scientistic attitude, are still possible. D. C. Dennett's *Elbow Room* is a good example, and I would recommend the reader to look through it. Secondly, my analysis has at its basis certain crucial notions, on which many arguments are built, that might require a sharper dissection. This is the case with the notions of reflection and commitment. Concerning them I have relied to some extent on intuition. But the reader should realize that intuitions sometimes do more work than they are entitled to and can be too hospitable to illusions. Finally, I have emphasized, especially against causal theories of intentional action, that reason and commitment do have efficacy of their own in our acting and that this efficacy is independent of that of desires, however closely related they are. But my arguments for this contention may be open to challenge. We can hardly claim to have proved that reason and commitment can influence our acting without a mediating and possibly indispensable influence of desires and more primitive causal factors. The Humean contention that only passions, and not reason, can move us to act retains its intriguing appeal and is supported by our seemingly undeniable character of physical, natural beings that are deeply rooted in the animal realm.

It might be further argued that our arguments rest upon an unwarranted confidence in our ordinary conceptual frame. Recall that one of our starting-points in defending human agency against reduction was the existence of some ordinary examples of actions which did not logically involve happenings, namely some specifically human types of meaningful actions. In fact, it is the *concept* of these actions that resists assimilation to happenings, and this concept is part of our ordinary conceptual frame and draws its virtues from it. In this sense, so the objection runs, having recourse to that concept begs the question by assuming the soundness of the conceptual frame that is threatened by reduction. I would answer in the following terms. First, something is gained if an *intuitive* distinction between actions and happenings is shown to rest on a *conceptual* structure that forbids the blurring of this very distinction. Most reductionist analyses do not seem to be aware of these conceptual difficulties. Secondly, I have no unwarranted confidence in our ordinary conceptual frame but, by the same token, I do not see why should I have a no less unwarranted distrust of it. I think it sensible to grant it the benefit of doubt and to assume its innocence unless proved guilty. Thirdly, I have not placed our ordinary conceptual frame in an unassailable position by unconditionally assuming its ultimate validity. As our last chapter shows, I take the possibility seriously that it might wildly misrepresent things. If strict determinism is true of all the physical world, the conviction that our actions can change things according to our will, independently of the previous states of the universe, would reveal itself as an illusion and the conceptual frame on which it rests would be shown to be a false representation of reality, even if, for psychological or practical reasons, we did not abandon it.

Deep, contrasting insights are in conflict in the philosophical field that this book has tried to explore once again. As I said in the Introduction, I do not think I have settled the questions, though in the end I do think I have plausibly argued that the case for our ordinary view of ourselves as free agents is strong, much stronger, as a matter of fact, than some naturalistic and scientistic tendencies seem nowadays to suppose.

Notes

Chapter 1 Actions and Happenings

1 A. C. Danto, 'Basic Actions', in *The Philosophy of Action*, ed. A. R. White (Oxford University Press, Oxford, 1968), pp. 43–58, esp. p. 51.
2 A. C. Danto, 'Freedom and Forbearance', in *Freedom and Determinism*, ed. K. Lehrer (Random House, New York, 1966), pp. 45–63, esp. p. 48.
3 Danto, 'Basic Actions', p. 45.

Chapter 2 The New Volitional Theory

1 See, for this distinction, G. H. von Wright, *Explanation and Understanding* (Cornell University Press, New York, 1971), ch. 3.
2 H. McCann, 'Volition and Basic Action', *Philosophical Review*, 83 (1974), pp. 451–73, esp. p. 452.
3 Ibid., p. 453.
4 Ibid., p. 454.
5 Ibid., p. 454.
6 Ibid., p. 456.
7 A. I. Melden, 'Willing', in *The Philosophy of Action*, ed. White, pp. 70–8, esp. p. 71.
8 McCann, 'Volition', p. 469.
9 Ibid., pp. 470–1.
10 B. O'Shaughnessy, 'Trying (as the Mental "Pineal Gland")', *Journal of Philosophy*, 70 (1973), pp. 365–86, esp. p. 369.
11 Ibid., p. 371.

12 Ibid., p. 373.
13 Ibid., p. 373.
14 Ibid., p. 375.
15 Ibid., p. 380.
16 Ibid., p. 378.
17 Ibid., p. 383.
18 Ibid., p. 378.
19 Ibid., p. 385.
20 See S. Shoemaker, 'Embodiment and Behaviour', in *Identity, Cause, and Mind* (Cambridge University Press, Cambridge, 1984), pp. 113–38.
21 J. Hornsby, *Actions* (Routledge & Kegan Paul, London, 1980). Her views are also connected with Prichard's. See H. A. Prichard, 'Acting, Willing, Desiring', in *The Philosophy of Action*, ed. White, pp. 59–69.
22 Hornsby, *Actions*, p. 4.
23 Ibid., p. 33.
24 Ibid., p. 14.
25 Ibid., p. 59.
26 Ibid., p. 130.

Chapter 3 Some Remarks about the Ontology of Actions

1 A. I. Goldman, *A Theory of Human Action* (Princeton University Press, Princeton, NJ, 1970), pp. 10ff.
2 Ibid., p. 10.
3 Ibid., p. 10.
4 Ibid., p. 21.
5 G. E. M. Anscombe, *Metaphysics and the Philosophy of Mind. Collected Philosophical Papers*, vol. II (University of Minnesota Press, Minneapolis, 1981), p. 212.

Chapter 4 Meaningful Actions

1 D. Davidson, *Essays on Actions and Events* (Clarendon Press, Oxford, 1982), p. 59.
2 Anscombe, *Metaphysics*, pp. 208–9.
3 See G. E. M. Anscombe, *Intention*, 2nd edn (Basil Blackwell, Oxford, 1979), pp. 11 and 45–6.
4 See Danto, 'Basic Actions'.
5 Goldman, *A Theory*, p. 25.
6 Ibid., pp. 25–6.
7 See C. J. Moya, 'Acción e Intención', *Quaderns de Filosofia i Ciència*, 9/10 (1986), pp. 213–20.

8 See R. M. Chisholm, *Person and Object. A Metaphysical Study* (Allen & Unwin, London, 1976), ch. 2.

Chapter 5 Agency and Intentional Action

1 See A. R. Miller, 'Describing Unwitting Behaviour', *American Philosophical Quarterly*, 17 (1980), pp. 67–72. See also Anscombe, *Intention*, p. 85.
2 Anscombe, *Intention*, p. 84.
3 Davidson, *Essays on Actions*, p. 229.
4 Hornsby, *Actions*, pp. 36–7.
5 See Moya, 'Acción e Intención'. See also Miller, 'Describing'.
6 See O'Shaughnessy, 'Trying'.

Chapter 6 The Intentionality of Mind

1 A. Rosenberg, *Sociobiology and the Preemption of Social Science* (Basil Blackwell, Oxford, 1981), pp. 144–5.
2 Ibid., p. 148.
3 See Anscombe, *Metaphysics*, pp. 209–10.
4 See Hornsby, *Actions* and Prichard, 'Acting'.
5 Anscombe, *Intention*, p. 52.

Chapter 7 Intentionality and Science

1 For a discussion of this claim in its Quinean form, see C. Hookway, *Quine. Language, Experience and Reality* (Polity Press, Cambridge, 1988), ch. 5.
2 One of the best collections of papers on identity theories is *The Mind/Brain Identity Theory*, ed. C. V. Borst (Macmillan, London, 1970).
3 Rosenberg, *Sociobiology*, p. 131.
4 W. O. Quine, *Word and Object* (MIT Press, Cambridge, Mass., 1960), p. 221.
5 For a discussion of Quine's eliminative position see Hookway, *Quine*, chs. 8–10.
6 See J. Fodor, 'Methodological Solipsism Considered as a Research Strategy in Cognitive Psychology', in *Representations. Philosophical Essays on the Foundations of Cognitive Science* (Harvester Press, Brighton, 1981), pp. 225–53.
7 See J. Perry, 'The Problem of the Essential Indexical', *Noûs*, 13 (1979), pp. 3–21.

Chapter 8 Laws and Explanation of Actions: P. M. Churchland

1   Some landmarks related to this discussion are the following: C. G. Hempel, 'The Function of General Laws in History', *Journal of Philosophy*, 39 (1942), pp. 35–48; P. Gardiner, *The Nature of Historical Explanation* (Oxford University Press, London, 1952); W. Dray, *Laws and Explanation in History* (Oxford University Press, London, 1957); C. G. Hempel, 'Explanation in Science and in History', in *Philosophical Analysis and History*, ed. W. Dray (Harper & Row, New York, 1966), pp. 95–126; W. Dray, 'The Historical Explanation of Actions Reconsidered', in *Philosophy and History: A Symposium*, ed. S. Hook (New York University Press, New York, 1963), pp. 105–35; C. G. Hempel, 'Reasons and Covering Laws in Historical Explanation', in *Philosophy and History*, ed. Hook, pp. 143–63.

2   P. M. Churchland, 'The Logical Character of Action Explanations', *Philosophical Review*, 79 (1970), pp. 214–36.

3   Ibid., p. 214.

4   Ibid., pp. 221–2.

5   Ibid., p. 222.

6   Davidson, *Essays on Actions*, p. 23.

7   C. H. Whiteley, 'Mental Causes', in *The Human Agent*, Royal Institute of Philosophy Lectures, vol. I (Macmillan, London, 1968), p. 98–114.

8   Churchland, 'The Logical Character', p. 225.

9   Ibid., p. 229.

10 See H. G. Frankfurt, 'Freedom of the Will and the Concept of a Person', in *Free Will*, ed. G. Watson (Oxford University Press, Oxford, 1982), pp. 81–95.

11 Churchland, 'The Logical Character', pp. 228ff.

12 Ibid., p. 236.

13 Whiteley, 'Mental Causes', p. 104.

14 Churchland, 'The Logical Character', pp. 234–5.

15 Ibid., p. 225.

16 Ibid., p. 225.

17 P. M. Churchland, *Matter and Consciousness* (MIT Press, Cambridge, Mass., 1984), p. 43.

Chapter 9 Laws and Prediction of Actions: Decision Theory

1   R. C. Jeffrey, *The Logic of Decision*, 2nd edn (University of Chicago Press, Chicago, 1983), pp. 3–4.

2 E. Eells, *Rational Decision and Causality* (Cambridge University Press, Cambridge, 1982), p. 4.
3 M. Hollis, *The Cunning of Reason* (Cambridge University Press, Cambridge, 1987), ch. 6.
4 Eells, *Rational Decision*, p. 30.
5 Hollis, *The Cunning*, p. 130.
6 Jeffrey, *The Logic of Decision*, pp. 210–11.
7 See Eells, *Rational Decision*, ch. 3, for a discussion.
8 Ibid., p. 33.
9 Ibid., p. 43.

Chapter 10 Davidson's Causal Theory of Intentional Action

1 Now in Davidson, *Essays on Actions*, pp. 3–19.
2 Ibid., p. 3.
3 Ibid., p. 5.
4 Ibid., p. 12.
5 Ibid., p. 15.
6 Ibid., pp. 16–17.
7 Ibid., pp. 149–62.
8 Ibid., p. 8.
9 Ibid., p. 17.
10 See, e.g., 'Freedom to Act', in *Essays on Actions*, pp. 63–81.

Chapter 11 Wayward Causal Chains

1 D. F. Gustafson, *Intention and Agency* (Reidel, Dordrecht, 1986), p. 37.
2 Davidson, *Essays on Actions*, p. 72.
3 Ibid., p. 87.
4 Ibid., pp. 7–8.
5 R. M. Chisholm, 'Freedom and Action', in *Freedom and Determinism*, ed. Lehrer, pp. 11–44, esp. pp. 29–30.
6 Davidson, *Essays on Actions*, p. 78.
7 Ibid., p. 79.
8 Goldman, *A Theory*, p. 62.
9 Davidson, *Essays on Actions*, p. 79.
10 See I. Thalberg, 'Do Our Intentions Cause Our Intentional Actions?', *American Philosophical Quarterly*, 21 (1984), pp. 249–60, esp. p. 253.
11 M. Brand, *Intending and Acting. Toward a Naturalized Action Theory* (MIT Press, Cambridge, Mass., 1984), p. 31.
12 Thalberg, 'Do Our Intentions', p. 256.

13 Ibid., p. 257.
14 H. G. Frankfurt, 'The Problem of Action', *American Philosophical Quarterly*, 15 (1978), pp. 157–62, esp. p. 158.
15 Brand, *Intending and Acting*, p. 18.
16 Ibid., pp. 18 and 23.
17 Ibid., pp. 31 and 35.
18 Ibid., p. 23.
19 Ibid., pp. 239 and 241.
20 Ibid., p. 241.
21 Ibid., p. 31.
22 Ibid., p. 23.
23 Ibid., p. 240.
24 Ibid., p. 25.
25 A. R. Mele, 'Intentional Action and Wayward Causal Chains: The Problem of Tertiary Waywardness', *Philosophical Studies*, 51 (1987), pp. 55–60, esp. p. 55.
26 Ibid., p. 59.
27 A. Donagan, *Choice: The Essential Element in Human Action* (Routledge & Kegan Paul, London, 1987).
28 J. R. Searle, *Intentionality* (Cambridge University Press, Cambridge, 1983), ch. 3.
29 Donagan, *Choice*, p. 91.

Chapter 12 Intention and Intentional Action

1   See Perry, 'The Problem of the Essential Indexical'.
2   See Gustafson, *Intention and Agency*, p. 184.
3   Ibid., p. 184.
4   Ibid., p. 63.
5   See G. Harman, *Change in View* (MIT Press, Cambridge, Mass., 1986), chs 8 and 9; M. Bratman, *Intention, Plans, and Practical Reason* (Harvard University Press, Cambridge, Mass., 1987), chs 8 and 10.
6   T. Nagel, 'Moral Luck', in *Mortal Questions* (Cambridge University Press, Cambridge, 1979), pp. 24–38.
7   See D. Carr, 'The Logic of Intentional Verbs', *Philosophical Investigations*, 7 (1984), pp. 141–57.
8   See, e.g., Gustafson, *Intention and Agency*, pp. 111–17, and H.-N. Castañeda, *Thinking and Doing* (Reidel, Dordrecht, 1982), ch. 6.
9   See, e.g., A. Baier, *Postures of the Mind* (Methuen, London, 1985), p. 198.
10 M. A. Robins, *Promising, Intending, and Moral Autonomy* (Cambridge University Press, Cambridge, 1984); A. C. Danto, *Analytical Philosophy of Action* (Cambridge University Press, Cambridge, 1973).
11 O'Shaughnessy, 'Trying'; Bratman, *Intention*.

12 Harman, *Change in View*; Bratman, *Intention*.
13 Harman, *Change in View*, ch. 8.
14 Bratman, *Intention*, p. 121.
15 Ibid., chs 1 and 2.
16 Harman, *Change in View*, p. 78.
17 R. Audi, 'Intending', *Journal of Philosophy*, 70 (1973), pp. 387–402, esp. pp. 395–6.

Chapter 13 Davidson's Theory of Intention

1 D. Davidson, 'Replies to Essays I–IX', in *Essays on Davidson. Actions and Events*, ed. B. Vermazen and M. B. Hintikka (Clarendon Press, Oxford, 1985), p. 195.
2 D. Davidson, 'How is Weakness of the Will Possible?', in his *Essays on Actions*, pp. 21–42.
3 Davidson, 'Replies', p. 196.
4 Ibid., p. 197.
5 Davidson, *Essays on Actions*, p. 88.
6 Davidson, 'Replies', p. 211.
7 Ibid., p. 214.
8 Ibid., p. 198.
9 Davidson, *Essays on Actions*, p. 93.
10 Davidson, 'Replies', p. 215.
11 Ibid., p. 197.
12 M. Bratman, 'Davidson's Theory of Intention', in *Essays on Davidson*, ed. Vermazen and Hintikka, pp. 13–26, esp. p. 17.
13 Ibid., p. 22.
14 Ibid., p. 22.
15 Ibid., p. 22.
16 Ibid., p. 23.
17 Ibid., p. 24.
18 Davidson, 'Replies', pp. 198–9.
19 See M. Bratman, 'Appendix: Davidson's Alternatives', in *Actions and Events. Perspectives on the Philosophy of Donald Davidson*, ed. E. LePore and B. P. McLaughlin (Basil Blackwell, Oxford, 1985), pp. 24–8, esp. p. 26.
20 See Bratman, *Intention*, ch. 8.
21 Ibid., p. 114.
22 Davidson, *Essays on Actions*, pp. 94–5.
23 Davidson would reply, however, that it is part of my *present* belief and desire that I want to buy *The Fixer* only if it is available, so that the case would be similar to wanting to leave the party if it is too noisy. But, as far as I can see, 'I want (desire) to buy *The Fixer* only if it is available' does not capture the content of my intention, for the fact is that I *desire now* to buy *The Fixer*, only I *will not be able* to buy it if it is not available. The condition, that is, affects my

178 *Notes on Pages 157–162*

future performance of the action, not its present desirability. Paraphrasing Davidson, we could say that my not being able to buy *The Fixer* is not a reason for or against my buying *The Fixer*. So, I still think that the two cases are different, the first involving a merely enabling condition of the performance of *independently desirable* actions, and the second a condition (loud noise) whose holding *presently increases* the desirability of an action (leaving the party). A merely enabling condition, such as the (unknown) availability of either book, cannot be a legitimate condition of a Davidsonian intention (present all-out desirability) of buying either book, or so it seems.

24 Bratman, 'Appendix'.
25 Davidson, 'Replies', p. 221.

Chapter 14 Agency and Physical Determinism

1 See D. Hume, *Enquiries Concerning Human Understanding and Concerning the Principles of Morals*, ed. L. A. Selby-Bigge, 3rd edn (Clarendon Press, Oxford, 1975), pp. 80–103. And see also J. S. Mill, *A System of Logic*, ed. J. M. Robson and R. F. McRae (University of Toronto Press and Routledge & Kegan Paul, Toronto and London, 1973), book VI, ch. 2.
2 A. J. Ayer, 'Freedom and Necessity', in *Free Will*, ed. Watson, pp. 15–23.

Bibliography

Anscombe, G. E. M., *Intention*, 2nd edn, Basil Blackwell, Oxford, 1979.

Anscombe, G. E. M., *Metaphysics and the Philosophy of Mind. Collected Philosophical Papers*, vol. II, University of Minnesota Press, Minneapolis, 1981.

Audi, R., 'Intending', *Journal of Philosophy*, 70 (1973), pp. 387–402.

Audi, R., 'Acting for reasons', *Philosophical Review*, 95 (1986), pp. 511–46.

Aune, B., *Reason and Action*, Reidel, Dordrecht, 1977.

Ayer, A. J., 'Freedom and Necessity', in G. Watson, ed., *Free Will*, Oxford University Press, Oxford, 1982, pp. 15–23.

Baier, A., 'The Search for Basic Actions', *American Philosophical Quarterly*, 8 (1971), pp. 161–70.

Baier, A., 'The Intentionality of Intentions', *Review of Metaphysics*, 30 (1977), pp. 389–414.

Baier, A., *Postures of the Mind*, Methuen, London, 1985.

Borst, C. V., ed., *The Mind/Brain Identity Theory*, Macmillan, London, 1970.

Brand, M. and Walton, D., eds, *Action Theory*, Reidel, Dordrecht, 1976.

Brand, M., 'The Fundamental Question in Action Theory', *Noûs*, 13 (1979), pp. 131–57.

Brand, M., *Intending and Acting. Toward a Naturalized Action Theory*, MIT Press, Cambridge, Mass., 1984.

Bratman, M., 'Two Faces of Intention', *Philosophical Review*, 99 (1981), pp. 375–405.

Bratman, M., 'Davidson's Theory of Intention', in B. Vermazen and M. B. Hintikka, eds, *Essays on Davidson. Actions and Events*, Clarendon Press, Oxford, 1985, pp. 13–26.

Bratman, M., 'Appendix: Davidson's Alternatives', in E. LePore and B. P.

McLaughlin, eds, *Actions and Events. Perspectives on the Philosophy of Donald Davidson*, Basil Blackwell, Oxford, 1985, pp. 24–8.

Bratman, M., *Intention, Plans, and Practical Reason*, Harvard University Press, Cambridge, Mass., 1987.

Burge, T., 'Intellectual Norms and Foundations of Mind', *Journal of Philosophy*, 83 (1986), pp. 697–720.

Carr, D., 'The Logic of Intentional Verbs', *Philosophical Investigations*, 7 (1984), pp. 141–57.

Castañeda, H.-N., *Thinking and Doing*, Reidel, Dordrecht, 1982.

Chisholm, R. M., 'The Descriptive Element in the Concept of Action', *Journal of Philosophy*, 61 (1964), pp. 613–25.

Chisholm, R. M., 'Freedom and Action', in K. Lehrer, ed., *Freedom and Determinism*, Random House, New York, 1966, pp. 11–44.

Chisholm, R. M., 'The Structure of Intention', *Journal of Philosophy*, 67 (1970), pp. 633–47.

Chisholm, R. M., *Person and Object. A Metaphysical Study*, Allen & Unwin, London, 1976.

Churchland, P. M., 'The Logical Character of Action Explanations', *Philosophical Review*, 79 (1970), pp. 214–36.

Churchland, P. M., 'Eliminative Materialism and Propositional Attitudes', *Journal of Philosophy*, 78 (1981), pp. 67–90.

Churchland, P. M., *Matter and Consciousness*, MIT Press, Cambridge, Mass., 1984.

Collingwood, R. G., *The Idea of History*, Oxford University Press, Oxford, 1946.

Danto, A. C., 'Freedom and Forbearance', in K. Lehrer, ed., *Freedom and Determinism*, Random House, New York, 1966, pp. 45–63.

Danto, A. C., 'Basic Actions', in A. R. White, ed., *The Philosophy of Action*, Oxford University Press, Oxford, 1968, pp. 43–58.

Danto, A. C., *Analytical Philosophy of Action*, Cambridge University Press, Cambridge, 1973.

Davidson, D., *Essays on Actions and Events*, Clarendon Press, Oxford, 1982.

Davidson, D., *Inquiries into Truth and Interpretation*, Clarendon Press, Oxford, 1984.

Davidson, D., 'Replies to Essays I–IX', in B. Vermazen and M. B. Hintikka, eds, *Essays on Davidson. Actions and Events*, Clarendon Press, Oxford, 1985, pp. 195–229.

Davis, L., *Theory of Action*, Prentice-Hall, Englewood Cliffs, NJ, 1979.

Davis, W. A., 'A Causal Theory of Intending', *American Philosophical Quarterly*, 21 (1984), pp. 43–54.

Dennett, D. C., 'Mechanism and Responsibility', in T. Honderich, ed., *Essays on Freedom of Action*, Routledge & Kegan Paul, London, 1973, pp. 157–84.

Dennett, D. C., *Brainstorms*, Harvester Press, Brighton, 1981.

Dennett, D. C., 'Beyond Belief', in A. Woodfield, ed., *Thought and Object. Essays on Intentionality*, Clarendon Press, Oxford, 1982, pp. 1–95.

Dennett, D. C., *Elbow Room. The Varieties of Free Will Worth Wanting*, Clarendon Press, Oxford, 1984.

Dent, N. H. J., *The Moral Psychology of the Virtues*, Cambridge University Press, Cambridge, 1984.

Diamond, C. and Teichman, J., eds, *Intention and Intentionality. Essays in Honour of G. E. M. Anscombe*, Harvester Press, Brighton, 1979.

Donagan, A., *Choice: The Essential Element in Human Action*, Routledge & Kegan Paul, London, 1987.

Dray, W., *Laws and Explanation in History*, Oxford University Press, Oxford, 1957.

Dray, W., 'The Historical Explanation of Actions Reconsidered', in S. Hook, ed., *Philosophy and History: A Symposium*, New York University Press, New York, 1963, pp. 105–35.

Edwards, R. B., 'Is Choice Determined by the "Strongest Motive"?', *American Philosophical Quarterly*, 4 (1967), pp. 72–8.

Eells, E., *Rational Decision and Causality*, Cambridge University Press, Cambridge, 1982.

Fishburn, P. C., 'Subjective Expected Utility: A Review of Normative Theories', *Theory and Decision*, 13 (1981), pp. 139–99.

Flanagan, O. J., *The Science of the Mind*, MIT Press, Cambridge, Mass., 1984.

Fodor, J. A., *Representations. Philosophical Essays on the Foundations of Cognitive Science*, Harvester Press, Brighton, 1981.

Fodor, J. A., 'Fodor's Guide to Mental Representation', *Mind*, 94 (1985), pp. 76–100.

Frankfurt, H. G., 'The Problem of Action', *American Philosophical Quarterly*, 15 (1978), pp. 157–62.

Frankfurt, H. G., 'Freedom of the Will and the Concept of a Person', in G. Watson, ed., *Free Will*, Oxford University Press, Oxford, 1982, pp. 81–95.

Gardiner, P., *The Nature of Historical Explanation*, Oxford University Press, London, 1952.

Goldman, A. I., *A Theory of Human Action*, Princeton University Press, Princeton, NJ, 1970.

Goldman, A. I., 'The Individuation of Action', *Journal of Philosophy*, 68 (1971), pp. 761–74.

Gustafson, D. F., *Intention and Agency*, Reidel, Dordrecht, 1986.

Hampshire, S., *Thought and Action*, Viking Press, New York, 1959.

Harman, G., *Change in View*, MIT Press, Cambridge, Mass., 1986.

Hempel, C. G., 'The Function of General Laws in History', *Journal of Philosophy*, 39 (1942), pp. 35–48.

Hempel, C. G., 'Reasons and Covering Laws in Historical Explanation', in S. Hook ed., *Philosophy and History. A Symposium*, New York University Press, New York, 1963.

Hempel, C. G., *Aspects of Scientitic Explanation*, Free Press, New York, 1965.

Hempel, C. G., 'Explanation in Science and in History', in W. Dray, ed., *Philosophical Analysis and History*, Harper & Row, New York, 1966, pp. 95–126.

Hollis, M., *The Cunning of Reason*, Cambridge University Press, Cambridge, 1987.

Hookway, C., 'Indeterminacy and Interpretation', in C. Hookway and Ph. Pettit, eds, *Action and Interpretation. Studies in the Philosophy of the Social Sciences*, Cambridge University Press, Cambridge, 1978, pp. 17–41.

Hookway, C., *Quine. Language, Experience and Reality*, Polity Press, Cambridge, 1988.

Hornsby, J., *Actions*, Routledge & Kegan Paul, London, 1980.

Hume, D., *Enquiries Concerning Human Understanding and Concerning the Principles of Morals*, ed. L. A. Selby-Bigge, 3rd edn, Clarendon Press, Oxford, 1975.

Inwagen, P., *An Essay on Free Will*, Clarendon Press, Oxford, 1983.

Janis, I. L. and Mann, L., *Decision Making*, Free Press, New York, 1977.

Jeffrey, R. C., *The Logic of Decision*, 2nd edn, University of Chicago Press, Chicago, 1983.

Kapitan, T., 'Deliberation and the Presumption of Open Alternatives', in L. Stevenson, R. Squires and J. Haldane, eds, *Mind, Causation & Action*, Basil Blackwell, Oxford, 1986, pp. 120–41.

Kenny, A., *Free Will and Responsibility*, Routledge & Kegan Paul, London, 1978.

Loar, B., *Mind and Meaning*, Cambridge University Press, Cambridge, 1981.

Locke, D., 'Beliefs, Desires, and Reasons for Action', *American Philosophical Quarterly*, 19 (1982), pp. 241–9.

McCann, H., 'Volition and Basic Action', *Philosophical Review*, 83 (1974), pp. 451–73.

McDowell, J., 'Functionalism and Anomalous Monism', in E. LePore and B. P. McLaughlin, eds, *Actions and Events. Perspectives on the Philosophy of Donald Davidson*, Basil Blackwell, Oxford, 1985, pp. 387–98.

McDowell, J., 'Singular Thought and the Extent of Inner Space', in J. McDowell and Ph. Pettit, eds, *Subject, Thought, and Context*, Clarendon Press, Oxford, 1986, pp. 137–68.

McGinn, C., *The Character of Mind*, Oxford University Press, Oxford, 1982.

Malcolm, N., 'The Conceivability of Mechanism', in G. Watson, ed., *Free Will*, Oxford University Press, Oxford, 1982, pp. 127–49.

Melden, A. I., *Free Action*, Routledge & Kegan Paul, London, 1961.

Melden, A. I., 'Willing', in A. R. White, ed., *The Philosophy of Action*, Oxford University Press, Oxford, 1968, pp. 70–8.

Mele, A. R., 'Intentional Action and Wayward Causal Chains: The

Problem of Tertiary Waywardness', *Philosophical Studies*, 51 (1987), pp. 55–60.

Mill, J. S., *A System of Logic*, ed. J. M. Robson and R. F. McRae, University of Toronto Press and Routledge & Kegan Paul, Toronto and London, 1973.

Miller, A. R., 'Describing Unwitting Behaviour', *American Philosophical Quarterly*, 17 (1980), pp. 67–72.

Moya, C. J., 'Acción e Intención', *Quaderns de Filosofia i Ciència*, 9/10 (1986), pp. 213–20.

Nagel, T., *Mortal Questions*, Cambridge University Press, Cambridge, 1979.

Nagel, T., *The View from Nowhere*, Oxford University Press, Oxford, 1986.

O'Shaughnessy, B., 'Trying (as the Mental "Pineal Gland")', *Journal of Philosophy*, 70 (1973), pp. 365–86.

O'Shaughnessy, B., *The Will: A Dual Aspect Theory*, 2 vols, Cambridge University Press, Cambridge, 1980.

Pears, D., 'Desires as Causes of Actions', in *The Human Agent*, Royal Institute of Philosophy Lectures, vol. I, Macmillan, London, 1968, pp. 83–97.

Pears, D., 'The Appropriate Causation of Intentional Basic Actions', *Critica*, 7 (1975), pp. 39–69.

Pears, D., *Motivated Irrationality*, Clarendon Press, Oxford, 1984.

Perry, J., 'The Problem of the Essential Indexical', *Noûs*, 13 (1979), pp. 3–21.

Popper, K. R., *The Logic of Scientific Discovery*, Hutchinson, London, 1980.

Prichard, H. A., 'Acting, Willing, Desiring', in A. R. White, ed., *The Philosophy of Action*, Oxford University Press, Oxford, 1968, pp. 59–69.

Quine, W. O., *Word and Object*, MIT Press, Cambridge, Mass., 1960.

Quine, W. O., 'States of Mind', *Journal of Philosophy*, 82 (1985), pp. 5–8.

Robins, M. A., *Promising, Intending, and Moral Autonomy*, Cambridge University Press, Cambridge, 1984.

Rosenberg, A., *Sociobiology and the Preemption of Social Science*, Basil Blackwell, Oxford, 1981.

Rotenstreich, N., *Reflection and Action*, Martinus Nijhoff, Dordrecht, 1985.

Ryle, G., *The Concept of Mind*, Hutchinson, London, 1949.

Searle, J. R., *Intentionality*, Cambridge University Press, Cambridge, 1983.

Shoemaker, S., *Identity, Cause, and Mind*, Cambridge University Press, Cambridge, 1984.

Stoutland, F., 'Davidson on Intentional Behaviour', in E. LePore and B. P. McLaughlin, eds, *Actions and Events. Perspectives on the Philosophy of Donald Davidson*, Basil Blackwell, Oxford, 1985, pp. 44–59.

Taylor, R., *Action and Purpose*, Prentice-Hall, Englewood Cliffs, NJ, 1966.

Thalberg, I., 'Do Our Intentions Cause Our Intentional Actions?', *American Philosophical Quarterly*, 21 (1984), pp. 249–60.

Tuomela, R., *A Theory of Social Action*, Reidel, Dordrecht, 1984.

Whiteley, C. H., 'Mental Causes', in *The Human Agent*, Royal Institute of Philosophy Lectures, vol. I, Macmillan, London, 1968, pp. 98–114.

Wilson, G. M., 'Davidson on Intentional Action', in E. LePore and B. P. McLaughlin, eds, *Action and Events. Perspectives on the Philosophy of Donald Davidson*, Basil Blackwell, Oxford, 1985, pp. 29–43.

Winch, P., *The Idea of a Social Science*, Routledge & Kegan Paul, London, 1958.

Wittgenstein, L., *The Blue and Brown Books*, Basil Blackwell, Oxford, 1958.

Wittgenstein, L., *Philosophical Investigations*, Basil Blackwell, Oxford, 1973.

Wright, G. H. von, *Explanation and Understanding*, Cornell University Press, New York, 1971.

Zimmerman, M., *An Essay on Human Action*, Peter Lang, New York, 1984.

Index

intentional action (*cont.*):
  and reflexivity, 85, 89, 141, 164,
    168
  strong and weak senses of, 59–60,
    66–7, 130, 167
  see also causal theories of action
intentional object *see* content
intentional states, 8, 61–2, 78, 129
  see also content
intentionality of mind, 7–8, 61–5, 71
  and science, 70–9, 110–12
  see also content
  see also under agency; intentional
    action
interactionism *see* mind and body

Jeffrey, R. C., 93, 99

Kant, Immanuel, 96

Lavoisier, Antoine-Laurent, 71
laws, 71
  and analytic statements, 82–3
  bridge laws, 74
  and *ceteris paribus* clauses, 82,
    83–4, 88, 89
  and explanation, 80–1, 87, 106,
    108–10, 162
  and prediction of actions, 6, 73,
    75, 100–4, 108, 160–2
  see also under explanation
Locke, John, 115
logical connection argument, 6, 106,
  110

McCann, Hugh, 19–22, 31, 35, 37
materialism *see* physicalism
meaningful actions, 38–48, 160–1
  and agency, 40, 170
  and basic actions, 40, 43–6, 47,
    48, 50
  and commitment, 46–7, 50–1, 67
  normative aspects of, 47, 48, 51, 67
  and the regress-problem, 4,
    38–41, 46–8, 49, 51, 66, 166
Melden, A. I., 20, 105
Mele, A. R., 126–7
Mill, J. S., 18, 68, 80, 95, 109, 115
mind and body, 21, 37–8, 68, 74

  see also behaviourism; functionalism;
    identity theory
  see also under reduction; tryings;
    volitions
moral conflict, 96, 136

Nagel, Thomas, 136
natural sciences, 5, 65, 70–1, 161,
  168, 169
naturalism, 5–6, 168, 169
  see also scientism
New Volitional Theory, 18–29, 44,
  115, 165
  see also tryings; volitions
normativity
  in decision making, 101–2
  and mind, 61–3, 71, 103
  see also under commitment; ex-
    planation; functionalism; future
    intention; intentional action;
    meaningful actions

ontology of actions, 30–6
O'Shaughnessy, Brian, 22–7, 34, 38

physicalism, 72, 111–12
  see also behaviourism; eliminative
    materialism; functionalism;
    identity theory
plans, 57, 122, 123, 125, 127, 129, 130
Popper, K. R., 80
practical reason, 95–6, 145–7
  see also rationalization
prediction of action *see under* laws
Prichard, H. A., 68
promises, 138, 139, 140
propositional attitudes, 62, 65
  see also intentional states
purpose *see* intention with which
    (purpose)

Quine, W. O., 75, 83

rationalization *see under* explanation
reasons
  and causes, 5, 6, 105–6, 107–13,
    141, 163, 168, 169–70
  and intention, 57, 140–1, 168
  see also under explanation

reduction
  of actions to bodily movements,
    32–3, 41–3
  of actions to happenings, 3, 16, 18,
    65–6, 68, 165
  of future intention to desires and
    beliefs, 7, 142–4, 148, 169
  of the mental to the physical,
    73–5, 98
reductionisn *see* reduction
reflexivity, 85, 89, 141, 168–9
  see also under desires: intentional
    action
regress-problem, 3–4, 12–17, 19, 37,
  53, 65–6, 165
  see also under meaningful actions:
    tryings: volitions
responsibility, 2, 67, 135, 136
result of action, 19, 31, 37, 38, 40–1
result-problem *see* regress-problem
Robins, M. A., 141
Rosenberg, Alexander, 65
Ryle, Gilbert, 4, 131

Schleiermacher, Friedrich, 80
scientism, 71–2, 168, 169
  see also causal theories of action;
    decision theory; extensionality;
    laws; physicalism
Searle, J. R., 127
Sellars, Wilfrid, 123
sense and reference, 42
social sciences, 5–6, 65, 72, 75
  see also explanation; scientism
subjective expected utility, 92–3, 96
  maximization of, 94, 100
subjectivity, 64, 71, 122, 168

Thalberg, Irving, 120–2, 124, 126,
  129
tryings, 22–3, 27–8, 34

content of, 24
and the mind-body problem, 23,
  28, 29, 38, 68
as ordinary intentional actions,
  24–5
as physical acts, 25–6, 28
and the regress-problem, 4, 17, 23,
  26–7, 29, 51, 165
see also volitions

unity of science *see* scientism

volitional theories of action, 4, 17, 44
  see also New Volitional Theory
volitions, 19–20, 114
  and agency, 17, 44, 48
  as basic actions, 17, 20, 115
  content of, 19–20
  as mental happenings, 18
  and the mind-body problem, 21,
    29, 37–8, 68
  and the regress-problem, 4, 17,
    19– 22, 29, 51, 66, 165
  see also tryings
wants *see* desires
wayward causal chains, 6–7, 114,
  115–28, 142, 168
  Brand's answer to the problem of,
    122–6
  Donagan's answer to the problem
    of, 127–8
  the 'right of way' of causation,
    118–19, 126, 157
  Thalberg's answer to the problem
    of, 120–2
weakness of the will, 146
Whiteley, C. H., 82–3, 86
will, 10, 68–9
Winch, Peter, 105
Wittgenstein, Ludwig, 50, 105, 124,
  125